Imagined Sovereignties

Imagined Sovereignties

Toward a New Political Romanticism

Kir Kuiken

FORDHAM UNIVERSITY PRESS

NEW YORK 2014

Library of Congress Cataloging-in-Publication Data is available from the publisher.

Printed in the United States of America

16 15 14 5 4 3 2 1

First edition

For my parents, Donald and Elisabeth

CONTENTS

ACKNOWLEDGMENTS

The impetus for this book began during my time in graduate school at the University of California, Irvine's Department of English and Comparative Literature. The seminars of Jacques Derrida provided an extremely challenging and fertile intellectual environment. Derrida's work and teaching has made an indelible mark on my thinking and writing. The research for this book began under the direction of Andrzej Warminski, who taught me how to read. Before him, Zsuzsa Baross at Trent University taught me how to think.

Friends and colleagues Branka Arsić, Rick Barney, Craig Carson, Jennifer Greiman, Paul Stasi, and David Wills all read my work at various stages and helped immeasurably with timely, thoughtful, and insightful suggestions. I am also strongly indebted to the conversations I have had with my colleagues Geoffrey Bennington, Pascale-Anne Brault, Michael Naas, Peggy Kamuf, and Elizabeth Rottenberg at the annual Derrida Seminars Translation Project.

The English Department at the University at Albany has provided me with nothing short of an intellectual community, and I owe a debt of gratitude to all of my colleagues. Mike Hill and Randy Craig as chairs have provided steadfast support throughout the writing process. Rick Barney, Helen Elam, and Charles Shepherdson have been a guiding presence as my faculty mentors. Liz Lauenstein, Lynn Beaurup, and Connie Barrett helped navigate the ins and outs of acquiring institutional support. I am grateful to the talented and hardworking group of graduate students in my Fall 2009 and Spring 2011 graduate seminars, whose engagement with some of the ideas in this book helped shape it. I am also thankful to be part of a community that is at once intellectual and social. For conversation, laughter, food, and drink I would like to thank Bret Benjamin, Donald Byrd, Pat Chu, James Lilley, Ineke Murakami, Tomás Noel, Helene Scheck, Ed Schwarzschild, Barry Trachtenberg, and Laura Wilder.

The University at Albany, State University at New York provided research support. I was able to complete the majority of the work on the manuscript thanks to a fall 2011 writing leave granted by the University at Albany English Department.

I would also like to express my deep appreciation for the tireless work of the entire team at Fordham University Press. Helen Tartar has been extremely supportive of the project, not only in taking time out of her busy schedule to meet with me but also in graciously and patiently seeing the process through to the end. Thomas Lay facilitated the whole process with similar care and attention. I would like to thank both Eric Newman and Erin Schwiderson for their incredibly diligent editing work. The book also owes much to the two readers Helen asked to review the manuscript. I am especially grateful to Jan Plug, whose extremely detailed and incisive comments helped to clarify a number of important points. A portion of Chapter 4 was published in the *Keats-Shelley Journal* 60 (2011) as "The Metaleptic Imagination in Shelley's *Defence of Poetry*" and is reprinted here in modified form with permission. Another portion of Chapter 4 was published in *Literature Compass* 8.2 (2011) as "Shelley's 'Mask of Anarchy' and the Problem of Modern Sovereignty." I would like to thank the Trustees of the British Museum for granting permission to use several plates of Blake's Illuminated manuscripts and Anselm Kiefer for permission to use his work *Osiris und Isis* for the cover of the book.

More personally, I have two families to thank. My parents, Donald and Elisabeth Kuiken, have supported me in every possible way, first by giving me a love of reading and writing, and then by helping to provide me with the means to turn it into a career. Their love and care at every step of the way has been unconditional. I owe them both a great deal more than can be expressed in these pages.

My other family consists of Branka Arsić, David Wills, and Emma Arsić-Wills. All along, they have been a refuge and a source of uncompromising moral and intellectual support. I thank them for their friendship and for raising Emma, a constant source of joy whenever I see her.

My wife and best friend, Vesna, has been an engaged and patient interlocutor for the entire time I was writing this book. I owe her boundless love for the beauty of a shared life.

Imagined Sovereignties

Introduction: Toward a New Political Romanticism

Among the great popular stories that followed Percy Shelley, or "Mad Shelley" as he came to be called after being expelled from Oxford for writing the *Necessity of Atheism*, was that while travelling with Byron in Switzerland, he would sometimes sign the hotel ledger under the name "Percy Shelley, democrat, great lover of mankind, atheist." Less fantastical than the tale about Edward Trelawny pulling Shelley's intact heart from his funeral pyre, it nonetheless conveys a familiar nexus of Romantic themes that connect immediately to the problem of politics. With the exception of the last descriptor—atheist—Shelley's signature could be read as the signature of British Romanticism more generally. Emerging coextensively with the great revolutions of the period that called divine right models of political sovereignty directly and violently into question, Romanticism sits at the crossroads of the modern era, which is forced to confront the task of reconstituting the political on new grounds. Shelley's triple signature, "democrat, great lover of mankind, atheist," opens a set of problems that would confront this modernity, along with all the *aporias* of the process of secularization that we are still familiar with today. These *aporias* produce a set of intractable questions: How does one construct a sovereignty no longer modeled on absolute divinity? Is there a conflicted relationship between secularized models of sovereignty and democracy? Does the substitution of Man for God as sovereign diminish in any way the threat of absolutism found in secularized conceptions of political theology? These fundamental paradoxes remain central to the mutation of the concept of sovereignty that Romanticism witnessed, and in which it also participated. It remains part of the prehistory of our own modernity, which is in the throes of its own specific crises and transformations of this concept.

Though readers of Romanticism have long understood that the revolutions of the period were fundamentally intertwined with it, exactly how remains an ongoing source of debate. Coleridge's early poem "Destruction of the Bastille" may serve as a good example of the lacuna within Romanticism's relation to the transformations in sovereignty that the revolution represents. The first stanza of the poem depicts freedom emerging as a volcano, "spreading its ruins," while the last witnesses "liberty succeed," flowing through every "pulse" and "vein." Since the middle stanzas are missing, it remains unclear how we get from the beginning to the end of the story. One could argue, however, that these missing stanzas have been filled with meaning by a growing critical literature that has sought to understand Romanticism in terms of its alleged indifference or naiveté in relation to politics. The last decade has witnessed a veritable explosion in studies devoted to the philosophical and political meaning of Romanticism. Having long ago surpassed the notion of Romanticism as a "visionary company"[1] unified around the liberating potential of the individual imagination, a number of "turns" have sought to understand the specific relation between the aesthetic imagination and the political that Romanticism inaugurated. As a result, all kinds of critical blindnesses or insights have been located in or projected onto its corpus, from claims about its displacement of history into the aestheticized realm of the imagination, to more recent identifications of Romanticism with ideology.[2] Its legacies multiple and contested, Romanticism remains either a moment that still determines our conceptions of literature and criticism, or a dangerous contemporary mystification that must be critically cast off.

This book is an argument about how key poets in British Romanticism position their poetics, their writing, and their philosophy in relation to the task of inventing a fundamentally modern form of sovereignty, one that would no longer rely on the absolute ground of the divine. It makes the case that the vague and still much misunderstood term "the imagination" is the site where this task is pursued, partly because it constitutes a source of power that is secular rather than celestial. But it is also the site where this reconsideration takes place because it offers a way of thinking about the *materialization* of power; it asks, in other words, how something unconditional (whether conceived as rights or otherwise) is given shape. The imagination, for the Romantics, is thus at once an *aesthetic* principle and a political one, a place where the conditional and the unconditional meet in a productive tension.

More recent attempts to understand the relation between the imagination and the political as something other than a mystification of history have tended to emphasize connections between the imagination and rhetoric, or the power of figurative language to engage a host of problems such as the integration of the individual with the collective, or the relation between politics and form.[3] Forest Pyle's seminal work *The Ideology of Imagination* long ago argued that the imagination was itself a political figure through and through, insofar as it acts as the site of an articulation between subject and society.[4] Arguing for a much more ambivalent understanding of the relation between imagination and politics, Pyle claims that while the imagination can certainly enact or produce powerful ideological mystifications, it also serves to undermine them by pointing out the fundamental disjunctions in the very linkages it makes between the individual and society, mind and nature, truth and beauty. Though the argument of this book concentrates on the construction of a new ground of political legitimacy through the imagination, which takes shape in the wake of the collapse of older models of political sovereignty, it keeps in mind Pyle's crucial insight that the imagination must be regarded as "the figural juncture of forces in conflict."[5] That is, for the Romantics themselves, the imagination is neither inherently ideological nor necessarily critical. It acts, rather, as a point of productive tension that troubles received ideas about the relation between political authority and representation.

My argument is not that the Romantics were able to resolve the tension between the conditional and the unconditional addressed by the figure of the imagination or that they were able to invent a truly modern form of sovereignty through it. Quite the contrary, notable Romantics such as Coleridge and Wordsworth tended to revert to positions late in life that restored much of the political theology they had spent their early careers challenging. I do claim, however, that Romanticism, precisely by considering the problem of political sovereignty through the imagination, unearthed fundamental tensions in the secularization of sovereignty. These tensions opened up spaces in which other forms of sovereignty than the choice between divine right or natural right could be imagined. Rather than view the Romantics as a mystified past that we must move beyond, I see Romanticism as a critical limit that unmasks our *own* reliance on oppositions that keep intact basic assumptions about the problematic relationship between aesthetics and politics, and about the nature of modern sovereignty itself.

If Romanticism opens an era to which we still belong, but the inheritance of which we are far from having settled, then perhaps the most contested of these legacies is the way that the Romantics center their attempt to reinvent the political on the aesthetic, or poetic, imagination. By and large, this connection has been understood as Romanticism's scandal, its political impotence or naïveté. Once aesthetics becomes a political model, so the story goes, it devolves into a form of aesthetic ideology that is either dangerously totalitarian or politically quietist. Historicist turns toward the politics of Romanticism have emphasized the latter position, focusing on how Romantic texts evade history or displace real-world political concerns into the abstract or purely individualized domain of the imagination.[6] In these readings, the Romantic fixation with the imagination is seen as an alibi, converting genuine historical struggles into purely internal contradictions that can be easily resolved since they have been removed from any contact with external reality. My interest, on the other hand, lies in the way Romanticism's investment in the imagination becomes a locus for its attempt to *reshape* the political. In these explorations, I am led to disagree with the notion that this investment yields nothing but a dangerously totalizing conception of the political, a reduction to the politics of liberalism, or a collapse into the whims of individual subjectivity. I treat the imagination as a site of contestation and of a critical ambivalence that begins to reshape some of the defining features of the political that the Romantics inherited from early modern and Enlightenment models.

The readings in this book also treat the texts of Romanticism themselves as a site of contestation, that is, as *texts* rather than as repositories of dated beliefs that can be demystified. The texts are riven by what they presume to say and what they do and do not control about what they say. My reading sometimes addresses the former, but equally so the latter since the notion of the political valence of the imagination in Romanticism was a topic of great ambivalence to the Romantics themselves. In some cases, they shied away from the radicalism of their own insights or sought to control their consequences. Coleridge, for example, would in the end restore the problem of *faith* at the heart of the sovereign's relation to the unconditional, thereby reconstructing a traditional political theology in his last major political treatise, *On the Constitution of Church and State*. But not before he had voiced the radical idea in the *Biographia Literaria* and *The Friend* that the unconditional must be subjected immediately, at its very origin, to the conditioned. It is between these two tendencies, both of which are represented in Coleridge's texts, that my reading operates, showing how, though he attempted to foreclose the radicalism of his earlier claims, the very rigor of his argument opens up different directions to his thought that are legible in the margins of his text.

A study focused on the political valence of the imagination in Romanticism, of course, runs up against the problem that there is hardly a consistent theory of the imagination at work there. What Blake means by "poetic genius" is not easily reconciled with Coleridge's conception of the productive imagination inspired by his encounter with German Idealism. However, the plurality of definitions of the imagination (within British Romanticism in particular) is precisely what makes it such a fecund place to explore how the Romantics thought a different model of sovereignty could emerge from it. While Blake's and Coleridge's conceptions of the imagination are quite far apart, they are in remarkable agreement on the fact that the imagination, in whatever form, has a political vocation that extends beyond the realm of purely aesthetic judgments. Although German Romanticism, following Kant, certainly conceived of aesthetic judgment as providing a model for political judgment, its understanding of the imagination as *Einbildungskraft*—the power of forming or producing images—does not associate aesthetic judgment and political judgment in the way British Romanticism does. Though some of the arguments offered here could certainly be brought to bear on the texts of German Romanticism, I concentrate on British Romanticism because their resistance to a broadly construed idealist understanding of the imagination is more acute—even in Coleridge, who generated his conception of the imagination through his understanding of Kant and Schelling. Further, I focus on British Romanticism because the canonical authors represented here—Blake, Coleridge, Wordsworth, and Shelley—are the ones most often targeted by the arguments seeking to show that their respective theories of the imagination are an evasion of history and politics.

How, then, does the question of political sovereignty come to be linked to the imagination in Romanticism? I proceed from the basic premise that the imagination in British Romanticism cannot be reduced to a simple subjective capacity. Though it is often described this way, Romanticism is linked to the problem of politics by way of a different dimension of the imagination, a collective one that the Romantics attempt to articulate. Even Wordsworth, whose resolute focus on the self would seem to necessitate a notion of the imagination that is a basic principle of interiority, indicates at the end of the *Prelude* that the imagination is a series of apparently mutually contradictory things. It is:

> another name for absolute strength
> And clearest insight, amplitude of mind
> And reason in her most exalted mood.[7]

As Simon Jarvis points out, "if imagination is 'absolute strength' *and* 'clearest insight' *and* 'amplitude of mind' *and* 'reason in her most exalted mood,' perhaps the only thing that does begin to become clear is that the imagination cannot possibly be a philosophical name for a clearly defined faculty, power or ontological region."[8] In other words, if, for Wordsworth, one of the dimensions of the imagination is its being a form of encounter with something that cannot be directly reconciled with the will or faculty of an individual, then its status must shift slightly, or at least take on the added component of being something that draws the individual out of himself. It not only has a collective dimension as one of its attributes, but is also a power or capacity that exceeds the individual.

This is why the imagination becomes a site where new forms of artistic and political authority are articulated. In lieu of an absolute starting point like divine or natural law, the imagination becomes for the Romantics a place to articulate the conditions of possibility for social transformation, whether this entails exploring how the individual is situated in relation to the community, or how existing forms of authority can be challenged. The imagination's connection with the motif of *poesis* and *auto-poesis* (making or self-making) is situated by the Romantics at the heart of the most central questions of politics in ways that are not immediately reducible to aesthetic ideology. The imagination often provides a figure for free creativity or auto-productivity that either becomes a counterpoint or a model for the radical inauguration that defines the modern sovereign. It also functions as the condition for the possibility of generating a sense of universality through the autonomy of aesthetic judgment. For both of these reasons, the imagination becomes a key touchstone for modern sovereignty in that it provides a quasi-secular alternative for the transcendence of the divine, which had hitherto been the basic condition of freedom, universalism, and political legitimacy.

In the chapters that follow, I read the imagination less as an original source of creativity than as the name for a set of fundamental questions that can no longer be resolved by reference to a pre-given ground or authority. These questions, naturally, include political ones: Who or what are the people that are sovereign? By what means do they exercise this sovereignty? In the wake of the collapse of divine right, a secular, collective power comes to define the sovereign. When sovereignty was secularized it began to undergo a mutation, splitting into multiple and contested sources of political legitimacy. The imagination, for the Romantics, was a way to articulate new sources of authority within an increasingly fragmented and democratized social sphere. One of its tasks was to mediate a whole series of oppositions—between exception and rule, or subject and object. In the construction of the modern sovereign, in whatever form, the imagination's main task was to realize the sovereign's exceptionality by articulating his privileged relation to his legitimating ground. The imagination thus "makes real" what would otherwise remain a purely formal law.

This creates a series of *aporias* and anxieties about the imagination's role. On the one hand, its auto-poetic structure threatens to make the forms of authority it legitimates indistinguishable from other kinds of arbitrary power.[9] On the other, the imagination's necessarily temporal character opens up the possibility of thinking a form of sovereignty that must come to terms with its own contingency, with the finite moment of its institution. Unlike the divine, the imagination is time-bound, divided between at least two internally differentiated moments: its *act* of production and *what* it produces. The question for the Romantics is whether these two moments can ever be reconciled so that the original positing act that institutes the sovereign can be identified as an act of his own will. If it cannot, a fracture develops between the ground of legitimacy and the act that sets the sovereign in place. It is this fracture that the imagination attempts to either heal or exacerbate, depending on the politics for which it is put to work. The internal division of the imagination gets carried over into the definition of the modern sovereign, producing a split between a legitimating ground and the figure that represents it. This split comes to be seen by the Romantics as either a temporary flaw that must be overcome or a constitutive feature of the sovereign himself.

The necessity of this "before" (the anterior act of production) and "after" (the products themselves) implies that the creations of the imagination—images or "laws" for Shelley, "vision of the infinite" for Blake—are the result of a prior structure of articulation. Though the imagination may appear to create *ex nihilo*, thereby constituting a prototype for the self-grounding sovereign, its temporal dimension opens up a relation to an anteriority that is not easily reducible to the indivisibility and autonomy that must, by definition, govern the sovereign's self-inauguration. Romanticism, in a sense, bears witness to a sovereignty that ceases to be itself the moment it is created. Having become its own ground of legitimation, the modern sovereign confronts the paradox of a continued need for an anteriority that is now presented as fundamentally its own, but which for that very reason threatens to undermine the sovereign by dividing him from himself. As Heidegger argues in his reading of Kant's transcendental imagination, the imagination does not simply *represent* an anteriority that lies beyond the sensuous, nor does it emerge *post-facto* to bridge it with its sensuous counterpart. Its task is precisely to "form transcendence."[10] If the transcendence or anteriority that the imagination must represent is created, set in place by the imagination itself, then an infinite regress unfolds, since the act that forms transcendence would have to precede what it sets in place. The Romantics' solution for this problem is to insist that this prior sovereign act *has already taken place* and the imagination is always catching up with it, constantly late for its own performance. It is thus always retrospectively giving shape to a sovereign whose source of legitimacy it may have itself invented.

The political concept of sovereignty is inherited from political theology,[11] where it denotes the incontestable ground of authority or legitimacy. Although Foucault has taught us to see the eighteenth and nineteenth centuries as inaugurating a shift from top down models of political authority and social control[12] to more mobile forms of power found in the various disciplinary practices and institutions organized around the care of the self, the problem of a central and basic organizing principle or source of authority that Hobbes identified in *Leviathan* nonetheless never entirely lost its significance. The transition from divine right to human rights cannot take place without the formal structure of a final or ultimate authority, whether this becomes either natural law or what Wordsworth and others will describe as an "inner divinity."[13] As Carl Schmitt has argued, "all significant concepts of the modern theory of the state are secularized theological concepts not only because of their historical development—in which they were transferred from theology to the theory of the state, whereby, for example, the omnipotent God became the omnipotent lawgiver—but also because of their systematic structure."[14] Sovereignty, even its secularized form, remains, as Jacques Derrida insists,[15] *onto-theological*, secular and theological at the same time, grounded by the desire for an antecedent transcendence or final authority, even if that final authority is no longer named God.

Nonetheless, there is a crucial contrast between divine right forms of sovereignty and secularized forms: whereas the monarch could lay claim to a divine reference, the people or the nation are a sovereign that generates itself. The finite or conditional moment of this constitution opens up new *aporia* not found in divine right theories of sovereignty because the monarch's legitimacy was always referred to an anterior and transcendent authority beyond him. Secularized sovereignty, on the other hand, exists in the absence of this reference. Because, by definition, sovereignty presupposes that it is *unconditional*—in other words, that there is nothing that precedes or supersedes it and that no instituting force or authority has been exercised prior to it—it must be radically self-inaugurating. This is why the Romantic appropriation of the motif of the imagination's auto-*poesis* is more than a question of poetics or just a nineteenth-century curiosity. Secular sovereignty is defined in terms of a relation to *itself* first of all, that is, to its own unconditionality and indivisibility. The absence of divine underpinnings provokes a crisis of legitimation, opening up the question of how the sovereign's unconditional ground comes to be represented or embodied in the political or juridical sphere. The imagination thus becomes a central point of an articulation between a definitive ground of sovereignty and its particular manifestation in the political realm. It acts both as the example of a radically self-inaugurating, self-grounding force and as the means by which that force can be felt in the world, represented, given shape, or incarnated into a fully fledged figure of the sovereign.

The modern sovereign, in order to be genuinely sovereign, cannot do without the invocation of a right, law, or ground that precedes him, even if this antecedence nonetheless belongs to him. In a curious sense that troubled the Romantics continuously, the modern sovereign (in whatever form) *precedes* himself, divides himself between a prior ground that legitimates him and the figure that incarnates this legitimation. The desire in Coleridge's *Kubla Khan* to reconstitute the moment of original composition that precedes the poem, and that, though lost, nevertheless continues to inform and direct the fragment that remains, is emblematic of precisely this problem. Coleridge is trying to represent the relation between an anterior ground that is still the imagination's own and poetry's presentation of the *effects* of this anteriority. *Kubla Khan* itself is the imagination's secondary reconstitution of its original act of creation. This state of being both before and after, figure and ground at the same time, is not only a predominant feature of the Romantic imagination, but a logic that characterizes the modern sovereign. Giorgio Agamben has argued persuasively that the modern "state of exception" emerges directly from the paradox of a sovereign who is both figure and ground, paradoxically before the law is instituted and emergent after it is instituted.[16] The sovereign is thus legitimated through a relation to something prior to the law that is materialized in the juridical or political order as a ground that is inside and outside the law at the same time.[17] This exteriority or anteriority is not illegal, since it is the sovereign himself who institutes the legal order; it is *a-legal*, since the law is not in place until it becomes the object of a sovereign decision.

The Romantics attempt to address this anteriority through the imagination precisely because it mirrors, represents, and formalizes an a-legal, unconditional ground. By being prior to laws of judgment, laws of nature, and political law, the imagination enters into a relation with what Agamben has called a "zone of anomie,"[18] a space prior to any particular determination of law. The presentation of this relation differs, of course, depending on the writer in question. In book eight of Wordsworth's *Prelude*, as I show in Chapter 3, the role of the imagination is in part to represent this space, to return to an anteriority that allows a genuine sense of community or collectivity to emerge that is anything but natural. In other works, such as Coleridge's *Biographia Literaria* and *The Friend*, as Chapter 2 makes clear, the imagination *itself* becomes the model for a force without law, a formative power that precedes law and acts as the condition of possibility for producing an unconditional sovereign who is no longer absolute. Coleridge builds on his understanding of Kant's development of the role of the imagination in aesthetic judgment, where the imagination does not operate according to previously instituted laws. As Kant clarifies in the *Critique of Judgment*, aesthetic judgments are reflective, not determinative; they imply an act of judgment that takes place in the absence of a given law or concept. Since reflective judgments, for Kant, bridge the realms of theoretical and practical reason, the conditions of experience and the conditions for moral (and political) action, the imagination constitutes the possibility of the *free creation* of law, both moral and physical. For other Romantic writers, the imagination doesn't just represent the sovereign or buttress his authority by generating the necessary emotive and aesthetic response that power relies on to produce subjects who recognize his legitimacy. It constitutes a prime *example* of a self-generating structure, an unconditional "Power seated upon the throne of the soul,"[19] as Shelley puts it.

This point helps explain the subtitle of my book: "Toward a New Political Romanticism." The notion of working toward this is a reference to one of Carl Schmitt's early books, *Political Romanticism* (1919), in which he claims that Romanticism prepares the way for the triumph of liberalism because it neutralizes—indeed, avoids entirely—the idea of the unconditional. Just three years later, in one of his best-known texts, *Political Theology* (1922), Schmitt famously defines the modern sovereign as "he who decides on the exception."[20] In a radical move, Schmitt insists that the *exception, not law*, grounds modern sovereignty, a claim that aggravates the *aporia* inherent to modern sovereignty by insisting that there is no prior ground to the sovereign's self-institution. There is only an exception that, by definition, is outside the law, a "zone of anomie" in Agamben's terms. Liberalism, according to Schmitt's argument, bypasses this *aporia* by substituting law, whether civil or natural, for God, thus suturing the fundamental incommensurability between the legal political order and the act that institutes it. For him, the claim that the sovereign is grounded on the exception does not simply mean that he locates all political authority in himself when an exceptional situation, such as a state of emergency, arises. It means, rather, that he has the sole right to decide *when* an exception takes place. By deciding on a relation to a space before the law that remains part of the legal order after the law, the sovereign constitutes the border or limit between that which is inside the legal system and that which is outside it.

Schmitt charges Romanticism with an attempt to avoid the exception as the proper ground of modern sovereignty and thus with an evasion of the political itself. In *Political Romanticism*, he locates this avoidance in the "aesthetic attitude" of Romantics such as Friedrich Schlegel and Adam Müller. Schmitt's few brief mentions of the British Romantics (Keats and Wordsworth in particular), though sporadic, do imply that the Romanticism he is considering is broader than just the German Romantics he focuses on more intently. For Schmitt, Romanticism as a movement is a form of occasionalism,[21] which holds that all finite entities are devoid of causal efficiency, and that God is the only true causality. Romanticism retains this basic attitude, according to Schmitt, but displaces its ultimate principle—God—with the free play of the aesthetic imagination. Romanticism, he insists, is "based, first of all, on a specific characteristic attitude toward the world; and second on a specific idea, even if it is not always conscious, of an ultimate authority, an absolute center" ("*einer letzen Instanz, einem absoluten Zentrum*").[22] The English translation, which renders "*letzen Instanz*" as "ultimate authority," obscures the fact that what Schmitt has in mind is not an authority that is already established, but an arbitrary instance or moment that interrupts the possibility of an infinite regress by constituting an absolute starting point. This "absolute center" subsequently organizes an entire field, an entire structure of law, while not itself being subject to the field it organizes.

The absolute center for Romanticism, according to Schmitt, is the free play of the individual imagination. The sovereignty of the aesthetic imagination colonizes every other domain, referring everything to the play of the subjective imagination, privatizing it, reducing every real and substantive opposition (good and evil, friend and enemy) to mere aesthetic contrasts. In short, the Romantics substitute the subjective imagination in place of real ethical and political commitments. Schmitt's argument, therefore, ultimately understands Romanticism as inaugurating a new understanding of the sovereign's relation to the unconditional, but only in the sense that the sovereign becomes sovereign by *refusing to decide*. Romanticism refers every decision to the infinite play of the imagination, which, rather than forming a model for judgment, reduces the groundlessness of decision to the abyss of endless possibility. The limitlessly creative potential of the imagination thus gives way to a total lack of commitment, obscuring a crucial wager over a genuine abyss that would require choice, a decision in which a particular form of the sovereign must emerge. The Romantic grounding of the "last instance" in the imagination, for Schmitt, gives way to an infinite proliferation of political forms, an actualization of potentially anything, which in the end produces no committed or determinate figure of the sovereign, no final authority. Evading the necessity of decision, Romanticism trades the illusion of autonomy for a subjection to the "strongest and most proximate power" ("*der nächsten und stärksten Macht*"),[23] that is, whichever sovereign happens to be in place at the moment. Romanticism's "sublime elevation above definition and decision" ("*die Erhabenheit über Definition und Entscheidung*") is transformed into a subservient attendance upon "alien power and alien decision" ("*fremder Kraft und fremder Entscheidung*").[24] For Schmitt, the sovereign's inability to decide on the exception, and to make that decision his own, is what gives it over to the other, to something outside the sovereign, ultimately destroying his genuine sovereignty. In this view, the Romantic endeavor to rethink modern sovereignty through the imagination ends in the reduction of politics to the whims of the individual subject, which in turn leads to the triumph of liberalism. Schmitt's argument also repeats a number of motifs that define much of what we understand as Romantic ideology, including a claim about its turn away from history toward the caprices of the aesthetic imagination, the production of an aestheticized politics that evades the question of the unconditional, and its passivity in the face of genuine political struggle.

This book contends that the Romantics do, in fact, relate the imagination to the exception that grounds the modern sovereign, but that they conceive of this relation, and of its consequences, very differently from

Schmitt. Indeed, the imagination institutes a relation between the unconditionality of the exception (i.e., something that is exterior to the order that it institutes) and the political. But this relation in Romanticism cannot always be reconciled to Schmitt's decisionist understanding of sovereignty. The relation to the exception that the Romantics articulate produces a theory of the sovereign as constituted by something that cannot be made the object of his autonomous will. Percy Shelley, for example, builds much of his conception of poets as "unacknowledged legislators of the world" on the posthumous dimension of their sovereign creative acts, of which they themselves are not fully aware. Poets are unacknowledged not only by the society that surrounds them but because of the genuinely sovereign nature of their productions. As Shelley puts it, poets are like "the words which express what they understand not, the trumpets which sing to battle and feel not what they inspire."[25] What makes them "sovereign" is not necessarily attributable to their conscious decision.

My readings in this book also show that the Romantics relate the imagination to an unconditionality that is unconditional only by being subject to division and to the finite moment of its institution. While the Romantics still ground sovereignty on the notion of the unconditional, they nonetheless invoke a relation to it that does not necessarily treat it as an absolute, which would in turn produce a figure of absolute sovereignty. Rather, the sovereign's relation to the exception or the unconditional exposes him to an exteriority that he cannot master and reveals that the very thing he requires for legitimacy exceeds his grasp. Romanticism, in other words, takes the need that the sovereign has for the unconditional to its logical extreme, revealing that there is always *more than one* unconditional, and thus always more than one representation of the unconditional. This relation to what is outside the sovereign, but which nevertheless determines him, invokes a logic built into the notion of modern sovereignty that Derrida calls "upping the ante."[26] To repeat: the sovereign by definition can have no instituting authority prior to him. In the absence of a final or absolute unconditionality such as God, however, this fact becomes a ubiquitous threat, which leads to a hyperbolization of sovereignty that radicalizes the status of the exception, placing it outside of any possible mastery.[27] If the sovereign is never able to constitute himself without reference to the finite moment of his institution, then he is always haunted by the figure of something more sovereign than himself, an anteriority that he cannot fully grasp as his own.

Romanticism's investment in the role of fiction and poetry for the construction of political sovereignty constitutes perhaps the most important element of its intervention into political theory. For the Romantics, fiction is what gives the sovereign his force and his right. He operates only by capitalizing on the effect that the work of the imagination offers, which is the image or simulation of an absolute anteriority, the representation of something before the law that he can appropriate as the force of the law's very origin. This is why, for the Romantics, sovereignty must be thought not in relation to the apodictic certainty of an absolute ground, but in relation to the effect of this ground's *fictionalization* or representation, which arises coextensively with the sovereign himself. As they each repeatedly suggest, without this "aesthetic-effect" there is no sovereignty.

The need for this aesthetic-effect has to do with the attempt to realize the exception within the political. The imagination does this by retrospectively delineating the unconditional, giving it a specific shape or form through which it can become the explicit property, the original act or identity, of the sovereign himself. Thus, on the one hand, the imagination acts to reinforce sovereign power and its monopoly over the presentation of a legitimating ground, while on the other, it exacerbates the logic of upping the ante, bringing to a point of absolute tension the internal conflict of the sovereign with himself. If sovereignty is nothing but a hyperbolic excess, something that is always more than or prior to the figure that serves as its representative, what becomes foregrounded is the way that the sovereign attempts to *appropriate* this anteriority, turning himself into its direct representative. It is this sleight of hand that Shelley, for example, will strive to demystify by showing how tyrants and absolute sovereigns derive their authority from masking the conflation of an arbitrary act of positing with an act of the (general) will. The problem, of course, is that the democrat makes the same claim to embody the general will. The fact that both tyrant and democrat alike derive their right to govern from an anteriority that each claims to embody means that Shelley is forced to distinguish the two by turning his attention to the problem of mediation. Hence, as Chapter 4 demonstrates, that which in Shelley's *Mask of Anarchy* separates the illegitimate form of the sovereign ("Anarchy") from its counterpoint ("Hope") is each figure's relation to the anteriority that legitimates it. Whereas the former attempts to identify itself with its own groundless self-assertion, the latter clearly distinguishes its authority from the ground that makes it possible. The alternative form of sovereignty that Shelley calls "Hope" thus openly maintains that the unconditional can only be realized through a purely contingent figure, one that puts the exception to work in ways that cannot necessarily be foreseen, regulated, or measured.

Central for the Romantics is the *form* that the mediation of this anteriority takes, so what often appears in their writing as an abstract meditation on poetry or the imagination carries in fact a significant political dimension. Since the Romantics focus on the *relation* between the sovereign and the (fiction of) anteriority that authorizes him, the *process* that produces authority through this transfer becomes essential. Rather than begin with the assumption that authority pre-exists the one who wields it, the Romantics insist that fiction plays the central role in the instantiation of the sovereign. This is why *Imagined Sovereignties* locates the Romantics' preoccupation with the problem of sovereignty in texts that do not appear at first glance to be straightforwardly political. Though it addresses some key texts of Romantic political theory, this book's main emphasis is on the poetic representation of sovereignty; it explores the concatenation of aesthetics with the unconditional. This involves repeated moments of diremption and displacement in the transfer of power from an unconditional ground to its presentation in the sovereign. The Romantics raise the possibility that the exception that founds the sovereign is no longer strictly identical with it, no longer something upon which it can "decide," in Schmitt's sense. The result, as I show, is that the sovereign becomes centered around what Claude Lefort calls the "empty place of power,"[28] a foundation specific to democracy that is entirely unfixed and indeterminate since democracy entails a mobile and ever-changing relationship between the ground of authority and its manifestation. This certainly means that Romanticism cannot be identified with liberalism, or with an attempt to ground modern politics on the rights and protections of the individual. Though many of the Romantics found common cause with radical liberalism and its emphasis on securing individual rights in the face of hereditary privilege, it is clear that they did not understand this project as the *end* of politics, its chief goal or mission. Describing how they might have conceived of the various possible forms of that end or goal is the task of this book.

Imagined Sovereignties attempts to dispel the prevalent idea that British Romanticism was plagued by various forms of political naiveté and to show that its concatenation of poetry, philosophy, theology, and politics reveals the extent to which aesthetics, or poetics in the classical sense (as "making" in general), is indispensible to a theory of modern sovereignty. The motifs of creation, composition, and production around which Romantic theories of the imagination are organized become analogies for the formations of politics: the creation of states, the founding of republics—indeed, for Shelley this is explicitly his claim. The Romantics witness a moment in which it becomes imperative to account for the sovereign's need for spectacle, for proxies, performance, even a theatrics of power.[29] They repeatedly demonstrate that, in the absence of an absolute ground, the sovereign's need for spectacle, for the imagination, and for the machine of aesthetics, with its desire for a sensuous presentation of the non-sensuous, grows exponentially.

The history of aesthetics and the history of sovereignty become more intimately intertwined after the Romantics. Rather than see the concatenation of aesthetics and the political as Romanticism's "scandal," its aesthetic or Romantic ideology, we can benefit from seeing it as a moment that frames our own modernity. The first two chapters of *Imagined Sovereignties* read how Blake and Coleridge articulate two different attempts to reconcile the vicissitudes of poetics with a reformulation of political theology. Though both remained committed to their respective theologies, the particular relation they establish between these doctrines and the political, as I suggested at the beginning, unleashes a set of *aporias* that are still in many ways "ours" and that continue to activate attempts to question the very precepts of political-theology from within its own edifice.[30] It is not my contention, however, that Romanticism is *the* break with older political forms or with political-theology more generally. Rather, I see it as staging a set of tensions, without resolving them, that point toward more than one alternative, more than one path toward the exit, as it were. It is incumbent upon "we moderns" to sift through this inheritance in order to better understand the outlines of a genuine choice. The texts of Blake's and Coleridge's are never straightforwardly progressive or conservative; instead, they are sites of contestation, often between more than one conflicting tendency. There is no legacy or inheritance without conflict, without the need to choose between different currents within a given tradition. It is this tension that makes Blake's and Coleridge's respective political theologies worthy of continued reexamination.

The last two chapters, on Wordsworth and Shelley, are my attempts to articulate Romanticism's understanding of the relation between poetics and allegedly secular forms of sovereignty. In the cases of Wordsworth and Shelley, this entails generating new models of sovereignty in the wake of the apparent failure of republicanism. Both writers place poetry front and center in their attempts to discover a presentation of the unconditional that will not simply collapse into absolutism. Once sovereignty is no longer reduced to the presentation of transcendence (whether conceived of as the divine or "the people"), the question for Wordsworth and Shelley becomes "what form can and should the sovereign take?" Wordsworth locates an answer in a poetics of the everyday that has as its aim the articulation of a form of community that is neither preexistent nor simply natural. His texts too are conflicted, sometimes returning to liberal republicanism and the concept of natural right that he nonetheless often tries to break with. In the end, however, he presents the conditions of possibility for conceiving a collective form of sovereignty that is irreducible to any natural community (or the *natio*) assumed by any conception of a nation. Shelley—who of the four authors I have chosen is the one perhaps most aware of the radicality of his attempt to wed poetics and politics—discovers a form of sovereignty that not only locates a rupture at the heart of traditional conceptions of the sovereign, but makes this rupture central to his attempt to think the possibility of a counter-sovereignty. In the closing chapter I show that Shelley's counter-sovereignty is more than simply an allegiance to a different absolute ground. It is a break with this very structure or necessity itself, even though he maintains a fidelity to the notion of an anteriority that every sovereign requires to legitimate himself.

The thread that weaves the chapters together, the book's common denominator, concerns this anteriority of the sovereign, its status, its relation to the sovereign, and the role of poetics in actualizing it. The reconceptualization of this anteriority is a quintessential Romantic motif: it constitutes the key to understanding Romanticism's particular intervention in the history of the concept of sovereignty and the various connections it establishes between politics and aesthetics. *Imagined Sovereignties* shows that Romanticism witnesses a critical mutation in the history of the concept of sovereignty. Not only does it intensify the possibility that there may be more than one anteriority that grounds the sovereign, but it also emphasizes that there is always more than one relation to this multiple *archē*. If the era of traditional sovereignty, as recent theorists have tried to demonstrate,[31] is slowly coming to an end, the beginning of this end coincides with Romanticism. A thinking of what comes after this end finds a powerful resource in its texts.

ONE

"Honest Indignation Is the Voice of God": Blake and Political Theology

> What Jesus came to Remove was the Heathen, or Platonic Philosophy, which blinds the Eye of Imagination. The Real Man.
>
> —BLAKE, *Annotations to Reynolds*

> If repetition is possible, it is due to miracle rather than to law. It is against law: against the similar form and the equivalent content of law. If repetition can be found, even in nature, it is in the name of a power which affirms itself against the law, which works underneath laws, perhaps superior to laws. If repetition exists, it expresses at once a singularity opposed to the general, a universality opposed to the particular, a distinctive opposed to the ordinary, an instantaneity opposed to variation, and an eternity opposed to permanence.
>
> —DELEUZE, *Difference and Repetition*

Blake's poetry is seemingly so esoteric that it might be deemed an unusual place to begin an argument about the contemporary valence of Romantic theories of the political imagination. The difficulty of his poetry has sometimes led to his dismissal as a mere eccentric. Coming from an inherited antinomian enthusiasm,[1] his work seems like an anachronism in relation to his own time, much less a continued resource for our own. Saree Makdisi's recent landmark study[2] has challenged this prevailing view of Blake, showing how Blake questioned many of the dominant orthodoxies of his time, including the tradition of radical liberalism and its notions of political, religious, and economic freedom. He was, in other words, far from a mere eccentric. As David Erdman demonstrated long ago, Blake was strongly influenced by the events of his time—particularly the American and French Revolutions—and sought to engage the question of what these events might mean, *post festum* or otherwise. The significance of Makdisi's insight consists in his reading of this aspect in Blake not as a rewriting of historical events into mythological terms, but as an engagement with the historical and political conditions that produced them. Although Blake's conception of what constitutes these conditions is very different from perspectives represented by contemporary political theory or history, his work is engaged, at a fundamental level, in an attempt to reconstitute what "politics" or "history" might mean. To do so is not to become apolitical or ahistorical, but to force the reader to suspend what he or she might understand these terms to signify. It is from this basic understanding of Blake's project that this chapter sets out to comprehend how he grappled with the transition from a form of sovereignty predicated on a specific conception of the divine to one that is grounded in what appears to be the secular foundation of Man. Blake's work is uniquely positioned in this context; not only does it make claims about the inherent divinity of Man—"the human form divine"[3] as he calls it—it also seeks to understand the connections between theological forms and their materialization in politics.

Blake's investment in the imagination (or, as he calls it early on, "poetic genius") is positioned at a crossroads. Seeing clearly that a particular conception of God, which acts as a figure of ultimate sovereignty, has helped perpetrate all manner of political repression, Blake is nevertheless unwilling to cede the notion of political freedom to a secularism he suspects is capable of reproducing many of the old forms of repression and giving them new names and justifications. What matters to him instead is a *reconstruction of the relation* between theology and the political, the *reinvention* of the understanding of this relation, and the problem of representation that goes with it.

Blake's early work in particular is concerned with this question. *America: A Prophecy*, set during the American Revolution, explicitly casts the rebel Orc against the forces of Urizen (linked with Albion's British imperial forces). Although Urizen takes many forms throughout Blake's work, on the whole he is taken to represent abstract Reason (the God of radical liberalism) or the traditional Christian God. Blake thus aligns specific forms of power—imperial, ecclesiastical, and civil—with the understanding of the divine, and the notion of transcendence, that Urizen represents. What interests Blake is the way in which any resistance to a politics that emerges out of a particular conception of the divine or the infinite *must nonetheless have recourse to another conception* in order to contest it. At stake is not just a critique of deism or traditional Christianity, but an attempt to show how the apparently radical distinction between a divinely ordained sovereign and a popularly ordained one requires a different political theology. Positioned at a crucial historical turning point in the concept of sovereignty, Blake recognizes that political theology cannot simply be overcome by a secularism that keeps the old structures intact and merely substitutes new names for them: Reason in place of God, the individual sovereign subject in place of the Monarch. For Blake these are all modes of perception, ways of understanding the world that, though apparently opposed, share basic formal structures that his work seeks to uncover and dismantle. Rather than attempt to reinvent a theology appropriate to Man's newfound political authority, Blake instead attempts to show the way these self-perpetuating structures are predicated on the forgetting of a prior conception of God, Man, and the Infinite. His work seeks to hasten the collapse of dominant forms of political theology by demonstrating how the structures of transcendence that authorize certain forms of sovereignty at the political and the individual levels are merely limited modes of a much wider theologically inflected understanding of politics. For Blake, it is a matter of twisting free of a dominant mode of political theology so that other connections between the theological and the political can be liberated. Poetic genius or the imagination, for the early Blake especially, constitutes the central site in which this reconceptualization of political theology takes place.

A full account of Blake's theology would be a daunting undertaking, one that cannot reasonably be offered here. This chapter is therefore less an interpretation of the specifics of Blake's theology, its influences and references, than an attempt to understand how Blake presents what one might call the *hyphen* in "political-theology." In other words, I will not address the question of how Blake's theology is developed or constructed, but concentrate instead on how Blake understands the *relation* between the mythology he constructs and the understanding of the political it necessitates.

What follows is a series of readings of four early texts by Blake: *The Marriage of Heaven and Hell* (1793), *The Book of Urizen* (1794), *America: A Prophecy* (1793), and his unillustrated poem *The French Revolution* (1791). These works contain some of Blake's clearest formulations of the relation between theology and politics. While the later epic poems begin to complicate and qualify this theme, their basic coordinates are established in the early works. *The Marriage of Heaven and Hell*, for example, provides some key images for Blake's conception of poetic genius, while *The Book of Urizen* establishes the relationship between certain forms of theological thinking and the kinds of authority they legitimate. *America: A Prophecy*, on the other hand, articulates a conception of how these forms can be contested by opening up, through the imagination, a relation to the infinite as an attempt to think something unprecedented or, in Blake's terms, "impossible." He famously writes later in *A Descriptive Catalogue* (1809) that what traditional historians fail to account for in their narratives, focused as they are on mere "probabilities," are "miracles": "Historians . . . who being weakly organized themselves, cannot see either miracle or prodigy; all is to them a dull round of probabilities and possibilities; but the history of all times and places, is nothing else but improbabilities and impossibilities; what we should say, was impossible if we did not see it always before our eyes" (DC, E543). The emergence of Orc in *America: A Prophecy* is one of Blake's first attempts to poetically represent the American Revolution as the emergence of such a "miracle or prodigy" and to understand it as the result of a transformed relation to the infinite. In his rendering, the American Revolution is not just a political revolution but a cultural and theological one as well because it challenges the imaginative structures of perception that make certain forms of authority and sovereignty possible. Blake effectively revises the meaning of the American Revolution by retrospectively insisting that it attempts to do more than simply replace one sovereign with another—it attempts to challenge the very nature of sovereignty itself. Blake's representation of Orc acts as a prophecy that the American Revolution is incomplete and that other forms of democracy are still possible. The chapter concludes with a reading of Blake's *French Revolution* to suggest that for him even secularism is infused with assumptions about the infinite that either underpin or destabilize its conceptions of political legitimacy and social organization. As with the American Revolution in *America: A Prophecy*, Blake revises the significance of the French Revolution, interpreting it as an attempt to imagine a new form of the body politic that might emerge in the wake of the collapse of absolute sovereignty. What is at stake in each case, I argue, is Blake's attempt to revise the relation between politics and the theology that informs it in order to redefine the very meaning of political theology itself.

Urizen and Absolute Sovereignty

In Blake's pantheon of recurring mythological figures Urizen represents at once a figure of reason, of limitation (his name itself is suggestive of "horizon"), deism, and the vengeful and moral God of the Old Testament. In short, he tends to encapsulate a variety of forms of power as creator of empire, domination, and uniformity. In *America: A Prophecy* he is linked with the British imperial project, with slavery, the repression of sexuality, and numerous other forms of control and limitation. What connects all these forms of oppression and dominance, for Blake, are the metaphysical structures that Urizen represents. He constitutes a figure for a transcendent ground that introduces binary oppositions into the world (body and mind, male and female, good and evil) while privileging one side of the opposition over the other. Common to all of these instances is the way Urizen abstracts himself from the process that he initiates. His creation of the world of oppositions, for instance, exempts him from their hold over him. Though he fashions a dualist world, he himself is above the dualism he creates. It is this process of abstraction and the creation of *exceptionalism* that constitutes Urizen's authority. By making himself the exception to the moral, juridical, or political order that he institutes he makes himself the ruler of that order, a judge whose exemption from the law is precisely what gives the law its force and alleged neutrality. No longer immanent to the world he has produced, Urizen creates a transcendent beyond with which he identifies himself and that confers on him an authority that nothing else can match.

It is the process of constructing this exceptionalism that Blake's *Book of Urizen* relates. The poem is an ironic rewriting of the book of Genesis[4] with Urizen in the position of the creator-God who fashions the world, and eventually Man, in his own image. It begins with Urizen's emergence out of the world of the eternals and relates not only how he generates the idea of transcendence that gives him power, but also how he begins the process of incarnation and the delegation of that power, producing the priesthood and other institutions of authority. Urizen is clearly, even early on in Blake's work, a figure for a specific form of the relation between the theological and the political. One of the major themes of the poem—Urizen's creation of divine transcendence—in fact, becomes the basis for religious and secular forms of domination and tyranny. The ultimate focus of the poem, however, is the conception of the infinite that Urizen enacts in this process. When he creates the notion of a transcendent beyond, he also begins the process of reconceiving the relation between the finite and the infinite. It is this quasi-theological problem that, for Blake, becomes the central pillar of Urizen's power, his hold on the imagination, and what must be broken if Urizenic forms of thought and religion are to be challenged. The poem finally demonstrates how Urizen cordons off the infinite from the finite, placing them in opposition to each other. This process outlines what, for Blake, is an unsettling relationship between the theological and the political, a relationship that ends up producing a form of absolute sovereignty. Urizen thus represent not just the Christian God, or Reason, but any form of absolutism, including its various political expressions.

Much of the poem focuses on Urizen's self-defining gesture and what results from it: the division of Eternity into the opposition between the finite and the infinite. Makdisi's suggestion that we understand Blake's conception of the infinite in terms of Deleuze's reading of Spinoza is critical for an understanding of this work[5] since it implies a theory of differentiation, individuation, and the conception of a "plane of immanence" that helps explain what Blake means by the "rending" of Eternity at the beginning of the poem. Rather than think of individuals or individual things as determinate forms, substances, or subjects, Spinoza conceives them principally in terms of the relation they have to each other and the position they have within a field of forces, affects, and bodies. What defines these relations is not external to the relations themselves—they are related to each other through their mutual belonging to a common immanent and divine body (which Spinoza calls "God"). Eternity in *The Book of Urizen*, prior to Urizen's emergence, likewise is an immanent plane, which Urizen irrevocably transforms in his first creative act by dividing Eternity from itself and by producing a transcendence that establishes something distinct from it. The first line in the first chapter describes a "horror" that has "risen/in Eternity! Unknown, unprolific! Self-closd, all-repelling" (BU 3:1–3, E70). Though the pronoun "he" that appears in stanza two clearly refers to Urizen, the speaker in the first stanza initially seems unsure whether the "abominable void" and "soul-sudd'ring vacuum" (BU 3:4–5, E70) are identical with Urizen. Its (or his) characterization as a "dark power" (BU 3:7, E70) has to do with the fact that he has become a "secret," something withdrawn from the Eternal world in which he was formed. The insistence on describing this process as the creation of a "void" or a "vacuum" suggests that Eternity knew no absence or negation prior to Urizen. What follows from it is the creation of time and space: "Times on times he divided, & measur'd/Space by space in his ninefold darkness/Unseen, unknown!" (BU 3:7–9, E70). Though the notion of measurement, which by definition suggests something finite, is seemingly already antithetical to Eternity, Urizen's capacity to measure the world is made possible by the fact that he himself stands outside of measurement and finitude, remaining "unseen" and "unknown." Measurement and finitude become possible through the creation and sacralization of something *beyond measure*.

Thus, while much of the poem appears to link Urizen with the creation of a fallen, finite world, his singular act appears to be an attempt to *exempt* himself from the very divisions that he unleashes. In chapter two, for example, when the Earth has yet to be formed, the solitary Urizen, who becomes the speaker of the poem for the first time, describes his motivation for dividing Eternity:

> From the depths of dark solitude. From
> The eternal abode in my holiness,
> Hidden set apart in my stern counsels
> Reserv'd for the days of futurity
> I have sought for a joy without pain,
> For a solid without fluctuation
> Why will you die O Eternals?
> Why live in unquenchable burnings? (BU 4:6–13, E71)

In his first speech, Urizen makes clear that what prompts his rending of Eternity is a desire to isolate oppositions from each other, to create a "joy without pain," and to stabilize something "solid without fluctuation." The last two questions from the passage address the other Eternals and, rather than constituting a threat, appear to want to entice them to his side. The "unquenchable burnings" he refers to in the final question concern the desire for solidity, for a world that does not contain all contraries in one "body." In other words, Urizen's desire here is for something much closer to what is usually understood by the word "eternity"—something outside of time, fluctuation, and decay. As Urizen insists, his emergence required that he fight "with the fire; consum'd / Inwards, into a deep world within" (BU 4:14–15, E72), suggesting that the "unquenchable burnings" of the previous line refer both to desire and to the basic composition of Eternity itself, which is made up of the elements but paradoxically has no solidity or stability. It is only once Urizen conquers its fluidity, repelling the "vast waves" and raising up "on the waters / A wide world of solid obstruction" (BU 4:22–23, E72) that he distinguishes himself from it by becoming sovereign, solitary, and separated from the unstable world of Eternity.

The image that accompanies plate four depicts Urizen revealing the "secrets of wisdom" (BU 4:25, E72) through his now universal "Book / Of eternal brass" (BU 4:32–33, E72). Urizen towers above his book, whose spine is aligned perfectly with the space between the double-column format of Blake's text below it. The image of Urizen's book depicts no text, but its juxtaposition with Blake's words below it is a contrast between the solidity of Urizen's new order represented by the book of brass and Blake's poetry. The image of the "book of brass" is highly suggestive, since its multicolored surface is reminiscent of the copper plates Blake constructed to compose his poetry, bringing to mind the image of an unevenly oxidized metal surface. The image sets in relief the relative stability and solidity of Urizen's "book" with Blake's text, revealing that what is about to emerge out of Urizen's division of Eternity is the world of representation and the difference between models and copies. Urizen's book of brass, like Blake's copper plates, constitutes an original to the text as copy. But in the case of Urizen's book, the model or original is a point at which all laws merge toward a single unified ground of authority, a single law that raises itself above the order it establishes, setting it into place. This is the act that Urizen represents: a point outside of Eternity, exempt from it, that organizes the world into a "solid world of obstruction," one of coherent laws that derive from the same origin:

> Lo! I unfold my darkness: and on
> This rock, place with strong hand the Book
> Of eternal brass, written in my solitude.
> Laws of peace, of love, of unity:
> Of pity, compassion, forgiveness.
> Let each chuse one habitation:
> His ancient infinite mansion:
> One command, one joy, one desire,

Figure 1. The Book of Urizen, copy D, plate 4 (Erdman plate 4). © Trustees of the British Museum.

> One curse, one weight, one measure
> One King, one God, one Law. (BU 4:31–40, E72)

The book that emerges out of Urizen's solitude introduces a set of laws that standardize, solidify, and govern a whole series of things. Presented as laws of "peace, love, and unity," their dominance becomes apparent in the ruse of "choice" that governs what has now become a single unified order. Rather than a multiplicity, Eternity has become consolidated around the repeated "one" of the final lines of the passage, which links political and legal authority ("one command"), moral or sexual authority ("one joy," "one desire"), the universalization of time and space ("one weight, one measure") with the notion of divine right: "One King, one God, one Law."

The establishment of Urizen's authority in Blake's poem is thus far more than a simple retelling of the book of Genesis from a dissenting viewpoint. Rather, it is a myth about the creation of a false universalism[6] that establishes itself as law through the materialization of a sacred exteriority, something transcendent to the order it establishes. *The Book of Urizen* allegorizes the construction of this exteriority, in whatever form it takes. Once it has been established, it can then act as a solid, absolute ground. Urizen, thus, represents not only the transcendence and sovereignty of a traditional Christian God, but also the notion of an unconditional universal ground more generally. Understanding Urizen as a figure that unites divine right models of sovereignty with more modern allegedly democratic ones aligns with Jon Mee's claim that the sources of Blake's radicalism must be located outside the dominant liberal tradition of the period. For Blake, the radical liberalism and deism represented by writers like Paine merely replaces reference to an abstract deity with an equally abstract form of Reason or Natural Law. As Mee suggests: "Where Reason is reified into an abstract God, as Urizen seems to do in the mythology Blake develops from the mid-1790s, then it too is no more than a delusive object of worship. If radical politics abstracted the individual from the sum of human brotherhood in its stress on the autonomy of the reasoning power, then it perpetuated a 'mystery' as destructive of human potential as the 'State Religion' it wished to displace."[7] Insofar as Urizen allegorizes a structure that includes the secular theology of reason, he represents any attempt to valorize political or religious authority through some form of transcendence.

Blake's poem continuously focuses not just on the abstraction necessary for Urizen to rule, but on the way in which this abstraction is given shape or materialized in the finite world of bodies. What follows from Urizen's self-declaration is his construction of a form of transcendence that is outside the world of Eternity, which is figured as either a "void," a "womb," or a "globe." Though the first image suggests an opposition between the plenitude that constitutes Eternity and a vacuum, a nothingness that nevertheless has shape and form, the latter two images suggest a form of self-enclosure, something turned in on itself, creating a form of interiority that did not previously exist. The womb image occurs first in the passage from plate four cited earlier, when Urizen declares that his battle with the "fire" of Eternity "consum'd" him "Inwards, into a deep world within" (BU 4:15, E72). It appears again just prior to the introduction of Los, who represents the creative imagination and who will in the end be the one that gives Urizen a body, a form, and a reality. Urizen, bounding the horizon of Eternity, builds:

> And a roof, vast petrific around,
> On all sides He fram'd: like a womb;
> Where thousands of rivers in veins
> Of blood pour down the mountains to cool
> The eternal fires beating without
> From Eternals; & like a black globe
> View'd by sons of Eternity, standing
> On the shore of the infinite ocean
> Like a human heart strugling & beating
> The vast world of Urizen appear'd. (BU 5:28–37, E73)

The transcendent void or womb that Urizen creates is indissociable from the distinction it introduces between exteriority and interiority. Prior to Urizen's construction of his separation from the world of Eternity, there is no concept of interiority and no valorization of identity. Urizen's construction of the void links the creation of his sense of sovereign self with the unified Law that closes chapter two. The "deep world within" that Urizen constructs leads not only to the "wide world of solid obstruction" without, but to a crucial sense of sovereign identity. Urizen's battle with the elements leaves him "self balanc'd stretch'd o'er the void / I alone, even I!" (BU 4:18–19, E72). This notion of an "I alone," a self that is independent and detached from its surroundings, is made possible by an act of division that creates the opposition between interiority and exteriority. Blake thus links at least two forms of sovereignty to Urizen's creation of transcendence: the universal laws that culminate chapter two, as well as the notion of a sovereign self. In both cases an authority or controlling force is created that, though it cannot be seen or known, remains hidden behind the external manifestations of its power.

Urizen's division is thus also what institutes the problem of representation in Blake. If the genuinely authoritative source is always unseen, couched in mystery, the question then is how it manifests itself—in other words, how it comes to be represented and how the force of its authority comes to be felt, seen, or heard. Urizen's power is partly generated by the extent to which his transcendence remains not only abstract but unknown, impenetrable to knowledge, since he is the one figure capable of embodying or granting access to it. His division of Eternity thus does more than create a fallen material world. It erects a structure of reference that organizes the world around an absent center that becomes the secret truth it embodies. Urizen writes the "secrets of wisdom" (BU 4:25, E72). The womb or "void" he produces is "fathomless" (6:5, E74), "unseen," and "unknown" (BU 3:10, E70). Once it has been produced, it becomes a source of authority because the question becomes who has the right to represent it or give it shape. The preludium to the poem, which is actually set after the events of *The Book of Urizen*, alludes to this problem in the "assumption" of power by Urizen's priests: "Of the primeval Priests assum'd power, / When Eternals spurn'd back his religion; / And gave him a place in the north, / Obscure, shadowy, void, solitary" (BU 2:1–14, E70). When the priests assume power, they do so in the name of Urizen's "obscure" and "shadowy" authority. As proxies, their power flows from Urizen's transcendence, as they in turn become ministers of his arcane secrets, official priests of his mystery.

Though the first part of the poem focuses on Urizen's division of Eternity and his construction of a unified source of authority, much of the rest of the poem concentrates on the means by which Urizen's "abstraction," his separation, conditions the material world. The introduction of Los, a figure for the imagination, is the crucial link between the formal structure of power that Urizen represents and its embodiment. It is the imagination that animates Urizen's machinations, giving him an (allegorical) body by realizing the "formless unmeasurable death" (BU 7:9, E74) that constitutes his source of power. The naturalization of Urizen's authority takes place when Los builds the "mind-forg'd manacles" that produce a series of links and chains that become time itself: "The Eternal Prophet heavd the dark bellows, / And turn'd restless the tongs; and the hammer / Incessant beat; forging chains new & new / Numb'ring with links, hours, days & years" (BU 10:15–18, E75). Los's creation of the chains of necessity does more than produce succession, it introduces a "forgetfulness," a sense of inevitability that things could not be otherwise: "Forgetfulness, dumbness, necessity! / In chains of the mind locked up, / Like fetters of ice shrinking together / Disorganiz'd, rent from Eternity" (BU 10:24–27, E75). Urizen embodies this "chain of necessity" by becoming a vast spine that slowly materializes into a human form trapped by his senses.[8]

The image on plate seven depicts Urizen as a skeleton who is slowly being given the contours of a body by Los, starting with the spine and ribs, which are clearly accentuated in the image, to which Los then adds the "branches" (BU 11:6, E76) of the nerves and muscles, the brain and heart (BU 11:11–12, E76), and eventually the organs of the five senses, which close themselves to Eternity and augur the division between the infinite and the finite.

A crucial element of Blake's allegory of Urizenic sovereignty is the fact that the imagination (Los) ratifies Urizen's authority by giving physical shape to his abstraction. The imagination, for Blake, is more than the power of recalling absent memories or images. It is fundamentally productive, capable of producing the material.[9] The imagination's incarnation of Urizen's formal abstraction is what gives his sovereignty shape and form, localizing it or representing it in a specific body, say, of a King. Once Los has formed Urizen's body, he looks back on his work only to encounter it as a "space undivided by existence" (BU 13:46, E77). This paradoxical phrase (since it is hard to conceive of a place or a body that is part of the spatio-temporal world but would not have "existence") suggests a physical manifestation of something without substance. Blake later calls Los's creation the "death-image of Urizen" (BU 15:2, E78), producing an image or mask that embodies an absence, something hinted at but never fully made manifest.

The end of the poem sees Urizen's children finally succumb to his "Net of Religion" (BU 25:22, E82), forgetting "their eternal life" (BU 25:42, E83)

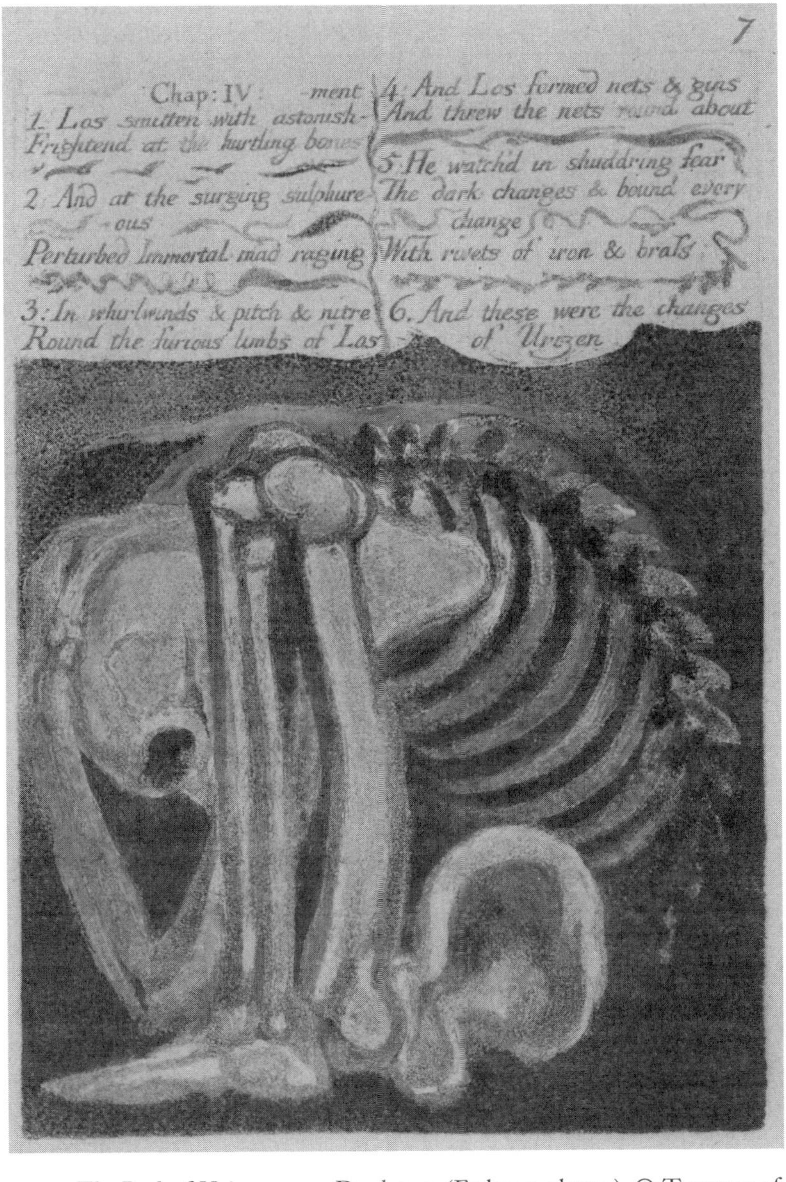

Figure 2. The Book of Urizen, copy D, plate 7 (Erdman plate 7). © Trustees of the British Museum.

and obeying the "laws of prudence," which they call "the eternal law of God" (BU 28:6–7, E83). One of these children—Orc—will eventually emerge to challenge Urizen's rule and will become a key figure for understanding how Blake conceives of resistance to Urizenic forms of sovereignty. Though Blake stages the confrontation between Orc and Urizen through a reading of the American Revolution, the allegory of Urizenic sovereignty in *The Book of Urizen* reveals a complex system through which his authority is maintained, even where it appears to be most seriously challenged. The sovereign is incarnated as the representation of a transcendence, an exteriority that can be given only in negative form through the opposition between a transcendent ground that acts as an "unseen" model and its visible copy. For Blake, a genuine challenge to this structure cannot simply seek to appropriate it for other ends; instead it must break with the static conception of the eternal or the infinite implied by it and destroy the system of representation or incarnation it relies on. Blake thus attempts to show that the imagination, potentially placed at the service of power, is also necessarily resistant to it because it remains in contact with a notion of the infinite that cannot be made to correspond with an absolute ground. As such, the imagination breaks with the monopolization of transcendence by a single figure or representative.

Between Two Infinites: The Space of the Political

Because Urizen's dominance has been materialized by Los, the temporal manifestation of the imagination, resistance to Urizenic forms of sovereignty requires a return to the moment at which the imagination naturalized the metaphysical structures that henceforth appear as "chains of necessity." Blake's poetry constantly gestures toward a moment prior to the one in which Urizen's logic became naturalized, attempting to overcome the "forgetting" of a different conception of the infinite. The imagination is the crucial site for this critique because it is what gives form and shape to the formless and therefore articulates the realization or instantiation of the very notion of an absolute ground. Because of its complicity in the ascendency of Urizenic forms of thinking, the imagination is not just the means for, but also the very object of, liberation.

However, this attempt to return back to a moment prior to the imagination's construction of the chains of necessity should not be read as a form of nostalgia. For Blake, there is no return back to the plenitude of an Eternity prior to the construction of the world of oppositions, and no apocalypse or final unveiling of truth.[10] His poetic intervention instead attempts to show that Urizenic logic is ultimately grounded on something irreconcilable to the system it erects. This externality is generated by the same logic of transcendence, a gesture toward something prior to, or *more sovereign* than, Urizenic forms of sovereignty. Blake's early conception of the imagination (what he initially calls "poetic genius") often appears to reduplicate the Urizenic notion of a transcendent ground that is the source of all oppositions. However, his notion of poetic genius and its relation to the particular figures it makes possible is irreducible to this logic in two significant ways. First, it disrupts any notion of incarnation that entails a synthesis of the visible and the invisible, challenging the hierarchy between figure and ground that this presupposes. Second, it calls into question a quasi-theological conception of infinity that could act as a solid ground, a stable origin, for the world or be represented by a political figure. For Blake, the infinite, properly understood, always includes and exceeds the finite, calling into question any act that would attempt to identify it as a static essence.

As always, the difficulty of discussing Blake's conception of the imagination is that it is not clear whether Blake ever embraced a single defining meaning of the word. In his late epic *Jerusalem*, for example, he comes close to suggesting that the imagination constitutes a condition of existence for all that is, since "All Things Exist in the Human Imagination" (J 69:25, E223). In the engraving to the Laocoön, Blake understands imagination as the mediation between divinity and Man: "The Eternal Body of Man is the Imagination, that is, God himself, The Divine Body, [Yeshua] Jesus we are his Members" (E273). In this view, the imagination not only links the divine and Man but in fact *is* both of them. When Blake writes in the *Annotations to Berkeley* that "Man is All Imagination God is Man & exists in us & we in him" (E664) this should not be mistaken for a humanization of what had formerly been the domain of a separate divine power. It is a claim about the coextension of God and Man—their indiscernibility. Early on in the development of his political theology in *The Marriage of Heaven and Hell*, Blake challenged belief in a God who acts as the sole, sovereign source of creation: "Some will say, Is not God alone the Prolific?" (MHH 16, E40). The reply counters: "I answer, God only Acts & Is, in existing beings or Men" (MHH 16, E40). Notably, the purported humanization of God as the imagination does not center itself in Man only, but in "existing beings" more generally. Like Spinoza's understanding of God, the Imagination is at once bodily *and* spiritual, human *and* divine.

Blake first spells out his notion of poetic genius in an early work (*All Religions Are One*), the form of which is a systematic presentation of principles. Blake's "first principle," the starting point for his system, is the notion of poetic genius. Following the opening argument that claims that the "true faculty of knowing must be the faculty which experiences" (ARO, E1), Blake goes on to define this faculty: "That the Poetic Genius is the true Man. and that the body or outward form of Man is derived from the Poetic Genius. Likewise that the forms of all things are derived from their Genius" (ARO, E1). Blake, in fact, articulates a complex relationship between the apparently transcendent origin of poetic genius and the infinite variety it makes possible. One way to interpret this relationship is to privilege the priority and unity of poetic genius and to designate it as the source of all that is, which results in a kind of poetic Platonism.[11] The trouble with this understanding of poetic genius is that Blake consistently contests this particular sense of its *a priori* unity. In *The Marriage of Heaven and Hell*, for instance, he critiques the system that was erected by the priesthood of ancient England after the poets had "animated all sensible objects with Gods or Geniuses" (MHH 11, E38). The priesthood's power was created when it "took advantage of & enslav'd the vulgar by attempting to realize or abstract the mental deities from their objects" (MHH 11, E38). Blake's claim, which follows from the principles of *All Religions Are One*, is that poetic genius and the "outward forms" that it makes possible cannot be dissociated or abstracted from each other. There is no realized unity of poetic genius prior to its animation and production of the infinite variety of sensible objects.

How, then, does one separate poetic genius from Urizenic transcendence? Blake emphasizes the way that each exemplifies a different relation between the finite and the infinite. Urizen grounds his authority on a conception of infinity that can be abstracted from the world and thus appropriated as a singular source of authority since it is distinct from, and superior to, the finite world. This abstraction, however, means that the infinite is defined by the finite, since it is thus understood as some *thing* that surpasses the finite. Poetic genius, on the other hand, conceives of the infinite as immanent to the finite. It does not exist outside of the finite—it is, rather, its very condition, and therefore no finite instance can ever have a privileged access or a more proximate connection to it. The task of his poetry, as Blake himself repeatedly affirms in *The Marriage of Heaven and Hell*, is to make the finite "appear infinite and holy, whereas it now appears finite and corrupt" (MHH 14, E39). This, however, involves more than simply revealing an infinite that lies "behind" the finite world.[12] The perception of the sensuous world as "finite and corrupt" is, in fact, what occurs when one understands infinity as separate from the finite, rendering any sensuous particular inadequate to it.

Blake's proposal in *The Marriage of Heaven and Hell* about "melting apparent surfaces away" to reveal "the infinite which was hid" (MHH 14, E39) must be read not as an apocalyptic claim, but as an attempt to invoke a different relation to what is "already the case," already "there" in the sensuous world. The famous line that follows—"If the doors of perception were cleansed every thing would appear to man as it is: infinite" (MHH 14, E39)—does not entail a departure from the senses but a return to them. The "doors of perception" must be "cleansed," not circumvented, and what must be removed is the notion that perception gives access only to finite objects, distinct from the infinity of God. The opening of Blake's "Auguries of Innocence" suggests that the infinite is a constitutive feature of the finite and the senses the only doors needed to access it: "To see a World in a Grain of Sand / And a Heaven in a Wild Flower / Hold Infinity in the palm of your hand / And Eternity in an hour" (AI 1–4, E490). Infinity can be felt and held precisely because it is not something separate from the temporal world. For Blake, one does not melt away the finite to pass into the transcendent realm of the infinite. It is rather the opposite: one is returned to a differently conceived *finite* world when it is no longer considered distinct from the infinite. In order to go back behind the moment at which Urizen's creation of a transcendent conception of the infinite was inaugurated, Blake attempts to indicate the way something can be both radically finite *and* infinite simultaneously.

Blake's use of the image of a vortex in his later epic poem *Milton* (1804) provides some insight into his early understanding of the interaction of two different conceptions of the infinite. In his descent to Earth, Milton passes through a vortex, an image that Blake uses to define Milton's opening toward a different conception of infinity:

> The nature of infinity is this: That every thing has its
> Own Vortex; and when once a traveller thro Eternity.
> Has passd that Vortex, he perceives it roll backward behind
> His path, into a globe itself infolding; like a sun:
> Or like a moon, or like a universe of starry majesty,
> While he keeps onwards in his wondrous journey on the earth
> Or like a human form, a friend with whom he livd benevolent.
> As the eye of man views both the east & west encompassing
> Its vortex; and the north & south, with all their starry host;
> Also the rising sun & setting moon he views surrounding
> His corn-fields and his valleys of five hundred acres square.
> Thus is the earth one infinite plane, and not as apparent
> To the weak traveller confin'd beneath the moony shade.
> Thus is the heaven a vortex passd already, and the earth
> A vortex not yet pass'd by the traveller thro' Eternity. (M 15:21–35, E109)

A vortex is a theory of the universe that involves the ". . . rotary movement of cosmic matter round a centre or axis, regarded as accounting for the origin or phenomena of the terrestrial and other systems."[13] In other words, a vortex constitutes the image of an absent center and as such provides a concise figure for Urizen's transcendent conception of the infinite. However, what initially appears to Milton as the "all" becomes an enclosed and limited "globe" once he has passed through it.[14] Milton moves from a conception of the infinite as a focal point or center to a realization of the partiality of that view of infinity. The image of the vortex thus becomes a figure for the mutual coexistence of two different conceptions of the infinite: the Urizenic conception that treats it as a stable locus around which "the many" is organized, and an infinite that is constantly displacing itself, fracturing into multiple loci. Once Milton passes through the vortex to reveal that what was initially considered infinite is, in fact, only a *partial* conception of infinity, the vortex "roll[s] backward behind his path" and becomes a series of "globes." Ronald Grimes correctly claims that this passage ". . . suggests that one can transcend any particular space-time situation, but to do so is not to escape being situated altogether."[15] The infolding of the vortex into a globe "like a sun" or "like a moon" suggests a shifting of perspectives from one center to another: from the sun, which makes the Earth peripheral, to the moon, which makes it central. The fact that the vortex also "infolds" like a "universe of starry majesty" reveals that this center is constantly displaced no matter what magnitude one views it from. There is thus no identity to the infinite, only an endlessly receding limit that gives way to a proliferating series at virtually every level of existence. As lines 21–22 suggest, "every thing has its own Vortex." Even the domains of Heaven and Earth are conceived as "infinite plane[s]" or vortices that have already been passed through or not yet encountered. If this is the case, then everything is at once finite and infinite, rather than divided between a finite (or Earthly) nature and an infinite (or Heavenly) beyond. And crucially, for Blake, without this division there is no transcendence for a sovereign to mediate or incarnate, only an endlessly receding limit that delocalizes the infinite as a ground upon which power or representation can erect itself permanently.[16]

The difference between the two conceptions of the infinite, then, is not essential or definitional, but has to do with whether the infinite can be grasped in a single identifiable figure, something stable and absolute, originating from a standpoint outside the particular. When Ezekiel, in *The Marriage of Heaven and Hell*, claims that he is never able to see or hear God "in a finite organical perception," but that his senses "discover'd the infinite in every thing," (MHH 12, E38) it is this very conception of the infinite in the finite that Blake is developing. Though God can never be *reduced* to a finite figure or representation, he can be found *only* in what Blake calls "minute particulars."[17] This term sometimes refers to individuals, or particular things, while at other times appears to indicate the smallest conceivable unit of time or space. In either case, Blake wants to stress that the infinite is immanent to the particular and thus fundamentally indissociable from it. A passage from Blake's later epic *Jerusalem* (1804) is useful for grasping the relation between the infinite and the "minute particular":

> Let all Indefinites be thrown into Demonstrations
> To be pounded to dust & melted in the Furnaces of Affliction:
> He who would do good to another, must do it in Minute Particulars
> General Good is the plea of the scoundrel hypocrite & flatterer:

For Art & Science cannot exist but in minutely organized Particulars
And not in generalizing Demonstrations of the Rational Power.
The infinite alone resides in Definite and Determinate Identity.
(J 55:58–64, E205)

A Blakean ethics is hinted at here, which bypasses the general altogether (and with it the quasi-utilitarian conception of the "general good"). The desire to do good must not be mediated by an abstract law or a command that comes from anywhere but the particular itself, and least of all from the dictates of a rational moral law.[18] The imagination, though corrupted, nevertheless contains the chance or hope that a return to the "minute particular" will not only challenge the basis of Urizenic universalism but open up an ethics and politics predicated on the recognition of each one's infinite otherness. Blake's notion of poetic genius entails an insistence that the infinite encountered in each "minute particular" is never the same. Since it "alone resides in Definite and Determinate Identity," it cannot become an exclusive foundation for the sovereign, but is in fact shared "equally" by everything finite. As a political-theological principle, this will necessitate a mode of commonality that is not organized by any identification with a single representative, or representative body, of a transcendent ground upon which a community or state might be formed. For Blake, the return to a conception of poetic genius is what gives rise to other forms of sociality yet to be imagined.

Poetic Genius as Counter-Sovereignty

Turning now to the question of how these seemingly abstract theological questions become political ones, it is important first to clarify why it is not enough to simply comprehend poetic genius as a theological counterpoint to Urizenic logic. Since Blake concentrates on "minute particulars," the challenge to Urizenic forms of thought, and the politics that result from them, cannot be waged solely on the level of immaterial conceptions of the infinite. The struggle against Urizenic forms of sovereignty is not a war of concepts, for Blake. Rather, it is a war at the level of the finite: specific struggles between particular groups and individuals. What interests Blake in these struggles is the way that the imagination is always indirectly involved, generating a particular conception of the infinite, and thus realizing a specific understanding of its relation to the finite or the particular. And realization or materialization always has a political dimension, for Blake. It produces different forms of hierarchy. It generates relations of power between individuals and groups. It accounts for the structure of the body politic itself. The notion of poetic genius is therefore not by itself an antidote to the forms of sovereignty, power, and oppression that develop out of the opposition between the finite and the infinite.

However, since there is always, for Blake, more than one reception of poetic genius, there is always the possibility of other social and political forms that might emerge from the same principle. Blake's early attempt to define poetic genius in *All Religions Are One*, for example, involved an attempt to comprehend it as a principle that might be able to unite a heterogeneous humanity around a single relation to the infinite. Blake claims in his fifth principle that "The Religions of all Nations are derived from each Nations different reception of the Poetic Genius" (ARO, E1). While this might sound like a Platonic idea, where the infinite remains identical with itself but is differently articulated by particular groups and nations, some of Blake's other principles complicate such a reading. Whereas the fifth principle implies that poetic genius is a universally shared essence, the second establishes a different relationship between difference and sameness, complicating the connection between the "infinite variety" of "outward forms" and the unity of poetic genius: "As all men are alike in outward form, So (and with the same infinite variety) all are alike in the Poetic Genius" (ARO, E1). The second clause of the principle suggests that sameness and difference are not, in fact, opposed "in the Poetic Genius." What characterizes it is not homogeneity (a single transcendent source from which all outward forms are derived), but infinite heterogeneity, "infinite variety." Just as the finite and the infinite cannot be differentiated, the "same infinite variety" that qualifies Man's "outward form" also qualifies poetic genius. Hence, there is no prior identity that various nations and religions share. What is allocated to each particular religion is the infinite differentiation that characterizes poetic genius, describing thus merely a *relation* to the infinite rather than a shared essence.[19] To claim that the infinite variety of the poetic genius is "received" by particular religions instead of "derived" implies that the relation between the particular (religion) and the universal (poetic genius) is not, in fact, *necessary* and can therefore be revised. There is always more than one relation to or reception of poetic genius and hence more than one conception of transcendence.

Blake begins to tease out of some of the religious and political consequences of this understanding of poetic genius already in *The Marriage of Heaven and Hell.* The question of the status of the infinity of poetic genius is fore-grounded when Isaiah and Ezekiel are asked about how they manage to assert that God spoke directly to them as prophets. As the mouthpieces of a divine transcendence, their potential misunderstanding of God's voice threatens to become a "cause of imposition" (MHH 12, E38) and therefore a source of power, since it is their own voice rather than God's that speaks. Isaiah, however, replies that the particular relationship he establishes between his prophecies and God is not one of direct encounter: "Isaiah answer'd. I saw no God. nor heard any, in a finite organical perception; but my senses discover'd the infinite in every thing, and as I was then perswaded. & remain confirm'd; that the voice of honest indignation is the voice of God, I cared not for the consequences, but wrote" (MHH 12, E38). Blake contrasts Isaiah's understanding of the divine with the stable unitary voice that he rejects as a source of authority for his prophecies. What Isaiah hears is not God's direct voice but the "voice of honest indignation," which suggests a critical relationship to a preexisting state of affairs. God, in this sense, is less a single exceptional voice pronouncing divine sanction or law than a form of address that challenges various kinds of *existing* injustice and authority. In Isaiah's prophecy, God acts more like a form of delimitation than a source of absolute authority. In fact, it is God as the "voice of honest indignation" that becomes the basis for Isaiah's discovery of the "infinite in every thing."

In *The Marriage of Heaven and Hell*, Ezekiel points out that when treated as a unifying ground or origin, poetic genius becomes the basis for the subjugation of others under the global banner of Christianity:

> some nations held one principle for the origin, & some another, we of Israel taught that the Poetic Genius (as you now call it) was the first principle and all the others merely derivative, which was the cause of our despising the Priests & Philosophers of other countries, and prophecying that all Gods would at last be proved. to originate in ours & to be the tributaries of the Poetic Genius. (MHH 12–13, E39)

Once poetic genius is treated as an identifiable "first principle," it becomes not only a source of religious dogmatism, but also the very basis of political tyranny: "it was this. that our great poet King David desired so fervently & invokes so patheticly, saying by this he conquers enemies & governs kingdoms" (MHH 12, E39). Once poetic genius is generalized from an abstract relationship to a localized "infinity," it becomes a particular religious dogmatism that authorizes various forms of political dominance and imperial expansion.[20] For Blake, there is an unacknowledged imperialism implied in the seemingly ecumenical claims that govern *All Religions Are One*. Once poetic genius forms into a single identifiable source of "all" religions, it becomes possible to privilege a specific relation to it and homogenize others accordingly. Thus, Blake articulates how a perversion in the reception of poetic genius produces a host of theological and political aberrations, from the notion of divine right to various other forms of moral and religious oppression.

What is less clear, however, is whether the "voice of honest indignation" could do more than protest such aberrations. How does Blake envision these notions having an effect on existing institutions, religious or political? One of his closest explorations of this question is found in his interpretation of the American Revolution in *America: A Prophecy*, to which I will turn shortly. Blake viewed this event as a happening of the "impossible," an idea that follows directly from his notion of poetic genius. In *There Is No Natural Religion* he suggests that a perception of the infinite requires an opening to the unforeseeable, a break with what is "already known." Here he counters that a reliance on precedent binds Man unnecessarily to an impoverished and invariable conception of reason or *ratio*. Poetic genius disrupts this stability: "Reason or the ratio of all we have already known. is not the same that it shall be when we know more" (NNR bII, E2). He adds in conclusion: "If it were not for the Poetic or Prophetic character. the Philosophic & Experimental would soon be at the ratio of all things & stand still, unable to do other than repeat the same dull round over again" (NNR b7, E3). In other words, the relation between poetic genius and the infinite constitutes an encounter with the unprecedented, with something that breaks with the known and with previous modes of foresight: "He who sees the Infinite in all things sees God. He who sees the Ratio only sees himself only" (NNR bVII, E3). To "see the Infinite in all things" is to open oneself to the exceptional and the unprecedented, to a non-foundation, which cannot be localized or reified. To "see the Ratio only" is to analogize or identify this exception with oneself and to erect one's own identity and sovereignty over its transcendent abyss.

Because poetic genius is not another concept that precedes its realization in the world, its effect on the political realm becomes, for Blake, the emergence of an unprecedented, unforeseeable event. Early on, he will link this event with two different revolutions. Although they appear to simply replace one foundation with another, one form of transcendence (divine right) with another (natural or civil law), Blake attempts to read the revolutions according to their specific relation to the infinite. This does not mean that he attempts to interpret them "mythologically," as abstracted from the particular historical processes that brought them about. Quite the opposite: since the infinite in Blake is not opposed to the finite, it does not allow one to take a position outside of time or history. Blake's claim, rather, is that the revolutions must be understood as the emergence or the taking place of the "impossible" that he indicates in the *Descriptive Catalogue* historians cannot account for (E543). Poetic genius is oriented not toward the solid ground of an infinite that comprehends history as the unfolding of what is already known, the "same dull round" (NNR b7, E3) that keeps existing relations of power in place, but toward something unprecedented that breaks with these relations.

Blake's insistence on the "impossible" happening in and as history may seem initially to be a digression, but it is in fact a necessary condition of his critique of Urizenic sovereignty. The "unforeseen" nature of poetic genius, if it is going to be able to contest Urizenic forms of sovereignty, must be realized or manifested as an unprecedented historical event, but in a way that is different from the realization of Urizenic transcendence, the incarnation of an abstraction. This is not just because, as Blake writes in *The Marriage of Heaven and Hell*, "Eternity is in love with the productions of time" (MHH 7:10, E36) but because the historian's causal understanding of history is both profoundly *anti*-historical and in league with Urizenic forms of power. Urizenic sovereignty is established, as *The Book of Urizen* puts it, by locking thought up in causal "chains of necessity" and a form of forgetting that willfully ignores the fact that its own particular reception of poetic genius is the result of a long historical development. This is why a purely theological reconceptualization of the infinite remains ineffectual unless it can be articulated through a theory and poetics of the event by becoming a historical *act* in Blake's sense. For Blake, the unprecedented emerges in extraordinary historical events, where the theological-political can be transformed and where the impossible takes place.

The Impossible and the "Act" of Revolution

Blake's early prophetic poems—including *America: A Prophecy*, *Europe: A Prophecy*, and *The Song of Los*—have long been the touchstone for historicists such as Erdman and, more recently, Mee, who seek to locate Blake's poetics in relation to the radical currents of his day.[21] A recent essay by Jon Mee[22] suggests that the tension between what he calls "the political Blake" and "the religious Blake" is a productive one, leading to an alternative radicalism grounded in Blake's millenarian enthusiasm. Even the apparent privileging of the Romantic imagination over the material world of politics, according to Mee, needs to recognize that Blake's mythology involves a response to the events of his own time: "Eternity may well have been the ultimate object of Blake's politics, but he was enough of a follower of Milton to believe that it was less likely to be gained in the cloistered virtue of Beulah than in the historical struggles of the wars of truth."[23] Though Mee's basic point is sound, the phrasing of his position implies a fundamental tension between eternity as the "ultimate object of Blake's politics" and Blake's concern with events in his own time. But as even a situated or politicized mythology is still a mythology, the claim about Blake's representation of the political events of his time seems to be at odds with his quasi-theological focus on the infinite and eternity. In a similar vein, Nicholas Williams's recent work on the notion of utopia in Blake[24] suggests that his poetry gestures toward an apocalyptic culmination or end point of history. In Williams's view, the problem for Blake is "how to retain the particulars of history while bringing them to utopian perfection."[25] The very notion of perfection achieved through political struggle seems to imply that Blake's position entails either a mediation of his conception of the infinite with the "fallen" historical world or a return to an incarnational model where the political would simply be the fallen realm in which the transcendence of the imagination is realized.

What hasn't been taken into account in attempts to understand the relationship between Blake's quasi-theological conception of poetic genius, the infinite, and its relation to the political, is that both remain *immanent* to the finite rather than opposed to it. If history and politics are not simply an incarnation of a transcendent anteriority, then this alters how we must view Blake's interest in and understanding of the relationship between poetic genius, the infinite, and the conception of the political that emerges from both. Blake's work certainly develops a form of political theology and to that extent remains tied to a tradition that could be broadly construed as "idealist," coming at the question of politics from the perspective of the metaphysics that buttress it. Yet, Blake's challenge to some of the metaphysical suppositions that underpin traditional political theology causes it to deviate enough from this tradition to suggest that there are still other ways of conceiving politics latent within it. Blake intently focuses on how the *relation* between the theological and the political might be reconceived. The two most important examples where this becomes visible in Blake's poetry are to be found in his representation of Orc, the figure that comes to challenge Urizenic forms of sovereignty most directly, and in his attempts to alter the way in which the metaphor of the body politic is used in the construction of the "new republic" of France. In the latter, Blake's reconceptualization of the imagination's ability to shape, form, or represent the body politic according to a unified image of a preexisting social body challenges traditional conceptions of the relation between the sovereign (as "head") and the body politic itself. In the former, to which I shall now turn, Orc represents a challenge to Urizenic sovereignty by posing the possibility of a counter-sovereignty grounded on its own lack of precedent, that is, on the unprecedented nature of its own historical act of defiance. Orc, linked to the American rebels during the American Revolution, challenges Urizen not only by allegorizing a human ground for sovereignty (as opposed to divine right), but also by taking shape as a highly unstable and ambivalent counter-sovereign that sometimes risks reproducing Urizenic forms of power, but represents at the same time an opening toward an infinite that challenges these forms of power. Orc, in other words, acts as an ambivalent manifestation of Blake's notion of poetic genius insofar as he challenges any claim to turn the infinite into a transcendent ground of authority, and insofar as he invokes something not yet known, something that cannot be foreseen[26] that breaks with the chains of necessity that constitute Urizenic power.

This is why the narrative of *America: A Prophecy* recounts a history that is not an ordered or rational progression toward freedom. Blake's poetics of the American Revolution is the presentation of an event whose meaning has not yet been decided, and whose impossibility comes to us from the future, not just the past. Part of the poem's focus is on the American Revolution's future repetition in other contexts (such as France in *Europe: A Prophecy*, or Africa and Asia in the *Song of Los*). As Ian Balfour has shown,[27] the prophetic nature of Blake's poem draws on the past through a structure of citationality that, paradoxically, marks the poem's turn toward the future. This citationality does not involve the simple repetition of a historical model, but rather a repetition of the unconditional emergence that constitutes the American Revolution from the start. Orc represents both the failed promise of the revolution and a moment prior to which, as Saree Makdisi puts it, the "impossible was assimilated and absorbed by the real,"[28] reinserted into a causal or historical narrative. Orc's emergence is unparalleled; he does not constitute a repeatable model of sovereignty or revolution, nor does he stand outside of time and history as the essence of a revolution that is exportable to any time or place. The poem's critical force resides in its exploration of both the possibility of repeating Orc's inaugural revolutionary energies and the difference that an opening to the impossible, or the infinite in Blake's sense, makes.[29]

Although *America: A Prophecy* has a narrative structure, including a "Preludium" that sets up the account of Orc's resistance to Urizen, one of the more difficult aspects of the poem involves identifying its locus of action. The poem is structured by a series of constantly shifting temporal indicators that make it difficult to situate a particular context for much of what takes place, even when it appears to refer to specific historical events. In a single line, Blake moves from the simple present, to the progressive present, to the past, making it arduous for the reader to find his or her bearings:

> Swelling, belching from its deeps red clouds & raging Fires!
> Albion is sick. America faints! enrag'd the Zenith grew.
> As human blood shooting its veins all round the orbed heaven

> Red rose the clouds from the Atlantic in vast wheels of blood
> And in the red clouds rose a Wonder o'er the Atlantic sea; (AM 4:3–7, E53)

This progressive disruption of temporal continuity often makes the action of the poem appear strangely without agency. Many of the verbs in the progressive present appear without a corresponding subject: "Reviving shake, inspiring move, breathing! awakening!" (AM 6:4, E53). In other cases, the verb is deliberately detached from the subject, even though it seems attributable to it: "They look behind at every step & believe it is a dream. Singing" (AM 6:12–13, E53). The poem presents a series of actions that are continuous, yet curiously dissociated from any particular subject-position, as though Blake were deliberately employing a poetic voice the temporal position of which is intentionally ambiguous in relation to the events depicted. This temporal confusion does not just give a sense of events that are taking place outside of time, but constitutes the poem's central temporal predicament: are these events in the past, are they ongoing, or are they yet to come? The fact that the poem contains the notion of prophecy in the title might suggest the latter, although it appears to build a variety of temporal narratives on top of each other: Orc's emergence and confrontation with Urizen, the confrontation between the American rebels and British soldiers, and the defeat of Albion (who denotes both ancient England and "Fallen Man").[30] Each of these perspectives on the event takes place "in time," but not always simultaneously or chronologically. Such presentation highlights the way the poem disrupts any causal understanding of the revolution from the beginning.

In the first plate of the poem, for example, Washington addresses the rebels who include both "brothers and sons of America" as well as other specifically named revolutionaries, such as Franklin and Paine. When his speech ceases, the Americans are addressed by Albion's "voice," but it is not clear that his voice and Washington's occupy the same time or space. As Albion transforms into a dragon, "His voice, his locks, his awful shoulders, and his glowing eyes / Appear to the Americans upon the cloudy night" (AM 3–4:16–17, E52–53). Albion's voice is not *heard* by the rebels, but in a strange synesthesia "appears" to them and does not yet utter anything, suggesting at least a temporary distinction between them. The only "voice" that responds to Albion's is Orc's on plate six, as he, Albion's angel, and Albion himself engage in a series of exchanges. Thus, in Blake's poem, multiple temporal dimensions or layers coincide, while at other moments they contradict one another. Yet, these divisions are all part of the same "moment." As the poem develops, it is sometimes unclear where or when the action takes place: in the inhuman domains of Albion and Orc or in the historical world of Washington and Paine. What emerges is not an atemporal mythic space in which past, present, and future coincide, but rather a space in which the past, the present, and the future *coexist* in mutually contradictory and fundamentally unstable ways. This accounts for the apparent reversals and repetitions in the poem: on plate six, for example, Orc's speech appears to have declared victory over Albion and Urizen, since the last line proclaims that "Empire is no more, and now the Lion & Wolf shall cease" (AM 6:15, E53). By the end of the poem, however, this victory is far from certain: even if Urizen is "unable to stem the fires of Orc" (AM 16:21, E58) he has not been fundamentally defeated.

Thus, while the poem itself eschews any clear sense of causal or narrative continuity, the point in the poem where Orc takes on the aspect of an unconditional counter-sovereignty to Urizen is in his appearance between the rebels and Albion. His emergence is described as a "wonder," a word linked closely with the "miracle" that Blake, in the *Descriptive Catalogue*, claimed historians were incapable of understanding. In the historical world of Washington, Orc is aligned with the rising up of America against the most powerful and well-equipped colonial army in the world, a war against seemingly impossible odds, but the impossibility of which actually takes place. Seen in part by Blake as a war against absolute monarchy, Orc personifies at once the possibility of another form of sovereignty and the very happening of the impossible itself.

At the same time, however, the imagery of fire and blood that characterizes Orc's emergence is also a citation of Albion's prior metamorphosis into a dragon, where he rends the clouds, unleashes "red meteors," and gazes menacingly on the rebels with his "glowing eyes" while "Solemn heave the Atlantic waves between the gloomy nations, / Swelling, belching from its deeps red cloud & raging Fires!" (AM 4:1–2, E53). The same imagery of fire and cloud heralds Orc's emergence:

> As human blood shooting its veins all round the orbed heaven
> Red rose the clouds from the Atlantic in vast wheels of blood

And in the red clouds rose a Wonder o'er the Atlantic sea;
Intense! naked! a Human fire fierce glowing, as the wedge
Of iron heated in the furnace; his terrible limbs were fire
With myriads of cloudy terrors banners dark & towers
Surrounded; heat but not light went thro' the murky atmosphere.
(AM 4:5–11, E53)

The repetition of imagery associated with Albion in the passages that detail Orc's initial emergence suggests more than just an "Orc cycle" that Northrop Frye first identified and that David Erdman historicized into a pattern of enslavement, liberation, and re-enslavement.[31] The passage above stresses a radical ambivalence that Blake continuously associates with Orc. His "impossible" emergence, its very unconditionality, is immediately threatened by the prospect that it can be reinserted back into a causality that forces it to appear as the very thing it defies.

As Orc appears to take the shape of what he opposes, Blake nevertheless distinguishes Orc from Albion (and later Urizen) in some key respects to highlight his status as the figure of a different relation to the infinite. Though the imagery of fire appears to link Orc with Albion, Blake asserts that Orc's fire is specifically "Human" (AM 4:8, E53). This identification contrasts with the celestial imagery of clouds and "red meteors" that defines Albion's initial appearance as a dragon and distinguishes Albion's superhuman status from his enslaved earth-bound subjects. Washington's first speech in the poem, for example, differentiates between Albion's "bended bow . . . lifted in heaven" (AM 3:7, E52) and the "Brothers and sons of America" whose "eyes [are] downcast, hands are work-bruis'd/Feet bleeding on the sultry sands" (AM 3:10–11, E52). The material oppression of the Americans is linked with the "heavenly" power that Albion wields against them from above, while the gazes and the labor of the Americans are directed toward the earth.

The image depicted on the second plate of the poem shows a human figure rising out of the earth, emerging coextensively with a tree's roots, which above ground become a coiled spiral reminiscent of the serpent image in the previous plate. This is contrasted clearly with the image of the dragon and Urizen on plate four, who descend on the cowering men, women, and children on the earth from above. Albion and Orc are distinguished by

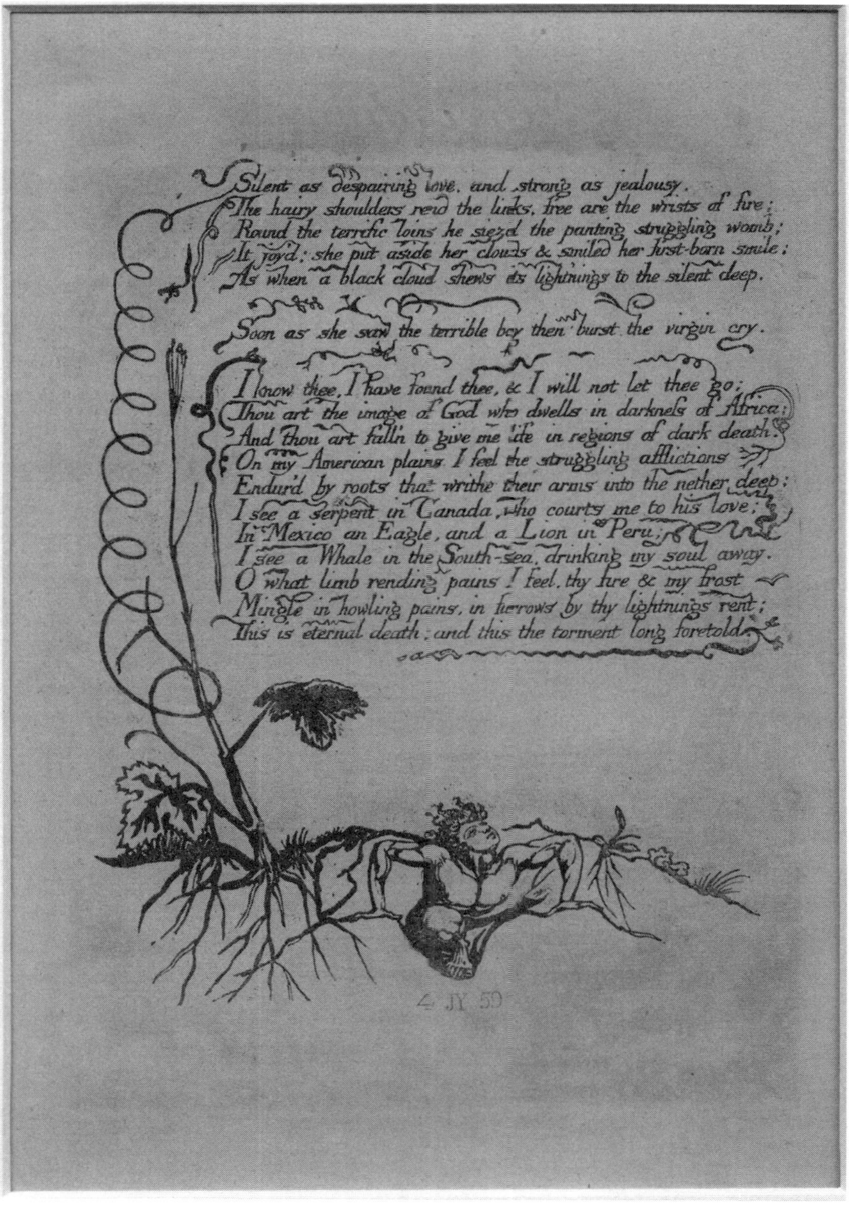
Silent as despairing love, and strong as jealousy,
The hairy shoulders rend the links, free are the wrists of fire;
Round the terrific loins he siez'd the panting struggling womb;
It joy'd: she put aside her clouds & smiled her first-born smile;
As when a black cloud shews its lightnings to the silent deep.

Soon as she saw the terrible boy then burst the virgin cry.

I know thee, I have found thee, & I will not let thee go;
Thou art the image of God who dwells in darkness of Africa;
And thou art fall'n to give me life in regions of dark death.
On my American plains I feel the struggling afflictions
Endur'd by roots that writhe their arms into the nether deep:
I see a serpent in Canada, who courts me to his love;
In Mexico an Eagle, and a Lion in Peru;
I see a Whale in the South-sea, drinking my soul away.
O what limb rending pains I feel. thy fire & my frost
Mingle in howling pains, in furrows by thy lightnings rent;
This is eternal death; and this the torment long foretold.

Figure 3. America: A Prophecy, copy H, plate 2 (Erdman plate 2). © Trustees of the British Museum.

a connection the poem makes between Orc and specifically earthly, human, or material forms of power. Not only is the fire that accompanies his emergence defined as "Human," but his form of resistance to Albion is figured as "human blood shooting its veins all round the orbed heaven" (AM 4:5, E53). Orc's "impossible" emergence appears to pit two different conceptions of the infinite against each other: Albion's celestial power from on high, which insists on the hierarchical opposition between heaven and earth, and Orc's specifically "human" fires, which challenge this opposition. Orc's materialization of the "human form divine" acts as a countersovereignty to the unified power of Church and State that Albion's metamorphosis into a dragon implies.[32]

At the same time, however, Orc's emergence resembles a reinstitution or even radicalization of divine right. He emerges in the poem after the "zenith" grows in response to America's submission to Albion. This "zenith," the highest point of the celestial sphere, suggests a relation to the absolute. The sublime language[33] in the poem of Orc as a "Wonder" is thus accompanied with imagery similar to the one that qualifies Albion's absolutism. Orc rises in the clouds over the Atlantic, attempting to surround heaven in order to usurp it, or perhaps substitute his "human fires" in its place. When Albion's angel identifies him as the "transgressor of God's Law," Orc replies with his second speech, which proclaims the "scattering" of religion:

> I am Orc, wreath'd round the accursed tree:
> The times are ended; shadows pass the morning gins to break;
> The fiery joy, that Urizen perverted to ten commands,
> What night he led the starry hosts thro' the wide wilderness:
> That stony law I stamp to dust: and scatter religion abroad
> To the four winds as a torn book, & none shall gather the leaves
> (AM 8:1–6, E54)

The tearing up and scattering of Urizen's book (which alludes to the "book of eternal brass" in *The Book of Urizen*) suggests that Orc begins a process that deconstitutes the very basis of Albion's and Urizen's power. If, as I suggested earlier, "the book of eternal brass" represents not just the Old Testament but Urizen's first attempt to reify transcendence into a codified law that can be disseminated, universalized, and conferred on others, Orc's response is to turn this dissemination into a torn "book" that can no longer be gathered together into a whole. Orc is thus a figure wherein two different relations between the theological and the political play out. While he often appears to simply repeat Urizenic forms of sovereignty, he also invokes an opening toward something else: an earthly conception of the infinite where "every thing that lives is holy" (AM 8:13, E54) and that dissolves and "scatters" the various forms of authority organized by the notion of the infinite as a hierarchical structure.

Orc opens up the possibility of another relationship to political theology, however, primarily by constituting the conditions for the advent of a truly historical *act*—the "happening" of the impossible. In other words, Orc's status as an ambivalent figure in the poem simply means that, like the revolution itself, he contains multiple possibilities, multiple tendencies. If, as Blake insists in *The Marriage of Heaven and Hell*, "What is now proved was once, only imagin'd" (MHH 8:33, E36), Orc represents the opening up of the imagination as a break with the "chains of necessity" that allows one to visualize the impossible and to conceive the conditions in which it might take place.

At first glance, Orc seems to "do" very little in the poem. His role is organized by a purely negative relation to what he opposes: he stamps the stony law to dust in plate eight, opens dungeon doors, and loosens chains in plate six, but without necessarily producing alternative forms of power. At best, Orc's appearance acts as instigator for some of the historical figures—like Washington, who gains strength and resolve from Orc's flames—entering history by organizing the "fierce rushing of th'inhabitants together" (AM 14:12, E56). The emergence of Orc in the poem is thus identified less with a specific form of sovereignty, the reconstitution of a new form of power, than with a fundamental shift in the understanding of the possible. Given the ambivalent status of Orc, and the ambiguous imagery that accompanies his emergence, he offers little guarantee that the impossible will happen, only that it *could*, or *might still*. Since Orc's resistance to Urizen can just as quickly collapse back into a repetition of Urizenic forms of sovereignty, Orc appears to represent merely a loosening or unlocking of the sense of natural order that prevents genuine change from occurring. Orc first makes possible a conception of the world in which Washington and the rebels can act, can defy the odds and institute alternative forms of political sovereignty. As such, unlike Urizen, there is no specific incarnation of Orc's power in *America: A Prophecy* other than the rebels themselves and the chance that they may not only defeat Albion (and British colonial power), but also destroy belief in the metaphysical abstractions that reinforce his power.

This is why on plate six of *America: A Prophecy* Orc is positioned as a repetition of an impossibility that awaits us in the future, as a potentiality internal to the American Revolution that has not yet been achieved. The passage's declaration of the eventual triumph of Orc and the American rebels over the colonial power represented by Albion and Urizen initially appears organized by a linearity that is not typical of the rest of the poem. It moves from a present ("The morning comes, the night decays, the watchmen leave their stations" [AM 6:1, E53]) to a euphoric retrospective ("The Sun has left his blackness, & has found a fresher morning" [AM 6:13, E53]) to a futural projection: "For Empire is no more, and now the Lion & Wolf shall cease" (AM 6:15, E53). Formally, the passage maps out what appears to be a "felicitous" performative,[34] invoking in the present a declaration that remains consistent with itself and that carries out the assurance of a future beyond Urizenic empire. This futural projection, however, is preceded by a series of other performative-style utterances that remain, in this context, undecidable, not yet "felicitous":

> Let the slave grinding at the mill, run out into the field:
> Let him look up into the heavens & laugh in the bright air;
> Let the inchained soul shut up in darkness and in sighing,
> Whose face has never seen a smile in thirty weary years;
> Rise and look out, his chains are loose, his dungeon doors are open.
> And let his wife and children return from the oppressors scourge;
> (AM 6:6–11, E53)

Though they take the linguistic form of divine creation in Genesis (e.g., "let there be light"), like Orc's fires on plate four, the passage emits "heat but not light" (AM 4:11, E53). The felicity of these pseudo-performatives remains decidedly futural, as the line that follows suggests by highlighting their prophetic nature: "They look behind at every step & believe it is a dream" (AM 6:13, E53). This line can be read as portending the hopeless unreality of the dream of freedom—its purely fictional status. Or it can be read as suggesting the exceptional nature of the dream: it appears "as a dream" though it is real because it conforms to no reality that would be capable of recognizing it.

This "declaration of independence," as Erdman calls it, and the fall of Urizenic order is thus merely provisional, a prophecy in the weak sense of a projection of something yet-to-be realized. But it is a possibility that emerges only because Orc first sets the stage for it. His arrival suspends, if only temporarily, every transcendent ground upon which a law or sovereign, human or divine, could legitimate itself absolutely. When Albion's angel responds to the vision of liberation evinced in plate six, he attempts to identify Orc as a serpent and devourer: "Blasphemous Demon, Antichrist, hater of Dignities; / Love of wild rebellion, and transgressor of Gods Law" (AM 7:5–6, E53–54). Orc is described here as a radical antinomian who refuses every determinate moral law or form of authority. Like the Hegelian skeptic who opposes the infinite to every particular and fails to recognize that his negation has a determinate content,[35] Orc's opening toward a different conception of the infinite merely stamps "that stony law . . . to dust" and "scatter[s] religion abroad / To the four winds as a torn book." In other words, he does not oppose Urizen's law with a law of his own but casts it into a dissemination or "scattering" that does not allow it to gather itself, letting it be consumed "in bottomless deeps" (AM 8:7, E54) by an infinity that rejects every foundation.

Orc, then, is merely a catalyst. His arrival institutes a break with existing structures of authority and opens up a space in which alternative forms of the political become conceivable. It is the rebels themselves, and even Urizen's guardians, who ultimately bring about his downfall. Their acts, however, are predicated on Orc's re-visioning of the relation between the infinite and the finite, and the destruction of political and religious forms of power grounded in transcendence. The opening of other imaginative possibilities is symbolized by the spreading of Orc's fires over the Earth: "Fires inwrap the earthly globe, yet man is not consum'd; / Amidst the lustful fires he walks" (AM: 8:15–16, E54). Orc's "fires" denote a shift in a way of seeing that defines a particular vision of the world. Blake elsewhere links the imagery of fire not just with the imagination but with the purging of false perceptions of the relation between the finite and the infinite. In *The Marriage of Heaven and Hell*, for instance, the speaker proclaims: "The ancient tradition that the world will be consumed in fire at the end of six thousand years is true," adding "the whole creation will be consumed, and appear infinite. and holy whereas it now appears finite & corrupt" (MHH 14, E39). This conflagration, as I have already suggested, is not the liquidation of the finite,[36] but a shift in outlook, a shift in how the finite appears: no longer *as* corrupt, but *as* infinite. The finite world still *appears* in both cases, underscoring the fact that it is "not consum'd."

In *America: A Prophecy*, Orc inaugurates the conditions in which a particular vision of the world can be challenged by others once they no longer recognize its claim on them. In plate eleven, for instance, "Bostons Angel," who is "burning with the fires of Orc" (AM 11:2, E55), repudiates Urizen's authority by questioning his divine origin: "Must the generous tremble & leave his joy, to the idle: to the pestilence!/That mock him? who commanded this? what God? what Angel!" (AM 11:6–7, E55). At the end of the plate, once he has declared that he can no longer recognize Urizen and the social and political order that he legitimates ("no more I follow, no more obedience pay" [AM 11:15, E55]), the angel casts away his own symbols of authority: "So cried he, rending off his robe & throwing down his scepter" (AM 12:1, E55). His disavowal of the robe and scepter, symbols of the power bestowed upon him by Urizenic sovereignty, signifies the breakdown of his recognition of the transcendence that gives them legitimacy. The angel's immersion in the fires of Orc, in other words, initiates his *abandonment* of the trappings of power. Once Albion's "thirteen angels" follow suit, rending "off their robes to the hungry wind" (AM 12:3, E55) and throwing down their golden scepters, it becomes clear that the earthly/celestial division that governs the beginning of the poem is collapsing. As the angels relinquish their symbols of authority, they "fall" from the heights of heaven to earth, joining the rebels: "indignant they descended/Headlong from out their heav'nly heights, descending swift as fires/Over the land; naked & flaming are their lineaments seen/In the deep gloom, by Washington & Paine & Warren they stood" (AM 12:4–7, E55). Unlike Satan and the angels of *Paradise Lost*, the angels' fall from grace is not predicated on their attempt to "equall the most High,"[37] but precisely the opposite: a relinquishment of the power afforded to them by the structure of transcendence that certifies Urizenic sovereignty.

As Orc's emergence inaugurates a context in which the angels divest themselves of their celestial power to join the resistance to Urizen's authority, the human actors of the poem, including the rebels, mirror them by relinquishing their sovereign individuality. On the one hand, the thirteen Governors "that England sent" fall down at the feet of Washington, as British soldiers throw down "their swords & muskets to the earth" (AM 13:7, E56) and run "From the grim flames; and the visions of Orc" (AM 13:9, E56). On the other, the inhabitants of America abandon the tools of their respective occupations to join together as a collective form of resistance to the "plagues" that Albion has unleashed from his dark heaven:

> And the red flames of Orc that folded roaring fierce around
> The angry shores, and the fierce rushing of th'inhabitants together:
> The citizens of New York close their books & lock their chests;
> The mariners of Boston drop their anchors and unlade;
> The scribe of Pensylvania casts his pen upon the earth;
> The builder of Virginia throws his hammer down in fear. (AM 14:11–16, E56)

As Saree Makdisi has suggested,[38] this relinquishment of individual interests is what makes possible the *collective* "fierce rushing of the inhabitants together." This collective also defends the revolution's opening toward an infinite that generates a sense of togetherness without becoming a transcendent unity that subtends each individual:

> Then had America been lost, o'erwhelm'd by the Atlantic,
> And Earth had lost another portion of the infinite,
> But all rush together in the night in wrath and raging fire (AM 14:17–19, E56)

Just as the angels cast off their trappings of power, the inhabitants of America band together, relinquishing their sovereign identities in order to save "another portion of the infinite," an odd phrase only if one thinks of a finite portion as being opposed to the infinite. If America is a "portion of the infinite," this suggests not only that the infinite is infinitely *finite* (an endless succession of finite differences), but also that this notion of the infinite is inherently resistant to the homogenizing intentions of imperial Urizenic rule. If the infinite is not one, but already many and therefore "portioned" by nature, it cannot become the basis of a false universalism.

What characterizes Blake's depiction of the revolution, then, from the angels to the rebels, is not only an assertion of a counter-sovereignty in the form of Orc, but also the relativization of Urizenic forms of sovereignty. Sovereignty, in Blake's political theology, need not take the form of a relation to a transcendent ground of authority. Orc's alternative understanding of the infinite, however, makes him an ambivalent representative of Blake's political theology. Since the infinite that he epitomizes does not act as a prior foundation, Orc can never incarnate it except by betraying it. The relation to infinity that he represents, therefore, constitutes an opening toward a non-transcendent basis for collective action no less inaugural than a state or sovereign organized and legitimated by an identifiable law (whether theological or natural). What Orc, as the emergence of the impossible in history, exemplifies for Blake is the prospect of a historical transition that does not involve the withdrawal of political theology, but instead initiates its radical reconstitution. No longer predicated on the incarnation of an absolute ground, the creation of a new political theology, in Blake's view, might give rise to a conception of sovereignty and the body politic that would no longer organize them around the assumption of a prior transcendent unity or unanimity. Though the theme of a new understanding of the body politic remained persistent in Blake even into his later epics such as *Jerusalem*, he first explored this question early on in his poem *The French Revolution*.

Desire for/as a New Body Politic

In *America: A Prophecy*, Orc constitutes a principle of rupture with the systems of power, including the British Crown, that are made possible by Urizenic forms of political theology. His role in other revolutionary contexts, however, is often less triumphant. In *Europe: A Prophecy*, for instance, which follows *America: A Prophecy* and deals indirectly with the French Revolution, it is not clear at all that Orc repeats his role as a catalyst for revolution. Having shifted time and place to France, *Europe* concentrates on Orc's mother, Enitharmon, who establishes her "moral law" as well as the false virtues of chastity, revenge, and the repression of desire. Though the poem appears to pick up where *America: A Prophecy* left off, since Orc's creation of the collective "fierce rushing" of the inhabitants also entails an unleashing of desire and its refusal to obey the laws of Urizen,[39] *Europe: A Prophecy* has shifted registers from the historical concerns of *America*—questions about how the impossible can emerge historically—to questions about the relationship between law, specifically moral law, and the desire that transgresses it. This shift may have to do with the fact that the events Blake is describing were unfolding at the time he was composing these poems and that in 1794, opposition to the strictures of moral law may have had a more ambivalent resonance given what was happening on the ground in France.[40] While the American Revolution already lay more than fifteen years in the past by the time Blake was writing his poem about it, the poems about the French Revolution deal with an event still in progress, the meaning and direction of which are even more uncertain, and that by 1794 showed troubling signs of an excessive and strict moralism. At the same time, Blake recognizes that the Revolution also involved the liberation of violent desires that confront even more fundamentally the metaphysical structures that propped up the *ancien régime*. This is perhaps why the focus of his interpretation of the French Revolution tends to be on the indissociability of law and transgression. If in *America: A Prophecy* Orc represents a relation to the infinite that opens up the possibility of a radical transgression of Urizen's "one law," in *Europe: A Prophecy* Orc is a figure of the uncertain relationship between what lies outside the law and the legal order itself, becoming an even more ambivalent figure as the revolution began increasingly to blur the lines between demonstrations of excessive passion and the defense of a newly constructed juridical system.

Thus, Blake's *Europe: A Prophecy* is in many ways a deeply pessimistic poem, suggesting that the revolutionary impulse can be turned back upon itself (the frontispiece includes an image of the serpent that Orc becomes when he is "bound" by his mother Enitharmon). Its focus is less on the revolutionary event itself, however, and more on the "eighteen hundred year sleep of Enitharmon" between the advent of Christ and the French Revolution. Blake's focus has thus shifted away from the future and the continuing legacy of the revolution Orc is able to catalyze toward the tradition or past that it must liberate itself from. But before we attribute Orc's devolution in *Europe: A Prophecy* to Blake's disillusionment with political revolution more generally,[41] it is important to consider the ways in which Blake's pessimism is directed also at the *new* regime's reconstitution of the same structures of sovereignty as the old under new guises. Blake's earlier poem, *The French Revolution* (1791) written during a period in which the revolution took on a somewhat different tone, concentrates much more on the question of the possibility of its continuing legacy. Absent the mythological characters that populate Blake's prophetic poems, it nonetheless situates the events of the French Revolution in terms of the political-theological claims that inspire them. Like *Europe: A Prophecy*, it understands the French Revolution through the lens of an opposition between desire and (moral) law, between antinomian forces and Urizenic conceptions of the universality of law.

One of its major themes is the question of how a new body politic might be created out of a differently conceived relation between the law, the political, and what remains exterior to law, which Blake calls "desire." If *America: A Prophecy* attempts to understand what a form of resistance to Urizenic sovereignty might look like, how it would need to be predicated on a different conception of the infinite, Blake's *The French Revolution* consists in an early attempt to comprehend what it would mean to reorganize the social according to this conception. In a sense, *The French Revolution* constitutes an early attempt to formulate a positive vision of a community founded on the immanent conception of the infinite that Blake first articulated in *The Marriage of Heaven and Hell.* If every minute particular is a portion of the infinite, but the infinite cannot be reduced to a single identity (it *exists* only through an infinite variety of finite particulars), then in what sense could it be said to organize a *collective* identity? These concerns are a constituent part of Blake's later epics, particularly *Jerusalem*, which attempts to understand community as the process by which every particular Man becomes "a Divine Member of the Divine Jesus" (J 91:30, E251). Yet these concerns receive an initial formulation in Blake's early conception of poetic genius. The relation between the one and the many, the individual and the common, is restructured by an imagination that can no longer posit a transcendent identity that precedes the community and allows each member to recognize itself as one with it, a constituent part of it. This naturally leads Blake to the question of how the imagination engenders a new form of the body politic, since it might appear that no sense of the common is possible without some form of identification, some privileging of the one over the many.

Blake approaches this question by attempting to break with the liberal tradition of understanding the emergence of the collective or general will as the simple accumulation of individual wills or desires. Because the infinite by definition is in excess of every representation, even if it is only found in "minute particulars," Blake has to articulate a way it can be situated inside the legal order as part of what binds the community together. If the body politic is no longer organized by a head (metaphorically or figuratively), something else must give it shape. For Blake, what does so is desire. His concept of desire is very much like the infinite insofar as it is in excess of every finite law that would prohibit it. It is also never fully realized or incarnated. Blake's ideal consists in positing desire as a non-juridical social bond, a force that shapes the social and that is integrative without privileging a particular part of the social body. Desire, for Blake, becomes what takes the individual out of himself and places him in relation to another. It is therefore always collective, never strictly individual.

One of Blake's earliest attempts to define a society predicated on this notion of desire is his early meditation in *The French Revolution* on the possibility of a new body politic emerging out of the fires of revolution. The poem consistently touches on the theme of liberated desire, focusing in particular on what appears to be an opposition between particular interests and the general good. Andrew Lincoln has argued that this poem not only rejects all legal forms of hierarchy, but also any "'democratic' alternative that erects the will of the majority as a limit to individual desire."[42] His analysis hinges on what he sees as an opposition between the individual desires of the revolutionaries and the consensus or will of the majority required for the national assembly to be able to write laws in the public interest. In this liberal reading of the poem, any limit to desire imposed by law would constitute a violation of its infinity and a step toward the hierarchization of tolerated desires on the way toward the creation of a general will.[43] However, "desire" must be understood in the poem as something other than an individual interest. It is a name for the possibility of social relations themselves. For Blake, no community can ever be produced strictly through a legal contract; it must be bound by something other than law. In *The French Revolution* desire is the name for another *form* of social relations, one that has yet to be fully articulated but the outlines of which become visible in the collapse of a previous social or legal order. *The French Revolution* attempts to present what it would mean to found a community according to a recovered sense of the infinite in which the infinite is not treated as a transcendent unity.

As Blake suggests throughout the poem, desire works to "suspend"[44] the law, but this suspension is, like Orc's emergence in *America: A Prophecy*, merely the opening toward another possibility. It is a state in which a previous law or social order has been suspended, or has already lost its legitimacy, but in which a new one has not yet been declared in its place. Blake presents desire's suspension of the law in *The French Revolution* in two key contrasting speeches, one by the archbishop of Paris, the other a reply by Orleans. As in the prophetic poems, Blake focuses here on the unprecedented nature of a historical moment in which "the triple forg'd fetters of times were unloos'd" (FR 4:62, E288), a period in which the old laws and hierarchies are being threatened. As the King initially suggests, the challenge to his power is at once political and theological: "The nerves of five thousand years ancestry tremble, shaking the heavens of France" (FR 4:70, E289). Once the Duke of Burgundy has finished giving his analysis of the situation, the archbishop of Paris rises to persuade the King to crush the National Assembly and restore order. The archbishop frames the conflict in terms of the need to defend law as the basic principle of social and religious harmony. Referring interchangeably to civil law and God's law, he opposes both to a form of desire that knows no bounds:

> My groaning is heard in the abbeys, and God, so long worshipp'd, departs as a lamp
> Without oil; for a curse is heard hoarse thro' the land, from a godless race
> Descending to beasts; they look downward and labour and forget my holy law;
> The sound of prayer fails from lips of flesh, and the holy hymn from thicken'd tongues
> For the bars of Chaos are burst; her millions prepare their fiery way
> Thro' the orbed abode of the holy dead, to root up and pull down and remove
> And Nobles and Clergy shall fail from before me, and my cloud and vision be no more;
> The mitre become black, the crown vanish, and the scepter and ivory staff
> Of the ruler wither among bones of death; they shall consume from the thistly field,
> And the sound of the bell, and the voice of the sabbath, and singing of the holy choir,
> Is turn'd into songs of the harlot in day, and cries of the virgin in night.
> They shall drop at the plow and faint at the harrow, unredeem'd, unconfess'd, unpardon'd

> The priest rot in his surplice by the lawless lover, the holy beside the accursed,
> The King, frowning in purple, beside the grey plowman, and their worms
> embrace together. (FR 8:137–50, E292)

For the archbishop, once the "bars of Chaos are burst," the very seat of ecclesiastical and monarchic authority is threatened; the miter, crown, and scepter become corrupted from within and wither. The resultant chaos of desire is described as an imaginative fire that razes limitations and the hierarchical relations that go with them, destroying all forms of stricture and structure. As in *America: A Prophecy*, when God's heavenly power is no longer recognized, the citizens "look downward and labour and forget my holy law," turning toward a material earth bereft of spirit, becoming, for the archbishop, mere laboring "beasts." He assumes that Law, specifically God's law, and the boundless infinity of desire are in opposition to each other. He presents a vision of desire loosed from its confinement by the law as chaos because the transgression of holy law threatens his unitary understanding of the nation, as well as his conception of the necessity of the order he is defending. Without this single unified law, there would be no order, no central pillar around which society could be organized. The threat that results from this chaos is a massive leveling: the priest "rots" beside the "lawless lover," the king beside the plowman and "their worms embrace together." There is more than a little parody in a line that assumes social hierarchies to be so natural that they would outlive death, where even the carrion would know the difference between a king and a plowman. The threat to clerical power is captured by the destruction of the hierarchy that follows from the transcendence of God's law, the "voice of the sabbath" that becomes transformed into "songs of the harlot in day, and cries of the virgin in night." What these concerns point to is a view of society and the body politic that must not only have a head, but a single undivided law that organizes it into a collective, assigning duties and functions to each part. For the archbishop, there is only law and what lies outside the law, order and its violation.

Orleans's response to the archbishop picks up many of these themes, but it positions desire in a much more ambivalent relationship to the law. Orleans opens his speech with the notion of multiple visions and potentialities that desire makes possible:

O princes of fire, whose flames are for growth, not consuming,
Fear not dreams, fear not visions, nor be you dismay'd with sorrows which flee at the morning;
Can the fires of Nobility ever be quench'd, or the stars by a stormy night?
Is the body diseas'd when the members are healthful? can the man be bound in sorrow
Whose ev'ry function is fill'd with its fiery desire? can the soul whose brain and heart
Cast their rivers in equal tides thro' the great Paradise, languish because the feet
Hands, head, bosom, and parts of love, follow their high breathing joy?
And can Nobles be bound when the people are free, or God weep when his children are happy? (FR 10:179–86, E294)

Proceeding through a series of rhetorical questions, Orleans first attempts to relativize the archbishop's vision, urging him and the nobles not to interpret the unleashing of desire as an existential threat. Bypassing entirely the question of the radical vision of equality that terrifies the archbishop, Orleans begins by attempting to persuade the nobles that their own well-being would follow from the relinquishment of privilege and that another vision of the body politic would become possible. When he asks "can the man be bound in sorrow/Whose every function is fill'd with its fiery desire?," Orleans is not only describing individual desires, but providing an image of the body politic whose "every function is fill'd with its fiery desire." Already cast in terms of the collective body, Orleans addresses the archbishop and the nobles as if they were either its heart or brain.

Rather than a chaos, however, Orleans imagines a body politic so radically egalitarian that it is no longer organized by particular functions: the "brain and heart" no longer dominate, but "cast their rivers in equal tides thro' the great Paradise" as the other functions, "hands, head, bosom and parts of love," independently "follow their high breathing joy." Orleans's speech imagines a moment *prior* to the application of law, a moment when the law is suspended and is no longer, or not yet, in force. This moment in the speech gives way to a collectivity predicated on the notion of a desire liberated from any homogenous origin of law. Desire, seen by the archbishop as *opposed* to the law, becomes an organizing principle unto itself. Displacing the transcendent unity of God's law, it reveals that the origin of the legal order and of community is never attributable to a single source.

Orleans speech then goes on to gesture toward an alternative vision of the body politic itself. What makes this particular body "healthful" is not the fact that each part works organically with the others, but that each part simultaneously expresses a collective desire and demonstrates the way that the fire of desire "delights in its form," each one particular. When the speech moves from the image of the collective as a vast desiring body to individual revolutionaries, Orleans emphasizes particulars that locate each of them in relation to the collective *and* in terms of their particular function within the body politic:

> Have you never seen Fayette's forehead, or Mirabeau's eyes, or the shoulders of Target,
> Or Bailly the strong foot of France, or Clermont the terrible voice, and your robes
> Still retain their crimson? mine never yet faded, for fire delights in its form.
> (FR 10:187–89, E294)

Neither the individual revolutionaries nor the collective itself form an identity in any traditional sense, though each is associated with a particular function within the body politic: the forehead, the eyes, the shoulders, the foot, and the voice. The image of "fire delighting in its form" implies that each of these functions, each without any privilege over the other, each with a different content, is nonetheless organized by a single "fire"[45] that gives them all shape. Orleans articulates an exceptional organization of the body politic, a vision of collectivity that does not presuppose an identity that subtends it:

> But go, merciless man! enter the infinite labyrinth of another's brain
> Ere thou measure the circle that he shall run. Go thou cold recluse, into the fires
> Of another's high flaming rich bosom, and return unconsum'd, and write laws.
> If thou canst not do this, doubt thy theories, learn to consider all men as thy equals,
> Thy brethren, and not as thy foot or thy hand, unless thou first fearest to hurt them. (FR 10:190–94, E294)

By the end of the speech the metaphor of the body politic has not vanished, just the organic or hierarchical structure implied in it. The desire that permeates this vast body along with each member also suspends the one law of monarchy and God, even as it articulates a desire that is collective but that does not yet take on a determined organicism or organization. Orleans's conception of desire links each member of the body politic through a radical incommensurability: first the "infinite labyrinth of another's brain," then the "fires of another's high flaming rich bosom." Though referring to other individuals, both of these images also refer to the centers of power—the brain and heart—of the body politic. Orleans insists on the idea that *each* "infinite labyrinth" of another person is irreducible to every other and is thus not generalizable into a common identity. There is no metaphorically common brain or heart that unifies the collective, and what shatters this myth is a conception of the infinite that does away with a single form or measure for the collective. The encounter with the infinity of the other must come, for Blake, prior to the construction of a universal body politic and the law governing the "circle" that others "shall run"—a reference to their place within the body politic. It is precisely *because* of the irreducibility of every other to each other[46] that radical equality emerges, forcing the archbishop to abandon his theories predicated on transcendent hierarchies. It leads, for Blake, to the possibility of a recognition of non-abstract, non-generalizing equality, an equality that does not homogenize each individual into a function, a foot or a hand of the social body, but treats each as genuine "brethren." Because this entirely fabulous body politic is no longer organized by a single head that commands the extremities such as the "feet and the hands" (FR 10:194, E294), equality no longer takes the form of abstract and interchangeable equivalence before a universal law.

The Futures of Political Theology

One might call this vision of collectivity utopic[47] so long as one does not understand this term in the usual way as taking us either nowhere or to an elsewhere separate from the present. For Blake, the possibility of this utopia, of another form of the body politic, is already present; it only awaits our discovery, a revelation that his poetry attempts to enact by taking us to a moment prior to the erection of the Urizenic world and Urizenic law. No doubt, this yearning appears to mimic the idea of a return to a paradise, or at least an alternative origin of law and power, prior to the fall. Yet it is also significant in that it represents an attempt to reinvent the role and status of political theology precisely at the moment when it was undergoing a critical mutation toward the secularization of the political concepts that had kept absolute forms of power in place for centuries. Blake's work confirms that political theology is not necessarily on the side of absolutism and that the secularization of political concepts inherited from this tradition, even when democratized, do not do away with the always latent possibility of a form of absolutism emerging from within democratic political forms. Blake's political theology points toward a "being-in-common" that acts as a buttress against this possibility. More important, however, his political theology invokes a gesture that would become an increasingly vital one in the aftermath of the gradual collapse of different forms of divine right: compressed into the question of how it is possible to think, without positing a necessarily absolute ground, the relation between law and what lies outside the law. If nothing by definition precedes the law, how does that anomic space or moment become represented inside the political, juridical, or religious order that it helps found? What political consequences emerge from the attempt to represent an unconditionality that is irreducible to the absolute? (In the next chapter, I explore these questions through a reading of Coleridge's own approach to the problem of political theology.)

Blake's attempt to create a fundamentally new, wholly invented political theology is framed by two different tendencies. The first involves his attempt to engage in a *critical* response to existing forms of political theology by challenging key assumptions and ruses that allow it to persist intact even when it is challenged or secularized. This is best demonstrated in the figure of Orc in *America: A Prophecy* where his role is to be a catalyst, an opening toward other possibilities that remain latent within a differently conceived relation between the theological and the political. The other tendency, which is represented by some of Blake's initial formulations in *The French Revolution* of a different form of the body politic structured by the infinity of desire, involves an attempt to offer a positive vision of what it would mean to found the state or the collective on an infinite or unconditional ground that cannot be reduced to a unique identity. These two tendencies are often in conflict with each other and are especially evident as Blake continued to develop these themes in his late epic poems. In a sense, they reflect two major tendencies at work in attempts to rethink political theology or ontology today.[48] One either begins by taking apart existing concepts, structures, and architectonics that belong to the tradition of political theology or ontology, showing their internal contradictions and subterfuges in order to gesture to other possibilities that lie dormant within them, or else one attempts a "positive" construction of a *new* political theology or ontology, with all the risks such an endeavor entails. As we will see in the chapters that follow, these two opposing tendencies were never quite reconciled in the conceptions of the political dimension of the imagination in most of the Romantic poets. Regardless of whether Blake's particular attempt to organize a new politics through a theologically inflected understanding of the imagination may or may not seem esoteric in its content, the form of its gesture remains a decisive one. He sets before us, in different registers, images, and poetics, a fundamental question for any attempt to think a modern conception of sovereignty: Is it possible to conceive of sovereignty without any determinate figure and without any *archē*? Blake's conception of poetic genius and the imagination constitutes a crossroads in the history of the attempt to do so.

TWO

The Blind Spot of Power: Sovereignty and Unconditionality in Coleridge's *Biographia Literaria* and *The Friend*

> It would be a question of critiquing, deconstructing if you will, one in the name of the other, sovereignty in the name of unconditionality. This is what would have to be thought, reasoned through, however impossible it might seem. Yet what is at issue is precisely another thought of the possible (of power, of the masterly sovereign "I can," of ipseity itself) . . .
>
> —DERRIDA, *Rogues*

> I asked, who then is at the head to guide them? He looked at me with ineffable contempt, not unmixed with an angry suspicion, and then replied, "No one." The string of blind men went on for ever without any beginning: for although one blind man could not move without stumbling, yet infinite blindness supplied the want of sight.
>
> —COLERIDGE, *Biographia Literaria*

Although the term "political imagination" has come to designate a variety of phenomena, in the case of Coleridge's theory of the imagination it could very well be considered a tautology. R. F. Storch's claim several decades ago that the "political function of the imagination precedes its literary function"[1] has yet to be fully developed in its consequences for understanding the interrelation between Coleridge's political theory and his aesthetics. Perhaps one of the reasons this articulation has not been developed is the fact that Coleridge's primary elaboration of the imagination takes place in the *Biographia Literaria*, a work that situates it within the context of what many commentators take to be Coleridge's main achievement: the development of the "practical criticism" of literature.[2] It is no accident, then, that the problem of the imagination, along with the symbol/allegory distinction, has been treated in relation to the discipline of literary studies.[3] In fact, the *Biographia Literaria*'s division into two volumes appears to repeat the structure of the ancient *agon* between philosophy and literature. For the philosophical articulation of the imagination that Coleridge advances with the help of interpretations of various German Idealists[4] in volume one is not easily reconciled with the specific readings of literary figures that become the focus of volume two. As a result, the imagination tends to be read as a transcendent aesthetic principle, just as the concepts of allegory and symbol are extracted from the specifically political aims that motivate the *Statesman's Manual* and its attempt to wed scriptural interpretation with the art of statecraft.

The nexus of texts that Coleridge published during the same period, including *The Statesman's Manual* (1816), *The Biographia Literaria* (1817), and the revised three-volume version of *The Friend* (1818) constitute a rich and varied set of works that are in dialogue with each other. Their interrelation provides important indications for understanding how Coleridge's metaphysics of the imagination evinces not just an aesthetic but a political dimension as well. Though many of these texts were composed much earlier (most of *The Friend* was originally published serially in 1810), the close proximity of their subsequent revision and publication suggests a set of concerns and theoretical arguments that cross multiple genres, evoking the interrelation of the philosophical, the political, and the literary. They also bear witness to the immediate aftermath of the historical crisis of political sovereignty that was emerging in post-Waterloo Europe. In the wake of the collapse of a conception of sovereignty grounded in divine law, coupled with the failure of its secular cousin, Reason, to vindicate anything other than the "self-willed" tyranny[5] of Napoleon, Coleridge responds to the historical exigency to find other principles that could ground the political (and the sovereign). It is in this exigency that the political dimension of Coleridge's conception of the imagination must be contextualized. The deduction of the imagination in chapter thirteen of *Biographia Literaria* anchors the various genres that he puts into contact with each other and acts as a center around which his political, literary, and aesthetic theory orbits.

To take seriously the politics of Coleridge's conception of the imagination is also to approach the question that a number of commentators have tried to answer concerning his political and religious convictions.[6] How is it that the political firebrand and religious dissident of the early 1795 *Lectures on Politics and Religion* came to seemingly endorse the status quo of

Church and State in his 1832 treatise *On the Constitution of Church and State*?[7] Various answers have been generated,[8] but a consensus has emerged that, although Coleridge's political views remain varied and independent, his conservatism is a consequence of his religious or theological convictions.[9] In this reading, the imagination as well as Coleridge's understanding of "Reason" are in the last instance theological concepts, functioning as substitutes for a God (whether Pantheist[10] or Anglican) who operates as the ground of political authority, moral order, and natural law.[11] Coleridge's "politics of the imagination" ultimately displaces the origin of authority from its theological foundations to the autonomous Subject (the "I am I") that Coleridge identifies with the imagination. If this is so, the question remains whether Coleridge's idealism simply repeats the transcendent structure of divine right by displacing and secularizing its origin as a divinity within Man. Nigel Leask makes a persuasive case that Coleridge's growing conservatism stems from his investment in a transcendental imagination that becomes a "spiritual consolation," a repository of cultural value sequestered from the growing "overbalance of the commercial spirit"[12]—or the commodification of social relations under capitalism. According to Leask, Coleridge's "politics of the imagination" starts out as an "overt and radical attack on both religious and political establishments, and especially a political tyranny endorsed by Anglicanism."[13] It later devolves into conservatism once it becomes transformed into the idea of a unifying cultural or poetic power "separated from material and social practice."[14] The imagination, thus, acts as an ideological category; it is divorced from history insofar as it mirrors the divine and inaugurates a realm of transcendent value. It is political only negatively because it remains detached from historical and political struggle, guarding "the political and moral virtue of the republic in a noumenal realm which [is] permitted to give the rule to conduct only by proxy."[15] According to this argument, Coleridge's attempt to find an alternative source of value to substitute for the discredited hierarchies of the *ancien régime* against the commodification of social relations ends up reinstating traditional structures of authority in a futile attempt to preserve the idea of a unified culture as a paradigm for civic behavior. This claim amounts to an equation of Coleridge's metaphysics with his conservatism;[16] his indebtedness to transcendental idealism accounts for his political recidivism, his theology for his political intransigence.[17]

In this chapter I do not disagree with these positions, at least as they apply to the notable divergences between Coleridge's early political positions and what comes to be evident in the late political treatise *On the Constitution of Church and State*. I do argue, however, that there is nothing *inherently* conservative about Coleridge's attempt to address the metaphysical bases of the political and that this was for him the very precondition for conceiving it otherwise.[18] While Coleridge's idealism certainly dovetailed with his theology, the particular connections he establishes between his deduction[19] of the imagination and the production of sovereign power cannot be easily reduced to a theological position. Thus, unlike Blake's attempt to redefine the limits of political-theology through a critique of the way political power originates in specific theological commitments, Coleridge's political theology attempts to understand this relationship without presupposing any particular theological commitments. What interests him instead is the question of how it is possible to move from an unconditional ground toward its manifestation in the political realm. To the extent that he remained a student of Kant, for whom the noumenal conditions of experience are always *immanent* to particular objects, Coleridge was an inheritor of a critical tradition that refused to posit knowledge of a purely transcendent ground without establishing the necessity of its deduction. This is why the famous "missing" deduction[20] of the imagination in chapter thirteen of the *Biographia Literaria* is crucial for an understanding of Coleridge's attempt to articulate morals, politics, and religion through "fixed principles" in his more politically-oriented work *The Friend*.

By "fixed principle" he means not simply faith in the divine, but the necessity of articulating the conditional in its relation to the *unconditional*. The fundamental question, at once metaphysical and political for Coleridge, is the following: How does a particular political arrangement ground itself by reference to an antecedent principle that cannot be given as such; what relation, in other words, does the sovereign (the king or the people) have to the ground of his sovereignty when he can no longer be understood as the realization of a simple transcendence? As we will see, these questions, for Coleridge, can only be answered by establishing specifically how the Subject is autonomous or self-grounding and by articulating how the unconditional comes to be represented in the political. Coleridge's focus on the imagination, reason, and the understanding in *Biographia Literaria*, and on their materialization in symbol or allegory in *The Statesman's Manual*, provide the crucial context for understanding his attempt to articulate a new principle of sovereignty in *The Friend*.

What emerges in these three texts is an *aporia* that arises from the attempt to articulate an alternative source of the political in a set of principles whose priority cannot, at least immediately, be given the imprimatur of a divine origin. That is why Coleridge insists they must be *self-grounding*. Unlike the monarch who asserts his authority by reference to an exteriority—the transcendence of God—Coleridge's fixed principles must authorize themselves *without* reference to something external to themselves precisely in order to be sovereign. The result is an unconditional sovereignty that cannot be separated from the necessity of its exposure to the conditioned. More concretely, in order to be absolute, sovereignty must *actualize* itself in a particular figure. This actualization introduces a radically finite, contingent moment into the sovereign's self-institution that cannot, in the last instance, be separated from his unconditionality. As Coleridge's well-known definition of the symbol suggests, the conditional and the unconditional, the finite and the infinite, are "consubstantial" (LS 29) with each other. This means that *neither of them is prior* and that therefore both together constitute the sovereignty of the sovereign.

This effectively places the problem of the "impersonation,"[21] incarnation, or representation of the unconditional, and thus the function of the imagination, at the heart of any contemporary notion of sovereignty. Put another way, the imagination, for Coleridge, constitutes the site both where the unconditional opens itself to the conditional and where the sovereignty of the sovereign is authorized, is given voice or, as Coleridge will put it in *The Statesman's Manual*, "ventriloquized."[22] This entails two different actualizations of the unconditional: a real literalization of it as its condition of possibility and a merely representational, figural relation to it as an absolute ground. The task for Coleridge's "politics of the imagination" is to thoroughly distinguish these two forms of actualization, since this distinction ultimately determines the sovereign's legitimacy. Coleridge develops a non-incarnational conception of sovereignty, along with a conception of the sovereign whose source of authority is irreducible to the political forms it makes possible. The result is a theory of sovereignty that attempts to reconcile the basic demand of traditional political sovereignty—that it be unconditional, without any authority that either precedes or supersedes it—with a conception of the sovereign that is entirely conditional and thus subject to endless variation. His theory, in other words, attempts to reconcile the threat of absolutism present in the theological-political with a democratic structure of shifting representations of sovereignty. Enlisting German Idealism and his theory of the symbol to rethink the relationship between sovereignty and the sovereign, Coleridge's understanding of the imagination is exposed to a more radical conception of how the unconditional comes to be incorporated into the political. Though he eventually retreats back to a theological position, I will argue that it is this other possibility that remains an important legacy of his interpretation of the political imagination.

In what follows, I begin by explicating the relationship Coleridge establishes between the various faculties of the Subject (Reason, the Understanding, and the Imagination) and the unconditional in the *Biographia Literaria* and *The Friend*. For Coleridge, politics must take into account the structure of Man's basic faculties, and his elaboration of the sovereign subject in turn provides a model for his conception of political sovereignty. I then focus on his deduction of the imagination in the *Biographia Literaria* since it becomes the central faculty for the *realization* or *representation* of Man's unconditional autonomy. I argue that Coleridge articulates a phenomenology of the unconditional and theorizes how it propagates authority. I then go on to analyze how *The Friend* applies the imagination's capacity for actualizing the unconditional to the political, producing Coleridge's specific conception of political sovereignty. I conclude with a meditation on how Coleridge's politics of the symbol opens up a different relationship between the unconditional and the sovereign, one that threatens to break finally with the threat of absolutism implied in attempting to embody the unconditional within the political.

The Unconditional, Reason, and the Imagination

The notion of the unconditional and its ability to found and organize morality, politics, and religion is the central guiding thread of Coleridge's political theory. Yet its role in his work is somewhat different from traditional attempts to ground the social on some basic apodictic certainty. When Coleridge insists in *The Friend* that he intends to "refer men's opinions to their absolute principles, and thence their feelings to the appropriate objects" and to "apply the principles thus ascertained, to the formation of stedfast convictions concerning the most important questions of Politics, Morality and Religion . . ." (FR 16), his task is different from the simple application of metaphysics to politics. Coleridge's task in *The Friend* is not merely speculative, but *critical* in the Kantian sense. Rather than propose up front a particular political program or moral system, Coleridge pushes the question of politics back to the *a priori* conditions in which political claims or institutions can be articulated in the first place.[23] The implication is that the "fixed principles" Coleridge refers to are *already at work* in the various political positions and philosophies he analyzes. The goal, then, is not the invention of new principles, but rather their discovery in the moral and political opinions already in circulation. What is needed, then, is a deduction of the principle that makes these opinions possible, which will confirm whether or not they are well founded. This means, first of all, as in Kant, defining the relation of Man's faculties to each other, their respective roles within various domains of knowledge. While Coleridge's presentation in *The Friend* could hardly be said to be systematic, it nonetheless displays a desire for systematicity,[24] a need to organize the question of politics, religion, and morality around a central point that unifies them into a coherent whole.

The same method that Coleridge employs to deduce the grounding principle of practical criticism—the imagination—is likewise employed in *The Friend* to deduce the "principles of political knowledge." In this section, Coleridge analyzes "all the different systems of political justice" and categorizes them according to their view of the "Human Being" and its faculties. The first system, based on Hobbesian contract theory, ". . . denies all truth and distinct meaning to the words, RIGHT and DUTY, and . . . affirm[s] that the human mind consists of nothing, but manifold modifications of passive sensation" (FR 166). Since, in this theory, it is man's defenselessness that forces him into society, the glue that holds the body politic together is *fear*, which, for Coleridge, neither legitimates law nor elevates man above his animal nature. There must be, he will go on to argue, a faculty within Man, inherent to him *as* Man, that prescribes him his social duties and rights. To develop this idea Coleridge details the taming of a mutinous crew aboard a ship commanded by Alexander Ball, who posts the rules of conduct such that "every individual of the ship should know and understand the code" (FR 169). The ship's crew, finding new discipline (and naval glory) as a result, is quelled by an "*invisible* power" of "LAW, acting on natures pre-configured to its influences. A Faculty was appealed to in the Offender's own being; a Faculty and a Presence, of which he had not been previously made aware—but it *answered* to the appeal!" (FR 171). This appeal of the law is to an "invisible combatant" whose power "is the same with that of my own permanent Self" (FR 171). Thus, Reason as lawgiver grounds social duties and obligations and provides the "true necessity, which compels man into the social state, now and always, by a still-beginning, never-ceasing force of moral cohesion" (FR 171). For Coleridge, Reason rather than fear is the basic organizing principle of society.

In Coleridge's argument, the function of Reason is to act as the sovereign ground of the common. It is the means by which an autonomous subject subjects himself to the law and thus locates himself within the social. In an earlier prefatory chapter Coleridge unveils the distinction between Reason and the Understanding that will later be crucial for his own political analysis. Reason, he argues, is "an organ bearing the same relation to spiritual objects, the Universal, the Eternal, and the Necessary, as the eye bears to material and contingent phænomena" (FR 155–56). The Understanding, by contrast, concerns the *a priori* conditions for the possibility of experience:

> Whatever is conscious *Self*-knowledge is Reason; and in this sense it may be safely defined the organ of the Super-sensuous; even as the Understanding wherever it does not possess or use the Reason, as another and inward eye, may be defined the conception of the Sensuous, or the faculty by which we generalize and arrange the phaenomena of perception: that faculty, the function of which contain the rules and constitute the possibility of outward Experience. (FR 156)

Coleridge is in familiar Kantian territory here. Reason, as super-sensuous faculty, is concerned with those things that cannot be objects of experience, the Understanding with the conceptual preconditions of any sensuous object. However, Coleridge departs from Kant significantly in his definition of Reason[25] since he insists that, unlike any other faculty, it is "identical with its appropriate objects" (FR 156), which would include "God, the Soul, Eternal Truth," all of which are "themselves reason" (FR 156).[26] This identification not only renders Reason a quasi-theological concept, but introduces the possibility that there are two distinct domains of the supersensible since both the Understanding and Reason are faculties concerned with laws *prior* to appearance. This problem becomes visible in Coleridge's later revision of the passage, which changes slightly the relation between the Understanding and Reason. Coleridge substitutes a phrase that indicates that Reason is "another and inward eye," suggesting that it is separate from the Understanding, with the phrase "*its* inward eye" (emphasis mine). Coleridge, in other words, vacillates between treating Reason as a heightened mode of the Understanding or as an entirely separate faculty. This vacillation can also be seen in Reason's non-transitive nature: "the Understanding and Experience may exist without Reason. But Reason cannot exist without Understanding; nor does it or can it manifest itself but in and through the understanding, which in our elder writers is often called *discourse*, or the discursive faculty" (FR 156). What follows from this is the necessity of the *ventriloquism*[27] of Reason *by* the Understanding, since Reason cannot act alone; it is in need of some form of articulation by something external to itself. It must speak itself through another, in a Coleridgean version of Hegel's "cunning of Reason."[28] Its newfound voice must discourse with itself through the Understanding, otherwise the force of its laws or edicts would be empty or blind.

The Understanding, then, is split between two functions: the "outward sense" that concerns the conditions of the possibility of objects of experience and thus deals with appearances and the aesthetic, and the "mind's eye" of Reason, a purely internal intuition whose immediacy bypasses the sensuous entirely. As Coleridge insists, the description of Reason as the "mind's eye" must be used "in its proper sense, and not as a mere synonyme of the memory or the fancy. In this way we reconcile the promise of Revelation, that the blessed will see God, with the declaration of St. John, God hath no one seen at any time" (FR 157). This reconciliation of revelation, appearance, and manifestation with the condition of *Deus absconditus* will be a crucial feature of Coleridge's elucidation of the nature of the manifestation of the sovereignty of Reason. What the Understanding establishes is the *presence* of Reason in its *withdrawal*, since it is radically incommensurate with any figure.[29] The sovereignty of Reason gives itself as the revelation of *Deus absconditus*, not as an incarnation.[30]

Thus, Coleridge's similar attempt to infer the fixed principles of political, moral, and religious judgments meets up with the problem of aesthetics, their conditions of appearance, and the basis for the transmission of Reason's authority in the figures it validates. Though symbol and allegory are not explicitly named, they are implied in the example Coleridge uses to depict the difference between forms of appearance reflective of the Understanding alone and forms of appearance specifically connected to the "mind's eye" (Reason):

> In this piece of *steel* I acknowledge the properties of hardness, brittleness, high polish, and the capability of forming a mirror. I find all these likewise in the plate glass of a friend's carriage; but in *addition* to all these, I find the quality of transparency, or the power of transmitting as well of as reflecting the rays of light. (FR 157)

Unlike the steel, which merely reflects or represents, the plate glass's "transparency" *transmits* Reason's authority through a medium that is not just reflective but capable of dissemination.

The problem of the actualization, impersonation, transmission, or ventriloquism of the unconditional is a key focus of the theory of the imagination that Coleridge develops in the *Biographia Literaria*. There, he first argues for the logical necessity of a principle within the Subject that is irreducible to appearances, ideas, or the passive reception of impressions. This is why Coleridge focuses for so long on English philosopher David Hartley's empiricist associationism, which reduces the Subject to sense-impressions or memories of sense impressions. Coleridge's critique of Hartley is essentially that he cannot account for the principle that organizes impressions and ideas except by positing a "soul." To do so, however, is to make Hartley's entire system profoundly self-contradictory since there is no corresponding "impression" that could verify the soul as the ground of the entire structure. As Coleridge suggests, the soul in Hartley's theory is a mere "*ens logicum*"[31] (BL I, 117); like Kant's transcendental unity of apperception, it acts as an empty formal placeholder for the unity of associations. In turn, it becomes, as Coleridge suggests, a "*caput mortuum*" (BL 117), the "dead head" of an organizing principle that cannot be reconciled with the structure it makes possible since it negates the idea that the mind is comprised entirely of associations. The soul reveals itself as a logical necessity, a "blind spot" within the Hartleian system, that it needs in order to constitute itself, but which institutes a fundamental contradiction at its core.

Coleridge turns this Hartleian blind spot into the object of his deduction of the imagination. He argues that associations, memories, impressions—in short, all forms of appearance—logically necessitate a principle that organizes them into a unity or single consciousness. Coleridge articulates the logical structure of this claim in chapter twelve of the *Biographia Literaria*, which calls for a principle that remains anterior to what it makes possible: "A system, which aims to deduce the memory with all the other functions of intelligence, must of course place its first position from beyond the memory, and anterior to it, otherwise the principle of solution would be itself a part of the problem to be solved" (BL I, 247). We see here a pattern that will repeat itself in various forms throughout Coleridge's philosophy, including *The Friend*. There must be a principle whose unconditionality is prior to what it makes possible. Unlike Kant's transcendental unity of apperception, however, this unconditional ground must also, from the beginning, implicate itself in the conditioned by actualizing itself there. It does so by passing from an "*ens logicum*," which remains a pure givenness not subject to further predication, into an "*ens reale*," something that acts in the world. Coleridge couches this problem initially as an attempt to intuit this principle as a *factum*, something immediately given to inner sense or the "mind's eye." In the end, however, this principle is not reducible to an intellectual intuition since, as he will go on to make clear, its actualization demands a certain perceptibility in order to be intuited.

Thus, Coleridge sets up the philosophical method that will not only lead to the logical deduction of a sovereign principle of pure unconditionality (from *ens logicum* to *ens reale*), but also to its unconditional self-grounding or realization; the method must contain both. The problem with a self-intuited starting point, however, is that "inner sense," unlike geometry, has no *content*—no "thing" to intuit:

> Philosophy is employed on objects of the INNER SENSE, and cannot, like geometry appropriate to every construction a correspondent *outward* intuition.

> Nevertheless, philosophy, if it is to arrive at evidence, must proceed from the most original construction, and the question then is, what is the most original construction or first productive act for the INNER SENSE. The answer to this question depends on the direction which is given to INNER SENSE. But in philosophy, the INNER SENSE cannot have its direction determined by any outward object. (BL 250)

Like the "mind's eye" from *The Friend*, the inner sense remains strictly non-sensuous. There is, in short, no *immediately* available intuition that inner sense has of itself, nor can its "first productive act" or "most original construction" be determined by anything outside of itself.

Yet this is precisely what Coleridge goes on to supply through an analogy with the geometrical figure of the line, which invokes the mere possibility of a purely self-grounded intuition of inner sense:

> To the original construction of the line, I can be compelled by a line drawn before me on the slate or on sand. The stroke thus drawn is indeed not the line itself, but only the image or picture of the line. It is not from it that we first learn to know the line; but on the contrary, we bring this stroke to the original line generated by the act of the imagination; otherwise we could not define it as without breadth or thickness. Still however this stroke is the sensuous image of the original or ideal line, and an efficient means to excite *every* imagination to the intuition of it. (BL I, 250)

The "stroke" in the sand or on the slate acts as an expedient; it is irreducible to the ideal line of geometry, which by definition is without breadth. The visible line merely "excites" the imagination toward an intuition of it, since the ideal line is already implied in the stroke that represents it. Coleridge's example here figures the infinite oscillation between objective and subjective knowledge out of which the reconciling finitude of the imagination emerges. Though the objective presentation of the line in the sand remains irreducible to the subjective ideal line, it nonetheless makes an intuition of it possible. Each, in other words, presupposes the other. This prefigures the "chiasmus"[32] between subjective and objective knowledge that Coleridge will insist requires the deduction of the reconciling "third" element (or "*tertium aliquid*") of the imagination: "During the act of knowledge itself, the objective and subjective are so instantly united, that we cannot determine to which of the two the priority belongs. There is here no first, and no second; both are coinstantaneous and one" (BL I, 255). Their co-instantaneity, Coleridge argues, requires a principle that "partakes of both" and that becomes antecedent to both, placing the imagination in the position of being at once the means by which two infinite unconditional principles are realized and the *a priori* unconditional principle that must itself be realized.

If this rather abstract excursion through Idealist philosophy appears to have left the question of the political behind, it is important to remember that Coleridge's elucidation of the faculties of the Subject become analogies for the autonomy of the sovereign in the political realm. This analogy is realized through the connection Coleridge makes between "inner sense" and the self-grounding act of freedom that is inaugurated through the imagination. When Coleridge poses the question of whether "there be found any means in philosophy to determine the direction of the INNER SENSE, as in mathematics it is determinable by its specific image or outward picture" (BL I, 250–51), he arrives at an enigmatic conclusion: "Now the inner sense has its direction determined for the greater part only by an act of freedom" (BL I, 251). This "act of freedom" is something Coleridge is at pains to distinguish from a representation, a "specific image or outward picture." As we will see, the possibility of the presentation of this outward picture will mark the transition to the political dimension of Coleridge's aesthetics.

Drawing on Kant's elaboration of the idea of freedom in the *Critique of Practical Reason*, Coleridge articulates the imagination not as a capacity of representation, but as the performative *actualization* of a force of law (Reason) that cannot be represented otherwise. As in Coleridge, the Kantian concept of freedom is precisely that which cannot be made an object of experience, since to do so would be to ensnare freedom's unconditionality within natural causality. Its *practical* application, however, is what gives freedom its reality, or its capacity to act in the world. As Kant insists: "Even though I have no intuition which would determine its [freedom's] objective theoretical reality, it nevertheless has a real application exhibited *in concreto* in intentions and maxims; that is, its practical reality can be pointed out."[33] The difference between Kant and Coleridge, however, hinges on the status of the possibility of an intuition of freedom, which Coleridge insists is the evidence of its practical reality. Kant's deduction of the concept of freedom in the *Critique of Practical Reason*, by contrast, makes the *lack* of any intuition of freedom the evidence of its reality: "Instead of the vainly sought deduction of the moral principle, however, something entirely different and unexpected appears: the moral principle itself serves as a principle of the deduction of an inscrutable faculty which no experience can prove but which speculative reason had to assume as at least possible. This is the faculty of freedom. . . ."[34] Arriving at the deduction of moral law, Kant insists that it "defines the law for a causality the concept of which was only negative in speculative philosophy, and for the first time it gives objective reality to this concept."[35] Having displaced the question of freedom from the domain of knowledge, Kant can claim that its deduction no longer obeys speculative-theoretical demands for evidence and that its mere possibility constitutes its reality for "beings which acknowledge the law as binding upon them."[36]

Unlike Kant, however, Coleridge maintains the unity of the speculative and the practical and thus has to account for the way in which the transcendent laws of Reason become immanent from the outset. Kant sequesters the unconditional within the realm of the intelligible, asserting that the sensuous world is structured as an ascent from the conditioned to the conditioned *ad infinitum*. He thus ultimately separates faith from knowledge. Coleridge, by contrast, seeks to produce the unconditional as the identifiable ground of the conditioned: "For as philosophy is neither a science of the reason or understanding only, not merely a science of morals, but the science of BEING altogether, its primary ground can be neither merely speculative or merely practical, but both in one" (BL I, 252). As a result, Coleridge's deduction of the imagination must be read as an attempt to finitize the unconditional, to reunite faith with knowledge, precisely at the "blind spot" of their compact.[37] More than just a model or an analogy of the efficacy of the unconditional, Coleridge's deduction of the imagination involves an attempt to move beyond a traditional attempt to represent it. It attempts to *enact* the unconditional within the conditioned, to give it a direct causality, and, in the end, to expose it to its own finite act of self-grounding.

It is here that the political import of Coleridge's metaphysics reaches its highest state of tension, at once confirming a desire for a real and effective absolute sovereignty, while at the same time exposing the unconditional immediately to finitude, dissemination, and fragmentation. This is why the "digressions," as Coleridge calls them, in chapter ten of the *Biographia* provide a crucial context for understanding the imagination's political vocation. This chapter, entitled "Opinions in Religion and Politics," repeats whole sections from the 1810 version of *The Friend*, describing the national unity displayed in Britain by both "reverers of the throne" and "honest zealots of the people" during the British wars against Napoleon. Coleridge explicitly attributes this unity to the unconditional principles it is the task of the *Biographia* to elucidate:

> If then unanimity grounded on moral feelings has been among the least equivocal sources of our national glory, that man deserves the esteem of his countrymen . . . who devotes his life and the utmost efforts of his intellect to the preservation and continuance of that unanimity by the disclosure and establishment of *principles*. For by these all *opinions* must be ultimately tried; and . . . on the knowledge of these all unanimity, not accidental and fleeting, must be grounded. (BL I, 190–91)

While one can detect a certain degree of defensiveness in this claim, given Coleridge's reputation for identifying earlier in his career with the "honest zealots of the people" *against* the "reverers of the throne," the larger point here should not be lost that the deduction of the principles of this unanimity awaits the reader in chapter thirteen in the form of the deduction of the imagination.

Coleridge's mapping out of the Subject and his focus on the deduction of the imagination is essentially framed by the question of the grounds for the possibility of social cohesion, organized on the collective universality of the dictates of Reason, which the imagination translates. The particular form of the "Self" or "self-consciousness" that Coleridge will go on to elaborate in the *Biographia* in turn becomes the form of the structure of self-grounding at the level of the social. Just as the Subject grounds itself in the opposition between objective and subjective knowledge, reconciled by the imagination, so the sovereign is grounded in the opposition between Reason and its manifestation in the Understanding. In both cases, it is a principle of actualization that acts as the point of articulation for an antecedent ground and its legitimate manifestation. As Coleridge insists: "every *principle* contains in itself the germ of a prophecy; and as the prophetic power is the essential privilege of science, so the fulfilment of its oracles supplies the outward and (to men in general) the *only* test of its claim to the title" (BL I,

191–92). His use of the language of entitlement to describe the oracular power of the unconditional places it within its proper context: the question of the transmission or manifestation (and continuity) of authority.

The oracular power of the imagination is not predicated on an absolute transcendence, however. Although Coleridge is clearly invested in the question of religion within the limits of reason alone, he strongly qualifies the nature and source of the imagination's oracular capacities. I will return to this question of the oracular capacities of the imagination in the section that follows. One of the main ways Coleridge circumscribes the capacities of the imagination is by remaining firmly rooted in Kant's distinction between "transcendent" and "transcendental" principles, which he mentions briefly in chapter twelve (BL I, 237), but which is implied throughout much of his philosophical writing.[38] Transcendent and transcendental principles both refer to something beyond experience. Transcendental principles, however, are always the *a priori* conditions of the sensuous, whereas transcendent principles eschew any reference to the sensuous whatsoever. In Kant, the inability to distinguish between the two leads to "transcendental illusion" and the antinomies of pure reason, where something that cannot be treated as an object of experience (such as freedom) is understood *as if* it were. The consequence of Coleridge's insistence on this distinction is that, for him, the transcendental antecedent ground of the sensuous is always necessarily referred to it; the unconditional is always the unconditional *of* the conditioned. There is no unconditional "as such," only the transmission of its authority in and through the conditioned.

Thus, Coleridge's idealism is not a subjective idealism insofar as it remains loyal to Kant's insistence on the necessary applicability of *a priori* conditions to the sensuous, which entails the constant collapse of the transcendental into the empirical. As we'll see, this distinction also proves helpful for understanding Coleridge's conception of the relation between sovereignty and the sovereign, since he sees a danger in the absolutism that he thinks results from the transcendental illusion of an origin of authority that is radically *other* to the sovereign. For Coleridge, genuine sovereignty implies a principle that is capable of grounding itself without reference to a transcendent authority that precedes it, and thus threatens to destroy it in advance. This principle, however, must present itself as a pure starting point—something without antecedent and therefore also without precedent. Drawing on Fichte's absolute positing of the "I am" in *The Science of Knowledge*,[39]

Coleridge will similarly posit an absolute origin, a "groundless ground" that is "groundless; but only because it is itself the ground of all other certainty" (BL I, 260). Fichte's opening gesture in *The Science of Knowledge* similarly attempts to establish a "primordial, absolutely unconditioned first principle of all human knowledge."[40] He asserts, however, that this starting point can "be neither *proved* nor *defined*, if it is to be an absolutely primary principle." This starting point thus expresses not an originary state of consciousness, but an "*Act* which does not and cannot appear among the empirical states of our consciousness, but rather lies at the basis of all consciousness and alone makes it possible."[41]

Unlike Fichte, however, Coleridge will imply that this act is identical with a pure intuition of itself. Thesis seven in chapter twelve of the *Biographia* insists that its status as an act has to do with the irreducibility of the Subject to its self-presentation in an object: "It has been shown, that a spirit is that, which is its own object, yet not originally an object, but an absolute subject for which all, itself included, may become an object. It must therefore be an ACT; for every object is, as an *object*, dead, fixed, incapable in itself of any action, and necessarily finite" (BL I, 278–79). Coleridge's emphasis on the morbidity and inactivity of the object shifts responsibility for the original act toward the opposite polarity of the subject.[42] This is significant for two reasons. First, it makes the absolute "I Am" identical with the founding "Act"[43] rather than something that emerges after reflection. The grounding principle of the "I Am," of course, becomes a key feature of Coleridge's definition of the imagination in chapter thirteen, where the primary imagination is defined as "a repetition in the finite mind of the eternal act of creation in the infinite I AM" (BL I, 304). Second, and most important, it turns the original act of the "I am" into an irreducible anteriority. The figure that would represent it, or the voice that would ventriloquize it, always comes too late and is thus always divided between the act and the need for its repetition, for its retrospective reconstitution as inaugural. The relation between figure and act thus takes on a different status in Coleridge. It becomes focused less on the *re*-presentation of transcendence and focused more on the process that is set in place by a structure that can only ever repeat an inaugural founding act *as if* it had already taken place.

Coleridge thus performs a subtle shift away from Fichte's and Schelling's principles of the "I Am," which, though playing a similar philosophical role, remain for Coleridge fundamentally immune to reflection. This is the point where Thomas McFarland's attempt to situate Coleridge within a tradition of philosophy that begins with the "I Am" as opposed to the "it is" breaks down:[44]

> We are to seek therefore for some absolute truth capable of communicating to other positions a certainty, which it has not itself borrowed; a truth self-grounded, unconditional and known by its own light. In short, we have to find a somewhat which *is*, simply because it *is*. In order to be such, it must be one which is its own predicate, so far at least that all other nominal predicates must be modes and repetitions of itself. Its existence too must be such, as to preclude the possibility of requiring a cause or antecedent without an absurdity. (BL I, 268)

The "I Am" is first of all an "it is," a pure act of positing that posits itself but that has initially no content. Like Fichte's unconditional first principle, it is purely tautological, having no predicates but itself. It is, as it were, folded in on itself, self-contained, and therefore whole and unscathed.[45]

What opens it up, and ultimately confirms its authority, is the necessity of its actualization by a key predicate that is not identical with it: namely, the will. The will is also a key feature of the "secondary imagination" whose repetition of the primary Imagination is defined in part by its coexistence with the will: "The secondary I consider as an echo of the former, co-existing with the conscious will, yet still as identical with the primary in the *kind* of its agency" (BL I, 304). The will differs from the original act "only in *degree*, and in the *mode* of its operation" (BL I, 304). While the original act of the "I Am" is prior to any empirical consciousness, the concept of the will is what completes the founding act through repetition. This marks another important difference between Coleridge and his German Idealist precursors. As David Ferris contends, Schelling makes the will a necessary moment within a larger system that only retrospectively attains completion once it has given itself the right to ground itself absolutely, whereas Coleridge "uses Schelling's principle as if it were an absolute fact, as if Schelling's principle and its exposition were the original series, and not merely its copy or perfect imitation."[46] While for Schelling, the completion of the system occurs only in a long, mediated detour that returns to its point of departure, Coleridge makes the will present from the very beginning, immediately divided from the inaugural act that it repeats. The relation to the founding act of the will is therefore always retrospective, never proleptic.

This deviation from his German Idealist predecessors introduces a problem, however. If the self-grounding of the "I Am" has already taken place, if it lies in an anteriority that always already withdraws, then the threat is that the unconditional becomes nothing but a ghost, like Hartley's "*caput mortuum*" of the soul. Such a principle would remain sovereign in itself, but not sovereign for others, a pure form whose self-identity renders it impotent. This is why the elaboration of the will in thesis nine and Coleridge's description of the transition from the "notional" thesis of the unconditional to its actualization are key moments in his account of the imagination, as well as for understanding how a legitimate form of sovereignty emerges in his political theory. In Schelling's *System of Transcendental Idealism*, the unconditional is realized in the final culminating moment of the aesthetic, which provides an objective and universal reflection of the original starting point.[47] For Coleridge, by contrast, the unconditional has already grounded itself *from the beginning*. The question then becomes what need the unconditional has for spectacle or figuration at all. If the starting point of Coleridge's system lies in an anteriority that always already withdraws from any presentation, any secondary act of the imagination will only ever be able to echo this withdrawal, confirming the primary imagination's anteriority through its own difference from it. It is only in and through this difference that it can retrospectively affirm the original founding act of the imagination.

Deductio Interruptus: *The Withdrawal of the Unconditional*

Before turning to Coleridge's application of these *aporia* to political theory, we must first approach the two solutions Coleridge proposes for how the unconditional effectuates itself through the conditional. Coleridge schematizes two very different solutions in the *Biographia* that account for his somewhat contradictory impulses in the exploration of authority. The first, which I will not be able to explore in detail though it is certainly a dominant tendency of Coleridge's thought, I will call the "theistic" solution.[48] Coleridge proposes a version of it in thesis nine. This thesis suggests that the "primary act of self-duplication" (between subject and object) implied in the will's repetition of the founding act of consciousness can be reduced to an "equatorial point," where "philosophy would pass into religion, and religion become inclusive of philosophy" (BL I, 283). As Coleridge puts it, we would "proceed from the SELF, in order to lose and find all self in God" (BL I, 283). The theistic solution, in short, locates faith at the original blind spot of the self-grounding unconditional principle. As Coleridge puts it in *The Statesman's Manual*:

> We (that is the human race) LIVE BY FAITH. Whatever we do or know, that in kind is different from the brute creation, has its origin in a determination of the reason to have faith and trust in itself. This, its first act of faith, is scarcely less than identical with its own being. *Implicité*, it is the COPULA—it contains the *possibility*—of every position, to which there exists any correspondence in reality. It is itself, therefore, the realizing principle, the spiritual substratum of the whole complex body of truths. This primal act of faith is enunciated in the word, GOD: a faith not derived from experience, but its ground and source, and without which the fleeting *chaos of facts* would no more form experience, than the dust of the grave can of itself make a living man. The imperative and oracular form of the inspired Scripture is the form of reason itself in all things purely rational and moral. (LS 18)

The unconditional has faith in its own reason precisely because it grounds itself, organizing the "chaos of facts" through the bond or oath it keeps with itself to believe in itself and to impart the solidity of this belief to what follows from it. As Coleridge asserts: "Here the immediate consciousness decides: the idea is its own evidence, and is insusceptible of all other. It is necessarily groundless and indemonstrable; because it is itself the ground of all possible demonstration. The Reason hath faith in itself, in its own revelations" (LS 32). Reason's faith in itself goes beyond its self-authorization. It passes into a "revelation" exemplified by the revealed Word, which requires only the requisite faith of the believer to give it authority.[49] It implies what Ian Balfour has argued so effectively: that Coleridge's theory of politics and rhetoric is "grounded in a theological metaphysics authorized by a certain ventriloquism of the divine word."[50]

Coleridge, however, proposes a second response to the *aporia* generated by the self-grounding of the unconditional, in what one might call its "fictional" resolution. This resolution is sketched in chapter thirteen of the *Biographia* in the deduction of the imagination itself. It privileges two elements that ground or legitimate the unconditional: the discovery of a necessary form of "finite generation" that cannot be dissociated from the unconditional itself, and the necessity of the interruption of its (self)-presentation.[51] The first has to do with what Coleridge calls the transition from the unconditional's purely "notional thesis" to its actualization. The second pertains to the staged interruption of the deduction of the imagination by a letter from a friend who advises Coleridge, in the name of his reputation, to dispense with an argument that would be required to "omit so many links" that it would appear "like the fragments of the winding steps of an old ruined tower" (BL I, 302–3). The letter is, of course, a conceit, but one that nevertheless plays an important role in what ends up being the deduction of a principle that is both an unconditional ground and the means by which this ground is deduced. The division between primary and secondary imaginations that emerges on the other side of the letter's interruption confirms the consubstantiality of the will with the fundamentally unverifiable act that precedes it. This other solution affirms a necessary fictionality to the withdrawal of the unconditional that remains internal to it, allowing it to operate, to disseminate itself. As I will suggest, the interruption of the deduction of the imagination actualizes the unconditional not by authorizing particular figures who personify it, but by constituting what Claude Lefort calls the "empty place of power,"[52] which involves the *withdrawal* of the unconditional from the space of representation. This withdrawal, in fact, guarantees that it cannot be fully instituted or materialized by any given figure and that its power is thus only ever partially presented.

In chapter twelve, the actualization of the "I Am" in its repetition by the will constitutes the *form* of the self-determining principle, the "primary act of self-duplication" (BL I, 281) inherent to it. Coleridge begins by articulating this "act of self-duplication" as a transition from a purely notional or logical necessity to an actual necessity:

> Now the transcendental philosophy demands; first, that two forces should be conceived which counteract each other by their essential nature; not only not in consequence of the accidental direction of each, but as prior to all direction,

> nay, as the primary forces from which the conditions of all possible directions are derivative and deducible: secondly, that these forces should be assumed to be both alike infinite, both alike indestructible. The problem will then be to discover the result or product of two such forces, as distinguished from the result of those forces which are finite, and derive their difference solely from the circumstance of their direction. When we have formed a scheme or outline of these two different kinds of force, and of their different results by the process of discursive reasoning, it will then remain for us to elevate the Thesis from notional to actual, by contemplating intuitively this one power with its two inherent indestructible yet counter-acting forces, and the results or generations to which their interpenetration gives existence, in the living principle and in the process of our own self-consciousness. (BL I, 299)

The "two forces . . . which counteract each other by their essential nature" are the principles of subjective and objective knowledge, neither of which can act by itself as an unconditional ground since each side of their polarity immediately implies the other. Thesis four insists that the very idea that there are two or more unconditional principles is impossible since each would have to "refer to some other, by which its equality is affirmed; consequently neither would be self-established" (BL I, 269). Each side's sovereignty is violated by its dependence on the other, necessitating reference to a "third" which is "neither subject nor object exclusively, but which is the identity of both" (BL I, 271). The imagination is thus already implied in the purely notional thesis Coleridge offers here. His insistence that the result of the opposing forces could not produce "arrest or neutralization" (BL I, 300) leads to the necessity of the "*tertium aliquid*, or finite generation" (BL I, 300) of the imagination. In other words, for Coleridge, the necessity of finite generation follows immediately from the necessity of the unconditional itself. The notional thesis of the imagination leads directly or *immediately* to the principle's actualization because finite generation is not external to the unconditional, but is consubstantial with it, a part of what makes it unconditional to begin with. This claim, however, takes Coleridge no further than the notional thesis established in chapter twelve, since all he has done is posit a series of logical necessities that follow directly from the *idea* of the unconditional. What Coleridge attempts to establish in the deduction of the imagination is its practical application, its elevation from notional to actual.

Just as Coleridge begins this task, however, the transcription of the deduction is interrupted by the arrival of a letter whose function has received a range of interpretations,[53] but has usually been understood either as an alibi for an argument that Coleridge cannot make, or a ruse that allows Coleridge to mask a sleight of hand for a principle that, fundamentally, cannot be presented. Another way to view the letter, however, is as a *form of the deduction* itself. Rather than understand it as a substitution, standing in place of an argument that cannot be made, the letter in fact exemplifies the only actualization of the notional thesis that could be offered.[54] Since what the unconditional is *not* is a transcendent principle separate from finite generation, and since its self-intuition, or self-grounding, is not the intuiting of an object, cognition, or appearance, what better way to exemplify its having already established its authority than through a practical intervention that hints at the possibility of a full presentation without actually giving it? In other words, the gap between the interrupted deduction and the resulting definition of the imagination *is* the principle's progression from the notional thesis to its actualization.

This actualization takes place through a formal dramatization or fictionalization of something that cannot become an object of experience, but which nonetheless is "given" in the interruption by withdrawing from the scene. The friend's letter hints at this reading in several ways, notably in its use of the image of a fragmented tower to describe the missing deduction: " imperfectly as I understand the present Chapter, I see that clearly that you have done too much, and yet not enough. You have been obliged to omit so many links, from the necessity of compression, that what remains, looks . . . like the fragments of the winding steps of an old ruined tower" (BL I, 302–3). One could read here the established Romantic trope of a fragment that is meant to evoke a whole of which it is a part, just as Coleridge's definition of the symbol in *The Statesman's Manual* implies a theory of incompletion that generates the symbol's synecdochal structure. The letter would then be understood as the substitution of a part (the prospectus) for a longer work yet to be written, namely the deduction itself. Yet the image of the ruined tower is not entirely synecdochal, since what is fragmented are the steps themselves, which represent access to the unity that the symbol is supposed to evoke. What it offers instead is a figure of the impossible, an apogee that cannot be reached, but whose hold on the imagination is all the more powerful for that very reason.

The structure of interruption that gives something withdrawn, hidden, or unpresentable is a recurring trope in much of Coleridge's oeuvre, particularly his poetry, whose use he imported to his prose works. It characterizes his famous fragment poem *Kubla Khan*, for example, whose preface tells the story of the composition of a longer original poem composed while asleep, which is described as having simply presented itself "without any sensation or consciousness of effort."[55] Upon waking, the speaker begins writing down the lines given to him in the dream, only to be interrupted by a "person on business from Porlock" who detains him an hour and causes the dream-poem to pass away "like the images on the surface of a stream into which a stone has been cast." The poem then builds a reference to this prior one into its very structure. While claiming to have a "distinct recollection of the whole," the poet produces a "fragment of a very different character"—*Kubla Khan*—which acts as a synecdochal repetition of the dream-poem.

The relation between *Kubla Khan* and its preface, however, is complicated by the fact that Coleridge's poem is also structured by the necessity of repetition in the relation between Kubla Khan's "decree" (line 2) in the first stanza and the poet's desire to revive it in the last. The poem is thus caught between two different relations to the unconditional: the pure givenness of the original poem, which arises through a passive synthesis, and the repetition of Kubla Khan's willful decree of the pleasure dome that inaugurates the extant poem. His unconditional decree in the first stanza frames the interior of the pleasure dome around the sacred river Alph, whose name suggests an "Alpha," a source or origin. Kubla Khan's position as the founder of a dynasty, and his status as a figure for the inaugural power of a political act, is juxtaposed with the "sacred river," whose path through "caverns measureless to man" (line 4) and "forests ancient as the hills" (line 10) suggests a natural anteriority that Khan attempts to reproduce or at least to cordon off inside the dome. What appears to be an inaugural act is in fact placed immediately in relation to something prior that the decree attempts to appropriate, encircle, and enfold, but whose measurelessness remains irreducible.

This is perhaps why Kubla Khan's fiat gives way in the second stanza to a wild turmoil and juxtaposition of opposites inside the dome. The imagery of the second stanza suggests something more than untamed nature or spontaneous creativity. Rather, it is characterized by a violent "tumult" (line 29) centered on the "Romantic chasm's" transformation of the sacred river:

> And from this chasm, with ceaseless turmoil seething,
> As if this earth in fast thick pants were breathing,
> A mighty fountain momently was forced:
> Amid whose swift half-intermitted Burst
> Huge fragments vaulted like rebounding hail. (lines 17–21)

The violence of this passage arises out of the imposition of the dome. The river's course toward the "caverns measureless to man" is briefly interrupted, forced into view through the sudden appearance of the fountain. Its materialization suggests less a spontaneous source of creative inspiration than an attempt to repeat, and appropriate, an anteriority that cannot readily become the object of a will or a decree. The poem thus stages the question of how the unconditional is *made* to appear and what role Kubla Khan's apparently arbitrary imposition plays in this process. The last stanza of the poem likewise contemplates the role of poetry and fiction in the attempt to reconstitute the force of his unconditional decree, a point I will return to shortly.

It is important first to understand the way in which the impossibility of the deduction of the imagination in chapter thirteen of the *Biographia Literaria* is reflected in the interrupting letter's emphasis on the shift from questions about the content of the deduction to the effects it has—on Coleridge's readers, on Coleridge's reputation, and on the friend himself. The friend confesses that Coleridge's method of argumentation is so new, and "so directly the reverse of all [he] had ever been accustomed to consider as truth," that "[he] should have felt as if [he] had been standing on his head" (BL I, 301). This feeling of inversion, like an image in a *camera obscura*, is translated into the friend's description of his "apotheosis":

> The effect on my feelings . . . I cannot better represent, than by supposing myself to have known only our light airy modern chapels of ease, and then for the first time to have been placed, and left alone, in one of our largest Gothic cathedrals in a gust moonlight night of autumn. "Now in glimmer, and now in gloom"; often in palpable darkness not without a chilly sensation of terror; then suddenly emerging into broad yet visionary lights with coloured shadows, of fantastic shapes yet all decked with holy insignia and mystic symbols. (BL I, 301)

The friend's elaboration of the effects of Coleridge's argument foregrounds the feeling of complete inversion, the interplay of oppositions intimated in the friend's sense of standing on his head. The entire passage describes a reversal, moving from "chapels of ease" to the "gloom" of the cathedral, from the "light" of knowledge to the "darkness," "terror," and obscurity of the Gothic. The reversal is completed only by another chiasmatic reversal, whereby the darkness of the cathedral is made the condition for the "colored shadows" and "fantastic shapes" that suddenly emerge. The friend's confession that Coleridge's argument induces the "reverse of all that [he] had ever been accustomed to consider truth" is given shape by an image that makes a *lack* of sight the condition for the emergence of the "holy insignia" and "mystic symbols" that portend a force or power beyond them. The friend's description involves an actualization of shadow into substance, through the obscurity of an initial lack of vision, a darkness that mobilizes it, giving it the force of reality: "In short, what I had supposed substances were thinned away into shadows, while every where shadows were deepened into substances" (BL I, 301).

The fact that it is a question of the power or effect of the non-arrival, or non-appearance of the deduction of the imagination, is confirmed by the friend's invocation, in the next paragraph, of the power of oracular vision. The friend's mention of the cave of Trophonius, named for the architect of the Oracle at Delphi, might at first glance appear to relate the missing deduction to Coleridge's conception of truth as a ventriloquism of the divine. However, the nature of this ventriloquism takes on a somewhat different resonance in the *Biographia*, given the way it operates in the friend's promise to await Coleridge's full presentation of the deduction: "Be assured, however, that I look forward anxiously to your great book on the CONSTRUCTIVE PHILOSOPHY, which you have promised and announced: and that I will do my best to understand it. Only I will not promise to descend into the dark cave of Trophonius with you, there to rub my own eyes, in order to make the sparks and figured flashes, which I am required to see" (BL I, 302). The allusion to the dark cave picks up on the imagery of the transposition of darkness into vision found in the friend's description of the Gothic cathedral. But it also adds an ironic comment on the authority transmitted by the missing deduction. Oracles, of course, are intermediaries for divine power, ventriloquizing the gods, allowing them to speak and thus presenting their will to mortals in the mask of an agent of divine authority. The difference between the oracle at Delphi and the oracle of Trophonius, however, is in how each oracle articulates a relation between authority and its mediation. The oracle at Delphi entailed the supplicant receiving its pronouncements through the *pythia* or priestess, whose inspiration was generated by the *pneuma*, the soul or spirit, that would emanate from the earth. Though the priestess's pronouncements required interpretation, her power operated according to an established relationship between source and ventriloquist. The supplicant descended into the chamber known as the *adyton* (or "the inaccessible") in order to receive a revelation mediated by the priestess whose ventriloquy of the divine transmitted its authority, giving access to the inaccessible, and speaking on behalf of a transcendent other. In the case of the Cave of Trophonius, however, the supplicant becomes *himself* the oracle. He descended into a cave, or in some accounts was dragged into it by an unknown force. According to Pausanias's account, the supplicant was required to drink from the rivers of *Mnemosyne* and *Lethe*, suggesting that the knowledge he received was also a form of forgetting. Once emerging from the cave, the supplicant was overwhelmed by either melancholy or madness and placed in the "chair of *Mnemosyne*" where, confused, half-mad, and terrified, his ravings were interpreted by a priest. Since the supplicant becomes the oracle himself, he can no longer testify to the truth of his own ventriloquy (a fact that the friend's letter reinforces in its suggestion that he would be required to "rub [his] own eyes" to induce the "sparks and figured flashes" of revelation). Unlike the mediation of the *pythia*, whose pronouncements may constitute partial, but nonetheless direct, "ventriloquy of the divine," the Trophonius reference places a constitutive form of forgetting at the heart of the conditions of possibility for the revelation of (divine) authority.

This blind spot internal to the birth of the imagination, figured in the interruption of its deduction, is precisely what allows it to become "a repetition in the finite mind of the eternal act of creation of the infinite I AM" (BL I, 304). Commensurate with its "finite generation," the interruption paradoxically actualizes the unconditional by instituting its withdrawal, its irreducibility to appearance. Thus, while keeping the possibility of its full advent alive in the promise of its realization, the imagination actualizes the unconditional by instituting it as a non-appearing ground, the *wo es war, soll*

Ich werden ("where it was, there I shall become")[56] of something that keeps itself intact and promises itself to the future. Hence, the very impossibility of the unconditional's appearance constitutes its power and authority. Like the darkness of the Gothic cathedral, or the madness induced by the cave of Trophonius, its authority is generated out of the blindness from which it originates, in the always already lost act of positing that produces its emergence. This is why Coleridge's deduction of the imagination is divided between a primary act that can never be reconstituted and its echo in the secondary imagination, where it is mixed with a conscious will that repeats its impossibility *as if* it were realizable. The secondary imagination retrospectively fictionalizes the antecedence to which it owes its birth and its authority by promising to recover the original voice that it echoes, even as it maintains the impossibility of doing so.

The last stanza of *Kubla Khan* similarly contrasts Khan's original political decree with the poet's secondary attempt to repeat its inaugural power. The vision of the "damsel with the dulcimer" that prompts the speaker's desire to "revive" her song, however, is radically provisional:

> A damsel with a dulcimer
> In a vision once I saw:
> It was an Abyssinnian maid,
> And on her dulcimer she played,
> Singing of Mount Abora
> Could I revive within me
> Her symphony and song,
> To such deep delight 'twould win me,
> That with music loud and long,
> I would build that dome in air. (lines 37–46)

This passage's emphasis on the conditional ("*could* I revive . . . to such deep delight '*twould* win me") suggests not just a capacity that the poet lacks, but an inability to know if the song can be revived without converting it back into a mere artificial "device" (line 35) like the pleasure dome, whose insubstantiality means that it can now only be built "in air" (line 46). This possibility of fictionalization, the production of a false paradise suggested in the reference to "Mount Abora" (which is an allusion to Milton's Mount Amara described in *Paradise Lost* as a "supposed True Paradise"), implies that the necessity of finite generation is both a condition of possibility for realizing, "reviving," or actualizing the unconditional and also a threat to it, since it simultaneously introduces the possibility that the unconditional is *nothing but* a fiction. Thus, *Kubla Khan*, formally a fragment poem, speaks of a break between the absolute unconditional authority of a decree and the condition of simulation or fictionalization required to consummate it. Like the *Biographia*, *Kubla Khan* insists that the unconditional and its fictionalization are inseparable—the former cannot exist without the latter—and that what is fictionalized emerges out of the *interruption*, the non-appearance, of the unconditional.

Primary and secondary imaginations, then, do not designate a logical or temporal before and after. They designate, rather, an unconditionality opened in advance to the conditional, divided within itself, and capable of incorporating within itself the *finite* moment of its institution. The unconditional, for Coleridge, is not an idea or an ideal that simply awaits its incarnation. It emerges through its (self-)interruption, which allows it to act as both figure and ground simultaneously, becoming an enabling limit across which it projects its own ventriloquized voice of authority

The Ventriloquism of Power

The political consequences of Coleridge's "fictional" solution to the impasse of an unconditional ground that can only authorize itself by exposing itself immediately to the conditional is developed further in *The Friend*. What the *Biographia* makes clear, and what *The Friend* and *The Statesman's Manual* translate into political terms, are the consequences of a notion of an unconditional that is no longer transcendent to what it authorizes. The unconditional as a principle of politics cannot do without a theory of its manifestation, including the manifestation of its impossibility, and it is this theory that *The Friend* and *The Statesman's Manual* elaborate. It is through the concept of the political application of the symbol in *The Statesman's Manual*, and the related notion of the "expedient" in *The Friend*, that Coleridge's articulation of his conception of sovereignty is developed. The symbol and expedient are attempts to account for the *non*-appearance of the unconditional through its partial representation. The partiality of the symbol, however, unlike allegory, is oriented by the *unique* withdrawal of the unconditional. This withdrawal articulates a synecdochal structure that, while not presenting the unconditional as such, nonetheless makes it a privileged figure by giving it the status of a legitimate offshoot, a figuration produced by the difference between it and the totality it strives to project. For Coleridge, as we'll see, the question of political sovereignty must pass through a notion of its figuration or "fictioning;"[57] the point of contact between the unconditional and the political is the finite generation that he describes in the deduction of the imagination. Without it, not only does the unconditional become an empty concept, but as a result genuine sovereignty becomes impossible. And since there is more than one pretender to the throne of the unconditional, the question will become not only how true sovereignty emerges as a political form, but how it articulates a relation to the antecedence that authorizes it. What these philosophical questions lead to, ultimately, is Coleridge's attempt in *The Friend* to demarcate a false ventriloquism of the unconditional from a genuine one.

Before considering Coleridge's politics of the symbol, however, it is important first to comprehend his recasting of the unconditional in terms of a perpetually self-renewing social contract that determines the individual's sense of duty to others. As we have already seen, Coleridge articulates Reason both as a quasi-theological concept and a quasi-faculty of Man, a "spiritual organ" (FR 158) capable of instituting laws, including the law of freedom and the laws of conscience. Once Coleridge moves from his description of the faculties to their application in the "Principles of Political Knowledge," the question becomes how Reason "determines our moral relations, as members of a body politic" (FR 174). Since, as we have seen, the imagination actualizes the unconditional through a presentation of its retreat from the space of representation, the interruption of its arrival gestures toward something akin to a regulative principle in the Kantian sense. A regulative principle, according to Kant, cannot be verified by the Understanding, but it is nonetheless directed toward "a certain goal by reference to which the directional lines of all the understanding's concepts converge in one point. And although this point of convergence is only an idea (*focus imaginarius*) . . . it yet serves to provide these concepts with the greatest unity."[58] This unity, Kant stresses is "only an idea," not something that can be inferred from experience, but something that nonetheless posits that *possibility* of a unity of the conditions of the sensuous.

Coleridge, however, while being careful to insist that the "*focus imaginarius*" not be considered an object, nevertheless allows the unconditionality of Reason to *act as though* it were constitutive. While not directly instituting the body politic, Reason nonetheless remains a constitutive force in the sense that it provides a directionality through which political progress and the legitimacy of different forms of social organization emerge. In other words, Reason provides more than a "*focus imaginarius*" for possible applications to politics or social organization. It is also the condition of possibility for structures of governance that derive their actuality from an idea that, in the end, never presents itself as such and can only ever be approximated. Perhaps the clearest example of this notion is demonstrated in Coleridge's conception of the constitution in his late work *On the Constitution of Church and State*. Though an idea that has not yet materialized, the constitution as the organizing principle of the body politic is nonetheless real:

> There is yet another ground for the affirmation of [the constitution's] reality; that, as the fundamental idea, it is at the same time, the final criterion by which all particular frames of government must be tried: for here only can we find the great constructive principles of our representative system (I use the term in its widest sense, in which the crown is included as representing the unity of the people, the true and primary sense of the word majesty); those principles, I say, in the light of which it can alone be ascertained what are excrescences, symptoms of distemperature and marks of degeneration; and what are native growths, or changes naturally attendant on the progressive development of the original germ . . .[59]

The notion of an "original germ" that unfolds itself, while withdrawing from view, suggests that something other than a simple return to a theistic origin of politics is at stake here. Even the monarch's reign is circumscribed not by divine right but by the "great constructive principles of our representative system." In other words, the monarch is just one figuration of an "original germ" whose potentiality remains open to re-elaboration and to the reconstitution of its sovereign power in other forms. The idea of the constitution is an attempt to deduce a principle of social cohesion, and of sovereign power, that remains supple enough to account for a variety of instances of the sovereign while being reducible to none of them.

While Coleridge fully worked out the political ramifications of a theory of the constitution in his late text, its original germ in *The Friend* more closely mirrors the structure of the deduction of the imagination at the end of the first volume of the *Biographia Literaria.* In *The Friend*, the term Coleridge uses to articulate the principle of social cohesion is an original "contract," whose basis is the "never-ceasing force of moral cohesion" (FR 171) that emerges out of Man's Reason, placing him in an original contract of mutual obligation with others.[60] The contract, like the imagination, is unconditional and fundamentally self-grounding and thus similarly requires the deduction of an act that presents the proper form of its groundlessness. The infinite regress that Coleridge tries to avoid in the *Biographia* thus rears its head again in *The Friend* through Coleridge's invocation of a contract that has already been presupposed rather than deduced:

> Before I proceed to the second of the three Systems, let me remove a possible misunderstanding that may have arisen from the use of the word Contract: as if I had asserted, that the whole duty of obedience to Governors is derived from, and dependent on, the *fact* of an original Contract. I freely admit that to make this the cause and origin of political obligation, is not only a dangerous but an absurd Theory; for what could give moral force to the Contract? The same sense of Duty which binds us to keep it, must have pre-existed as impelling us to make it. (FR 173)

Coleridge's denial that an actual contract exists, or was once entered into at some specific historical moment, puts him in the company of most contract theorists who treat the movement out of the state of nature as a necessary fiction that allows us to comprehend the nature of the social bond. As Coleridge insists, "I myself regard the supposition as no more than a means of simplifying to our apprehension the ever-continuing causes of social union" (FR 174). The lack of its reality, of its factuality, however, introduces what for Coleridge will become a cornerstone of his political philosophy: the reference to an "expedient" that can *realize* this fiction in a partial manifestation:

> For what if an original Contract had *really* been entered into, and formally recorded? . . . In after times it could be appealed to only for the general principle, and no more, than the ideal Contract, could it effect a question of ways and means. As each particular age brings with it its own exigencies, so must it rely on its own prudence from the specific measures by which they are to be encountered. (FR 174)

Though not directly named, the principle of "prudence" will become, like the finite generation that grounds the unconditionality of the imagination, the means to an impossible end.

Moving from the ideal contract to the necessity of its "*est demonstratum*" (FR 174) (as opposed to its *ens logicum*), Coleridge is faced with the task of dealing with distinguishing the two systems of government that are based on reason rather than fear. Having dispensed with Hobbes's system as "inconsistent with the facts revealed to us by our own mind" (FR 173), Coleridge moves to distinguish his own understanding of a system grounded on the unconditionality of Reason from the system he labels simply "Jacobinism." Since this system is based on Rousseau's philosophy, Coleridge's tries to distinguish his own claims about the political force of the unconditionality of Reason from Rousseau's, whose premises mirror his own in significant ways. Coleridge, in effect, attempts to develop a system that is the middle point between two extremes. He reads Hobbes's theory as embedding the social contract within Man's purely instinctual or sensual appetites, in a philosophy of *pure* expediency. Rousseau, on the other hand, locates the social contract entirely within the abstract realm of Reason. Between the radically sensuous and the radically non-sensuous, Coleridge will try to stake out the finite generation of a sovereignty that hovers between these two possibilities and that relies on articulating a reconciliation between a sensuous expedient and the non-appearing principle of unconditionality that determines it.

When Coleridge begins to articulate the system of government to which he ascribes, he starts by naming the faculty within human beings on which it is based: the Understanding. As Coleridge insists:

> The second system corresponds to the second point of view under which the human being may be considered, namely, as an animal gifted with understanding, or the faculty of suiting measures to circumstances. According to this theory, every institution of national origin needs no other justification than a proof, that under the particular circumstances it is EXPEDIENT. (FR 176)

Aware that the reader might find him inconsistent in advocating this system given his repeated insistence that society must be organized by fixed principles rather than the merely expedient, Coleridge attempts to distinguish this position from Rousseau's. What will distinguish them is not just Coleridge's definition of Reason, but how this ground is materialized or embodied in the body politic. Though Coleridge can more clearly demarcate his own position from Hobbes, since that system's main fault lies in predicating society on Man's sensuous capacities rather than on the invisible laws of his conscience, he has a harder time distinguishing his theory of sovereignty from Jacobinism because it too predicates society on the invisible, immutable laws of Reason.

The key difference between the two, according to Coleridge, is that Jacobinism assumes that Reason is capable of directly instituting its laws, without delay or mediation, bypassing the Understanding completely. In a long footnote to the chapter, Coleridge reminds the reader of how he understands this distinction:

> Under the term SENSE, I comprise whatever is passive in our being, without any reference to the questions of Materialism or Immaterialism; all that man is in common with animals, in *kind* at least—his sensations, and impressions, whether of his outward senses, or the inner sense of imagination. This in the language of the Schools, was called the vis receptiva, or *recipient* property of the soul, from the original constitution of which we perceive and imagine all things under the forms of space and time. By the UNDERSTANDING, I mean the faculty of thinking and forming *judgments* on the notices furnished by the sense, according to certain rules existing in itself, which rules constitute its distinct nature. By the pure REASON, I mean the power by which we become possessed of principle, (the eternal verities of Plato and Descartes) and of ideas, (N.B. not images) as the ideas of a point, a line, a circle, in Mathematics; and of Justice, Holiness, Free-Will, &c. in Morals. (FR 177)

If each of the three systems of government that Coleridge analyzes privilege one of Man's faculties over the others—sensation in the case of Hobbes, pure Reason in the case of Rousseau—Coleridge's own theory hinges on the necessity of the Understanding, which "suits measures to circumstances," and plays out the distinction between transcendent and transcendental principles at the level of the political. Reason is transcendent to experience, whereas the Understanding is already directed toward the world of Sense and is thus a transcenden*tal* faculty that suits the universal demands of Reason to a particular instantiation in the social realm.

Coleridge summarizes the fixed principles that underpin Jacobinism, on the other hand, by focusing on its privileging of Reason as the source of law's legitimacy:

> The following then is the fundamental principle of this theory: Nothing is to be deemed rightful in civil society or to be tolerated as such, but what is capable of being demonstrated out of the original laws of the pure Reason. Of course, as there is but one system of Geometry, so according to this theory there can be but one constitution and one system of legislation, and this consists in the freedom, which is the common right of all men, under the controul of that moral necessity, which is the common duty of all men. Whatever is not *every where* necessary, is *no where* right. (FR 178)

Coleridge's critique is directed at the unforgiving radicality of the immediate demand for the realization of the universal. For Coleridge, there is, or can be, only *one* voice of Reason since it cannot demand contradictory things. A sovereignty predicated entirely on the unity of Reason, however, nullifies the possibility of politics itself, not just by disqualifying all other contending claims to sovereignty, but by eliminating the need for any modification of the political order it establishes. A republic of pure Reason entails the immediate instantiation of the universal, without delay, and without reserve.

More important, however, a government based on pure Reason identifies its impersonation of the unconditional with the sovereign himself, giving him a fully transcendent right or authority. Since there is only one voice of Reason, the figure through which it speaks inherits Reason's unconditionality by collapsing its antecedence into a realized image, one that incarnates rather than mediates. If Reason *itself* speaks through the sovereign, then the sovereign becomes the universal as such, rather than a particular or partial figure for it. The absolute realization of Reason's absolute demands leads, for Coleridge, to political absolutism, precisely because "Reason is not susceptible of degree. For since it merely decides whether any given thought or action is or is not in contradiction with the rest, there can be no reason better, or more *reason*, than another" (FR 190). Since there can only ever be *one* Reason, "laws obligatory on the conscience" (FR 192) are identical with the laws that govern the constitution, "during which the general will arising from the general Reason displays itself" (FR 192). Coleridge thus moves from a general discussion of Reason in politics to the actual target of his attack: a line of descent that leads from Jacobinism to Napoleon, which "dimmed the recollections of democratic phrenzy in the minds of men" and replaced it with "the detestable maxims and correspondent crimes of the existing French despotism" (FR 180). Coleridge attempts to determine how this progression took place. How is it that we move inevitably from the great thinker of democracy, Rousseau, to his realization in the despotism of Napoleon?[61] For Coleridge, this involves the urgent need to apply Jacobin principles to their proper object and thus avoid repeating the French collapse into despotism: "by detecting the true source of the influence of these principles, we shall at the same time discover their natural place and object: and that in themselves they are not only Truths, but most important and sublime Truths; and that their falsehood and their danger consist altogether in their misapplication" (FR 185).

The problem with Rousseau, then, as opposed to Hobbes, for Coleridge, is not the principles behind his theory of the social contract, but in the way those principles are applied to the social body to produce a particular form of the sovereign. Coleridge begins by pointing out the "undeniable truth" (FR 189) that Rousseau's theory rests on. Like the deduction of the unconditional ground of the imagination in the *Biographia*, this principle entails an "important deduction" that is "equally undeniable." Starting with the principle that "morality is grounded in the reason" (FR 189), the deduction that follows is an assertion of a freedom of the *will*: "as the faculty of Reason implies free-agency, morality (i.e., the dictate of Reason) gives to every rational being the right of acting as a free agent, and of finally determining his conduct by his own will, according to his own conscience" (FR 190). None of this Coleridge contests, and in fact these claims mirror almost identically not only his own assertion of the centrality of Reason in moral and political matters, but his earlier discussion of the role of the will in the deduction of the imagination in the *Biographia*.

The error of the application of the unconditional principles of Reason to the political realm happens, according to Coleridge, in Reason's passage from the freedom of the individual will to the production of Rousseau's "general will." Though Coleridge misrepresents somewhat Rousseau's argument in *The Social Contract* by declaring that the principle of reason implies that "no individual possesses the right of prescribing any thing to another individual" (FR 191), he accurately defines how Reason articulates the moment at which a collection of individuals following their consciences is transformed into the general will of the people, the very principle of their sovereignty. The "people's will" is not defined by the pure aggregate of individual wills (tabulated by vote, for example), but by the integration of the individual will with the collective will through Reason: "If therefore society is to be under a *rightful* constitution of government, and one that can impose on rational Beings a true and moral obligation to obey it, it must be framed on such principles that every individual follows his own Reason while he obeys the laws of the constitution, and performs the will of the state while he follows the dictates of his own Reason" (FR 192). Thus, both individual conscience and the laws of the constitution flow from the same source. The self-sameness of Reason, which grounds both positive and natural law, ventriloquizes itself by speaking itself through a variety of forms, materializing itself in—and as—Rousseau's general will, which "arising from the general Reason, displays itself" (FR 192). This display can take multiple forms, but Coleridge's concern is clearly that it extends the unconditionality of Reason into a *direct* ventriloquism of truth. Insofar as reason obligates, it does so by remaining identical with itself, even if it is ventriloquized by multiple voices: "Laws obligatory on the conscience, can only therefore proceed from that Reason which remains always one and the same, whether it speaks through this or that person: like the voice of an external Ventriloquist, it is indifferent from whose lips it appears to come, if only it be audible" (FR 192). The problem, for Coleridge, is in the *identification* of the collective will with a purely transcendent ground whose unity induces a transcendental illusion that makes Reason *as such* the source of authority.

No matter how much a governmental system may attempt to build checks and balances into its structure to protect against the usurpation of the general will by a particular interest, for Coleridge, the identification of the general will with Reason opens it to a dangerous proliferation of ventriloquisms. Citing Edmund Burke, who invokes "the fullness, the freedom, and publicity of discussion" as a way to distinguish "what are acts of power, and what the determinations of equity and reason,"[62] Coleridge retorts that these mechanisms and determinations do not originate directly out of any necessity of Reason. The fact that the general will can be swayed by passions or remain "under the dominion of a common error" (FR 193) means that it must be "sacredly distinguished from the pure will which flows from universal Reason" (FR 193). It is not hard to see an anti-populist stance in these assertions located in the worry that the enthusiasm and passion of the masses will overwhelm Reason's moral and political effects. But there is a more pressing concern on Coleridge's part: countering the threat that the ventriloquy of Reason will introduce an even more powerful despotism into the heart of democracy by identifying Reason with the unconditionality of the sovereign. This identification would in the end make it impossible to tell the difference between "acts of power" and "determinations of reason" and would give way (for Coleridge) to the absurd situation of a principle of absolute morality inevitably producing a radical absolutism. It would, in short, invoke a Reason that is no longer purely universal, has become divided against itself, and is thus capable of speaking in more than one voice.

To protect the sacrality of Reason from this threat, Coleridge insists once again on its withdrawal from the space of representation. Its *non-appearance* and purely regulative status within the political are what constitute its proper sovereignty, marking the distinction between the unconditionality of Reason and the unconditionality of the sovereign who reigns in its name. For Coleridge, the consequence of Rousseau's development of the general will out of the individual will that follows the dictates of Reason is that the "sovereign will, to which the right of universal legislation appertains, applies to no one Human Being, to no Society or assemblage of Human Beings, and least of all to the mixed multitude that makes up the PEOPLE: but entirely and exclusively to REASON itself, which, it is true, dwells in every man *potentially*, but actually and in perfect purity is found in no man and in no body of men" (FR 193–94). The fact that Coleridge emphasizes that Reason is only *potentially* found in "every man" highlights once again its purely regulative function. Reason does not appear as such, but acts as a general guide for morality. Coleridge, in fact, refers to Kant's categorical imperative, emphasizing that the object of morality is not "the outward act, but the internal maxim of our actions" (FR 194). This internal maxim is never fully revealed in the act itself, since individuals can only act "as if" the maxim of their action "should be the law of all intelligent Beings" (FR 194) without this motive ever being finally verified. Reason dictates that one guides one's actions as if one were a purely rational being, when in fact one is not. The crucial dimension of the fictionality of Reason (it can become a motive of human action only by passing through the fiction of an "as if") is lost by Rousseau once he equates the general will with Reason itself. What is missing in Rousseau, for Coleridge, is the necessity of the unconditional's *fictionalization* or mediation. Reason, as guiding principle, can never be impersonated absolutely or as such, it can only be a potentiality.

This conflation of the unconditionality of Reason with the unconditionality of the sovereign is precisely what the Jacobins, according to Coleridge, turn into their central error:

> This distinction the latter disciples of Rousseau chose completely to forget and . . . the constituent legislators of France forgot it likewise. With a wretched *parrotry* they wrote and harangued without ceasing of the *Volonté generale*—the *inalienable sovereignty* of the people: and by these high-sounding phrases led on the vain, ignorant, and intoxicated populace to wild excesses and wilder expectations, which entailing on them the bitterness of disappointment cleared the way for military despotism, for the satanic Government of Horror under the Jacobins, and of Terror under the Corsican. (FR 194)

The key term in this passage, which posits a necessary progression from Rousseau to Napoleon, is the "parrotry" of the general will as the "inalienable sovereignty of the people." The disciples of Rousseau do not just "parrot," repeat, or ventriloquize Rousseau, they introduce a secondary ventriloquism of the unconditionality of Reason that aligns it with the unconditional sovereignty of the people itself. This parrotry, then, must be distinguished from the way in which Reason, in Coleridge's preliminary formulation of his preferred system of government, does not and cannot act alone, but must "clothe itself in the substance of individual Understanding and specific Inclination, in order to become a reality and an object of consciousness and experience" (FR 201). Coleridge's principle of expediency, like the finite generation of the deduction of the imagination, actualizes Reason while insisting on its irreducibility to the voice or dignitary that gives it shape.

This is why the figure of Napoleon becomes so crucial for Coleridge's attempt to differentiate his own conception of sovereignty from Jacobinism. His insistence that the logical conclusion of Rousseau's theory of sovereignty is Napoleon, stems from his interpretation of Napoleon's nightmarish parroting of legitimate sovereignty. In a false ventriloquy of Reason, Napoleon appropriates to himself the *appearance* of its principle through an identification with it that gives him an "unlimited authority" (FR 197). Like the divinely ordained despots before him, he identifies his own voice as the direct manifestation of Reason's transcendence:

> REASON is the sole sovereign, the only rightful legislator; but Reason to act on man must be impersonated. The Providence which had so marvellously raised and supported him, had marked HIM out for the representative of Reason, and had armed him with irresistible force, in order to realize its laws. In Him therefore, MIGHT becomes RIGHT, and HIS cause and that of destiny . . . HIS cause and the cause of God are one of the same. Excellent postulate for a choleric and self-willed tyrant! (FR 197)

The figure of Napoleon thus opens up a critical ambivalence between the figure of the sovereign and the invisible power of law that grounds him. Napoleon introduces the possibility of a *retrospective substitution* of this ground, a ventriloquy of reason not authorized by it, that threatens to become lost in the parrotry of a "ventriloquism of the divine" that substitutes its own voice for the withdrawal of a transcendence from which it claims to derive its authority.

In other words, Napoleon's despotism, like the despotism of the sovereigns before him, is derived from a transcendental illusion: his identification with an abstract source of (quasi-divine) authority that remains fundamentally other to him. Coleridge goes on to suggest that the Jacobins and supporters of divine right are in fact two sides of the same coin and end up "playing the same game with different counters":

> If the Jacobins ran wild with the Rights of Man, and the abstract sovereignty of the people, their antagonists flew off as extravagantly from the sober good sense of our forefathers, and idolized as mere an abstraction in the Rights of *Sovereigns*. Nor was this confined to the Sovereigns. They defended the exemptions and privileges of all privileged orders on the presumption of the inalienable *right* to them, however inexpedient they might have been found, as universally and abstractly as if these privileges had been decreed by the Supreme Wisdom, instead of being the offspring of chance or violence, or the inventions of human prudence. (FR 216)

In both cases, the relationship between the rights that underpin each conception of sovereignty share the same logic. Both "idolize" an abstraction, and both derive their authority from the representation of this abstraction in either the "Rights of Man" or the rights of Sovereigns, both of which entail treating them as if they "had been decreed by the Supreme Wisdom" when in fact they are the products of contingency, chance, and violence. Coleridge's insistence on the "inexpediency" of the rights declared by the monarchists should not be interpreted as a claim about their utility, as if they had once served a purpose that they no longer do. Rather, the notion of the expedient in Coleridge's development of the system of government he advocates entails an attempt to expound a model of authority that no longer realizes or materializes an abstraction, even as it maintains a relationship to an antecedence that grounds its legitimacy or right.

Symbolic Fictions: Mobilizing the "Blind Spot" of Power

Coleridge's notion of the expedient attempts to articulate a figure that is the symbol to Napoleon's allegory, consubstantial with Reason as an antecedent ground, but not because it manifests it as a transcendent abstraction. To understand what is at stake in Coleridge's attempt to conceive a different relationship between the sovereign and its ground of sovereignty, a return to the distinction he makes between symbol and allegory in *The Statesman's Manual* is necessary, since this distinction helps to define the two different relations between figure and ground that qualifies the differences between Jacobinism and the system of government Coleridge advocates. When Coleridge argues in *The Statesman's Manual* that the symbol entails a "translucence of the Eternal through and in the temporal" (LS 30), the implication is not that the infinite is *itself* manifested in the finite or that the finite is the sensuous presentation of the non-sensuous. The notion of "translucence," as I have already suggested, implies a level of refraction of the light that it emits. The symbol's reference to transcendence[63] thus always entails something withheld, obscured, withdrawn from the sensuous, held in reserve.[64] But this reserve is not some *thing* that awaits its manifestation. Coleridge can thus effectively insist on the inseparability of the exigency of sovereignty from the unconditional while simultaneously invoking the imperceptible difference[65] between an allegorical figure and a symbolic figure of the sovereign, in order to qualify his relation to the invisible ground that authorizes him.

The necessity of understanding the difference between symbol and allegory as essentially a political distinction is explicit in *The Statesman's Manual* and implied in *The Friend*. In *The Friend*, Coleridge critiques what he calls the progressive "sensualizing" of the minds of men, whereby the unconditional was progressively treated as a hidden *object*: "all fixed principles, whether grounded on reason, religion, law or antiquity, were to be undermined, and then, as now, chiefly by the sophistry of submitting all positions alike, however heterogeneous, to the criterion of the mere understanding, disguising or concealing the fact that the rules which alone they applied, were abstracted from the objects of the senses" (FR 439). The language used here parallels Coleridge's description of allegory in *The Statesman's Manual* as "a translation of abstract notions into a picture-language which is itself nothing but an abstraction from the senses" (LS 30). An allegory represents its transcendental ground as an abstraction, that is, as essentially other to the "picture-language" that signifies it. Both the figure it provides and the unconditional ground it represents are derived from the senses. This means that both figure and ground are treated in allegory as objects or appearances, since both emerge (*a posteriori*) first through the senses and are then retrospectively projected backward as an antecedent ground. Allegory is the equivalent of Kantian transcendental illusion, treating what cannot be an object of experience as if it were. Symbol, on the other hand, is no mere representative "phantom proxy," but "partakes of the Reality which it renders intelligible" (LS 30) and, like the deduction of the imagination in the *Biographia*, articulates finite generation with the infinite, the conditioned with the unconditional. Its synecdochal structure, however, which "abides itself as a living part in that Unity, of which it is the representative" (LS 30) installs at its heart an opacity that allows the translucence of its anteriority to be intimated rather than accomplished.

The Coleridgean symbol is therefore not what one traditionally calls an *image*. It neither represents nor strictly reproduces the antecedence with which it is consubstantial. Its closest philosophical equivalent is the Kantian "schema,"[66] which Kant calls an "image" but which remains irreducible to representation in the more traditional sense. When Kant in the *Critique of Pure Reason* divides knowledge into two stems, the intuitions of sensibility and the pure concepts of the understanding, he has to account for how they together produce experience. What unites them is the "schema-image," a fulcrum without which the concepts of the understanding would be empty and the intuitions of sensibility would be blind. Insisting several times that the schema-image "cannot be called *noumenon*"[67] or be "separated from the sensible data,"[68] Kant goes on to claim that schema-images entail more than an abstract meeting point between the sensible and the conceptual. They *form* (rather than present) the rules governing the applicability of concepts to the sensuous, presenting not an image in place of an ideal abstraction but "the presentation of a method for presenting."[69] That is, they present the rule whereby a concept could potentially refer to a particular empirical intuition. When Kant claims that "a schema of a pure concept of the understanding . . . is something that one cannot bring to any image whatsoever,"[70] this is not because the schema is transcendent to the sensible. It is because it constitutes the *a priori* unity through which concepts are *applied* to the phenomenal and the point at which the opposition between noumenal and phenomenal, infinite and finite, collapses. This is why no example of a schema-image is possible, since an example implies the distinction between itself and what it exemplifies, whereas the schema-image constitutes the very *condition of exemplification*, the rule for the presentability of a concept.

I refer here to Kant's schematism in order to suggest a precursor to Coleridge's understanding of the symbol that is not strictly theological. Debate has raged about whether Coleridge's definition of the symbol involves the importation of a theological concept into the realm of poetic language.[71] As Ian Balfour has demonstrated, Coleridge's notion of the symbol cannot be transposed from the theological domain to the realm of poetic language without being allegorized.[72] It is not entirely clear, however, that it remains purely theological once it gets there.[73] Coleridge's immersion in German Idealism and its investment in the category of the aesthetic suggests that his conception of the symbol is as much phenomenological as it is theological. So, while Coleridge will inevitably push the symbol toward a ventriloquism of the divine, the detour his elaboration of this ventriloquism takes in order to avoid a repetition of the theological-political (in, say, Napoleon's self-crowning as emperor) introduces a divergence with it. Like the Kantian schema, Coleridge's definition of the symbol is not simply concerned with the adequation of form and content. Rather, it depends on the notion that symbols are "educts" (LS 29) of the Imagination.

An "educt" can be defined either logically, as the result of an inference or judgment, or chemically, as a substance disengaged from a compound in which it previously existed intact. In a sense, this term attempts to capture the unity of the transition from the notional to the actual that Coleridge outlines in the deduction of the imagination. What it amounts to is the end result of a process that is no longer identical with its point of origin, but that is produced by something not fully present in the end result. This *non*-appearance constitutes the source from which the result is derived. Certainly, Coleridge's chief model for the symbol is found in Scripture: "In the Scriptures they are the living *educts* of the Imagination; of that reconciling and mediatory power, which incorporating the Reason in Images of Sense, and organizing (as it were) the flux of the Senses by the permanence and self-circling energies of the Reason, gives birth to a system of symbols, harmonious in themselves, and consubstantial with the truths, of which they are the *conductors*" (LS 29). In one of the manuscript copies of *The Statesman's Manual*, however, Coleridge crosses out the word "produce" and replaces it with "educt," adding in a note that ". . . perhaps these μορφωματα (constructs) of the mechanic Understanding as distinguished from the 'ποιησειζ' (poesis) of the imaginative Reason might be named *Products* in antithesis to *Produce*- or Growths" (LS 29). A sentence earlier Coleridge proclaims that the "political economy of the present" is a "product" of the "unenlivened generalizing Understanding" (LS 28). An educt thus appears to designate a form of production that flows organically from the producer and that cannot be separated from the act that produces it. A "product," on the other hand, entails a relationship to an act of making or forming that precedes it.

This distinction will, of course, yield all sorts of aesthetic consequences, among them a concept of organic form. But there is another dimension of Coleridge's claims about the symbol that extends it beyond its consubstantiality with what it represents or its status as an educt. Like Kant's schema-image, the symbol has an architectonic dimension. What tends to be bypassed in most commentaries is Coleridge's claim that the histories found in the Scriptures institute a *system* of symbols, not just a single instance of one. This system is explicitly designated as a systematic *fiction* in the definition of the symbol above. When the Imagination incorporates Reason in an image, or organizes the flux of the senses through the "self-circling energies of Reason," it does so only "as it were," a phrase that Coleridge places in parentheses, but which makes it clear that it is not the unconditionality of *Reason* that produces the symbol, but the unconditionality of the imagination. The imagination fictionalizes it in the Kantian mode of the categorical imperative, acting as if Reason produces the system of symbols. What is educed from this is a tropological system, a system of symbols consubstantial with the truths they conduct, but grounded by an original metaphoric transposition. Coleridge's example of the symbol, the "wheel of spirit" referenced in Ezekiel, is,[74] as Ian Balfour has pointed out, a metaphor of metaphor since the chariot that the image invokes is a figure for the transfer of sense from one locus to another. Certainly, Coleridge downplays the figural dimension of Ezekiel's insistence that the image of the chariot is "the appearance and *likeness* of the glory of God,' since a "likeness" entails the notion of translation associated with allegory. But the reason this is downplayed is that Coleridge wants to emphasize another dimension of the symbol, which insists precisely on its fictional nature, the fact that the symbol only functions "as it were" (i.e., figurally) and by doing so opens up a purely *virtual* dimension proper to the unconditional. Coleridge comments on his example by situating the chariot, the symbol of the symbol, at the crux between truth and its representation:

> The truths and the symbols that represent them move in conjunction and form the living chariot that bears up (for *us*) the throne of the Divine Humanity. Hence by a derivative, indeed, but not divided influence, and though in a secondary yet in more than a metaphorical sense, the Sacred Book is worthily intitled *the* WORD OF GOD. Hence too, its contents present to us the stream of time continuous as Life and symbol of Eternity, inasmuch as the Past and the Future are virtually contained in the Present. (LS 29)

The difficulty of Coleridge's presentation becomes evident in the quasi-negative diction he is forced to use in order to avoid turning the symbol into yet another representation of an abstract transcendence. It is indeed "derivative," but not "divided," "secondary," but "more than a metaphorical sense." The unconditional's *non*-appearance is precisely what gives way to its virtualization, which allows it to contain "Eternity" within the "stream of time" and make the two "continuous" by reference to the way that the past and future can be seen as being contained "virtually" within the present. For Coleridge, it is this virtuality that constitutes the unconditional, which here becomes something more akin to a regulative ideal, a directionality that organizes appearances around it, *precisely by remaining virtual*, by *not* identifying itself with the unconditional that it can do no more than promise.[75]

How does one tell the difference, then, between Jacobinism and the model of sovereignty that Coleridge articulates? It is, indeed, an imperceptible difference, since no manifestation represents sovereignty as such. And yet out of this imperceptible difference emerge two very distinct relationships between the figure of the sovereign and the unconditional sovereignty it represents. Napoleon appropriates the unconditionality of Reason by ventriloquizing it not as if he were its impersonation, but its direct manifestation. Napoleonic allegory operates by abstracting from the senses, conjuring a transcendent unconditional that it can then reappropriate as its copy. It treats the antecedence of the unconditional as an object, which is what allows its ventriloquy to analogize the unconditional's transcendence, making itself the phantom proxy of an incomparable.

Against this allegory, Coleridge's insistence on both the consubstantiality of the symbol with its ground and the *non*-appearance of the unconditional has two results. The first is that it opens up a means to the resacralization of the unconditional; Coleridge's theological commitments push him to articulate the unconditional's constitutive non-appearance in religious terms, placing faith at the site of the inherent blindness of the imagination. Its other effect, however, is to open up a fundamental dehiscence between the sovereign and the unconditional, since no expedient will ever be capable of realizing what, in essence, is a regulative principle. Furthermore, the unconditional's necessary and immediate subjection to the conditional causes it to speak in a voice that is simultaneously its own and not its own, opening it to the difficulty of how to establish a ventriloquism that is *insistently* a fiction. The symbol is never the appearance *of* the unconditional, but is instead the sign or the injunction that *there is* the unconditional, and that it is operative. The symbolic sovereign can only act as if he were an educt of the unconditional, which opens him immediately to potential delegitimation (which is, in fact, an explicit consequence of Coleridge's theory since no particular sovereign figure can be absolute). The fact that no one will ever be able to verify the difference between an allegorical and a symbolic sovereign perhaps explains why Coleridge resorts to faith as a way out of the necessary "blindness" at the heart of the unconditional.

Coleridge, then, is both encountering and addressing an impasse in the history of the relation between the unconditional and the political. With the advent of modern parliamentary democracy, a tension begins to emerge between the unconditionality of sovereignty and the fact that liberal democracy necessitates a sovereign whose autonomy is limited not just by a division of powers, but by the fact that the representation of the will of the people is periodical, temporal, and thus never achieves a finality that could produce an absolute sovereign. As Claude Lefort suggests, "modern democracy is . . . the only regime to indicate the gap between the symbolic and the real by using the notion of a power that no one—no prince and no minority—can seize."[76] Coleridge's development of the (non)-manifestation of the unconditional through the symbol becomes, in the end, a continuously receding horizon of the political that transforms into a regulative principle forever beyond any identification with a particular sovereign. Infinitely replaying the crucial gap between primary and secondary imaginations, Coleridge's insistence on the inherent difference between sovereignty and the sovereign should be read as an attempt to overcome every form of sovereignty that attempts to appropriate the unconditional to itself by opposing it to a sovereignty that takes up a different relation to the antecedence that authorizes it.

In an early chapter of *The Friend* that deals with the question of treason, Coleridge offers a glimpse into the consequences of his attempt to propose a system of government grounded in expediency that envisions a détente between unconditional sovereignty and the instantiation of an asymptotic regulative principle: "though every government subsisting in law must, and ought to, regard itself as the life of the body politic, of which it is the head, and consequently must punish every attempt against itself as an act of assault or murder, i.e. sedition or treason; yet still it ought so to secure the life as not to prevent the conditions of its growth, and of that adaptation to circumstances, without which its very life becomes insecure" (FR 71). Coleridge, thus, does not question the absolute right of a government, by law, to punish an act against it as an act against the "life of the body politic."

At the same time he acknowledges that this right, the identification of the government with the "life of the body politic," could itself produce an autoimmune[77] reaction that threatens it from within by limiting its capacity for "growth" and "adaptation." Its openness to "circumstance," to changing conditions, is what keeps it supple enough to survive.

Coleridge's notion of expediency, then, is an attempt to address the tendency within democracy (in whatever form) to realize itself in an absolutism (such as Napoleon's). It attempts to stave off this possibility by developing a conception of sovereignty that maintains a relation to the unconditional—the *non*-appearing, impossible guiding principle of all sovereigns and all forms of the body politic. This guiding principle constitutes a virtualized holism, caught between the contradictory demands of totalization and differentiation. On one hand, Coleridge stresses the *ideal* of the body politic as an organic whole: "as a multitude of parts and functions make up one human body, so the whole multitude of his countrymen may, by the visible and invisible influences of religion, language, laws, customs, and the reciprocal dependence and re-action of trade and agriculture, be organized into one body politic" (FR 298–99). On the other, Coleridge cautions against this ideal's realization: "But much as he desires to see *all* become A WHOLE, he places limits even to this wish, and abhors that system of policy, which would blend men into a state by the dissolution of all those virtues which makes them happy and estimable as individuals" (FR 299). The same hovering between the ideal and its facilitating expedient is found throughout Coleridge's political theory, though in ways that become increasingly theological. Part of its appeal is that the content of the ideal is not what matters since it has none. What matters is its *form*, which grounds the political by situating it in relation to an unconditional that is nondenominational and even potentially secular. The "Principles of Method" that close out *The Friend* invoke the synecdochal structure of the symbol as the basic structure not just of science, but of the body politic: "Between the purpose and the end the component parts are included, and thence receive their position and character as means, i.e. parts contemplated as parts. It is in this sense, we will affirm, that the parts, as means to an end, derive their position, and therein their qualities (or character)—nay we dare add, their very existence—as particular things—from the antecedent method, or self-organizing PURPOSE . . ." (FR 499). The self-organizing purpose, which Coleridge applies to his politics, his science, and his aesthetics, provides an image of a purely regulative totality. The fact that the unconditional never presents itself as such is precisely what gives it such sway, making it the hidden secret of each part of the social body.

Lest one think that a relation to a purely regulative unconditional has no teeth, no force of law behind it, Coleridge articulates various forms of expediency that invest this secret in the social realm, through the imagination and the will: "But neither can reason or religion exist or co-exist as reason and religion, except as far as they are actuated by the WILL . . . which is the sustaining, coercive and ministerial power, the functions of which in the individual correspond to the officers of war and police in the ideal Republic of Plato" (LS 65). The imagination and the actuating principle of the will are, in Coleridge's account, in a state of "immanence or indwelling" (LS 65) with respect to Reason, which means that the conditioning of the unconditional is immediate: "Reason as the science of All as the Whole, must be interpenetrated by a Power, that represents the concentration of All in Each—a Power that acts by a contraction of universal truths into individual duties, as the only form in which those truths can attain life and reality" (LS 64). The expedient, for Coleridge, does not just facilitate the "contraction" of the universal into the particular "duties" of the individual; the universality of reason, in fact, already implies that it will have an effect, that it will *act* in the world of morality and politics, even if this act never becomes the object of cognition.

Yet this contracting is never complete, and its incompletion produces at least two different results that are analogous to the theistic and fictional resolutions to the aporia of the unconditional that I discussed above. The first, which Coleridge will pursue in *The Statesman's Manual*, and later more forcefully in *On the Constitution of Church and State*, is to translate this incompletion into a cipher for faith. In *The Statesman's Manual*, Coleridge identifies the power of contracting the universal into the particular as the proper domain of religion: "Now this is RELIGION, which the EXECUTIVE of our nature, and on this account the name of highest dignity, and the symbol of sovereignty" (LS 64). The equation of religion with the imagination's implementation of the unconditional demands of Reason is further concretized when Coleridge finally proposes the creation of the intellectual and social class he names the "National Clerisy" in *On the Constitution of Church and State*. In this case, Coleridge's conservatism restores a post-divine-right form of the theological-political where, though the sovereignty of Reason is no longer located in a single figure of the monarch, it is nonetheless dispersed into an entire social class: "men of faith" charged with administering the moral and cultural demands of Reason throughout the body politic. In this respect, Nigel Leask is correct that the imagination eventually becomes, for Coleridge, the desire for a repository of cultural value immune from other forces of social cohesion (or fragmentation).

But the other result of Coleridge's rethinking of the relation between the political and the unconditional makes his elucidation of the imagination more ambivalent in its political implications. His insistence on the irreducibility of an unconditional whose power is propagated by its non-appearance implies an unconditional ground that cannot in the end be appropriated to any traditional figure of sovereignty. From the autonomous subject to the secular dictatorship of Napoleon, Coleridge's unconditional exempts itself from figuration. This withdrawal is at once what protects it, immunizing it against a more radical division, while at the same time articulating an unconditionality that can no longer be concentrated into a single point of indivisible sovereignty (whether as the monarch or the people). Coleridge's political theory, in its attempt to advance a theory of sovereignty grounded in the unconditional, touches on a relation to it through the imagination that severs it from absolute sovereignty and grounds the sovereign on something that it cannot appropriate. As Coleridge insists in *The Statesman's Manual*, something radically other speaks through the sovereign in the name of Reason because: "It [Reason] cannot in strict language be called a faculty, much less a personal property, of any human mind! He with whom it is present, can as little appropriate it, whether totally or by partition, as he can claim ownership in the breathing air, or make an inclosure in the cope of Heaven" (LS 70). This same sentence is found in the last essay of the "Principles of Method" in *The Friend*, prefaced by a remarkable passage on the irreducibility of Reason to the sovereignty of the subject, and by extension, to other forms as well:

> The idea itself, which like a mighty billow at once overwhelms and bears aloft—what is it? Whence did it come? In vain would we derive it from the organs of sense: for these supply only surfaces, undulations, phantoms! In vain

> from the instruments of sensation: for these furnish only the chaos, the shapeless elements of sense! And least of all may we hope to find its origin, or sufficient cause, in the moulds and mechanism of the UNDERSTANDING, the whole purport and functions of which consists in the individualization, in outlines and *differencings* by quantity, quality and relation. It were wiser to seek substance in shadow, than absolute fulness in mere negation.
>
> We have asked then for its birth-place in all that constitutes our relative individuality, in all that each man calls exclusively himself. It is an alien of which they know not: and for them the question itself is purposeless, and the very words that convey it are as sounds in a unknown language, or as the vision of heaven and earth expanded by the rising sun, which falls but as warmth on the eye-lids of the blind. To no class of phenomena or particulars can it be referred, itself being none; therefore, to no faculty by which these alone are apprehended. As little dare we refer to it as an abstraction or generalization: for it has neither co-ordinate or analogon! It is absolutely one, and that it IS, and affirms itself TO BE, is its only predicate. And yet this power nevertheless, is! In eminence of Being it IS! (FR 514–15)

The radical otherness of the unconditional to any faculty of the subject, as well as to any object, any abstraction or generalization, constitutes a radicalization of the unconditional that threatens to push it outside the scope of the political altogether. Or rather, it threatens to ground sovereignty, including the sovereignty of the subject, on a non-sovereign, non-subjective agency, the voice of a nothing, or a no one, a "phantom." Coleridge's counterexample, Napoleon, ventriloquizes Reason (and thus "freedom") only by appropriating the voice of the other, giving himself the legitimacy of the other's transcendentality, just as the monarch once gave himself the right to his authority by the divine decree of a transcendent God whose otherness to the political grounds his sovereignty absolutely. Before giving way to the temptation of re-essentializing the unconditional, Coleridge's theory of the imagination touches on an antecedent ground that will fundamentally call into question the self-present agency of Reason, thus invoking a sovereignty that fundamentally eludes the sovereign, dividing him from himself in his very singularity. Coleridge provides a figure of a sovereign attuned to a voice that speaks through him, for better or worse, but whose relation to the unconditional always threatens to overthrow his self-sufficiency, while rendering him inimitable.[78]

Perhaps this is the most significant legacy of Coleridge's political theory emerging out of his idea of the imagination: rather than insist that the unconditional and the imagination have no place in politics, or that the imagination simply reproduces a sovereignty grounded in a secularized version of divine right, Coleridge holds firm in his insistence that the political, and for that matter the aesthetic, can only be understood in relation to the unconditional. And yet what he introduces, along with a reinstitution of the theological-political, is a glimpse of a notion of sovereignty that takes shape through the imagination, in relation to an antecedent ground that the sovereign cannot appropriate as his ground of legitimation. Coleridge's political theory of the imagination testifies to a radical *aporia* in the relation between sovereignty and the unconditional that remains to be thought today. If it is the unconditional that defines the indivisibility of sovereignty, then it is also this self-same unconditionality that divides the sovereign from himself, opening the possibility of a non-sovereign politics. Coleridge's political theory of the imagination would thus present a particularly pointed moment in the task of attempting to rethink the relation between the unconditional and the political that remains the task of our own modernity.

THREE

"To the Great Ends of Liberty and Power": Community and the Problem of Sovereignty in Wordsworth's *Prelude*

Wordsworth's *Prelude* has been something of a bellwether for debates in Romantic studies for the last half-century. One or another school of interpretation has found itself reflected in it or has read it to uncover the critical errors of its interpretive predecessors. From the visionary and transcendentalist readings of Harold Bloom and Meyer Abrams in the 1960s and '70s, to the deconstructive critique of the transcendental or apocalyptic Wordsworth, to the more recent historicist turn, the *Prelude* has been made to emblematize Romanticism itself, or at least to put on display what are considered some of the movement's or period's more problematic tendencies. In it can be demonstrated everything from the Romantic interest in the revival of epic, to Romanticism's political and philosophical idealism, to its alleged focus on interiority, the self, and the imagination's development out of its relation to the external world of nature. Its sheer scope and ambition at least partly explains its status: the Romantic devotion to the problem of the self could presumably find no better illustration than a poem of over eight thousand lines devoted entirely to the autobiography of its author. While one or more of these approaches has privileged a particular book, or even a particular scene to make its case, there is a prevailing view that the sections on the French Revolution and its aftermath, which comprise roughly a third of the poem, are framed by Wordsworth's interest in the production of his own autonomous individuality. Abrams long ago suggested that the *Prelude* should be read as a story about how "the external means" for bringing about social transformation "was replaced by an internal means for transforming the world."[1] The slightly updated version of this claim advanced by McGann and other historicists[2] entails an indictment against Romanticism generally for its focus on interiority and the production of poetic form, or on its practice of a form of historical revisionism symptomatic of a turn away from political concerns. Commenting on Wordsworth's "Intimations Ode," for example, McGann asserts "that the poem annihilates its history, biographical and socio-historical alike, and replaces these particulars with a record of pure consciousness."[3] This kind of claim seems easily transposable to the *Prelude*, given that the sections on the Revolution are couched explicitly in terms of the "poet's progress" back toward the imagination out of the disappointment of its failure to achieve lasting change in politics or at the level of history.

The argument of this chapter articulates a reading of Wordsworth that demonstrates why this is an insupportable conception of what is at stake in Wordsworth's *Prelude*. I argue that the *Prelude* moves against these claims not only by explicitly concentrating on political themes, but in part by reflecting on the materiality of poetic *form*.[4] This reflection is not a retreat to a hypostatized or aesthetic sphere cut off from the political.[5] Rather, it is an attempt to rethink the conditions in which *poesis*, in the ancient Greek sense of "making" in general, engages with the formation of the political itself. While the *Prelude* is autobiographical to the extent that it presents the emergence and development of the poet's imagination, this very development engages urgent political questions, not the least of which is what role the imagination plays in the production of a community and an emergent democratic sovereignty. The *Prelude*, in fact, reflects continuously on the political capacities of the imagination in its role as the mediator and *poesis* of a new form of community or collectivity. Granted, it turns away from the direct representation of history in order to do so, but it does so in order to interrogate the conditions in which a particular conception of history, of collectivity, and of popular sovereignty arises in the first place. What results, I will argue, is a *poetic politics*, that is, a politicization of the relationship between images of collectivity and the production of community or democratic sovereignty. Thus, whereas the first two chapters were concerned with Romantic attempts to articulate the imagination as a source of authority with the *aporias* bequeathed to modern sovereignty by the legacy of political theology, this chapter and the one that follows are concerned with Romantic attempts to elucidate the imagination in relation to new forms of collectivity and popular sovereignty.

Like his friend Coleridge, Wordsworth understands the imagination not just as a subjective capacity, but as a structure of production that mirrors the problem of a source of power and authority that is not just given, but must be founded retrospectively. Wordsworth shows that the intervention of the imagination in the construction of community introduces a strictly formal dimension that produces the social through the temporality and contingency of the *image*, rather than through any form of organicism. My argument begins by focusing on perhaps the most discussed section of the *Prelude*, the crossing of the Alps in book six, and its emblematic implications for the structure of the poem as a whole. I argue that this first "missed crossing"[6] between nature and the imagination points toward a dimension of the imagination that cannot be integrated into a "record of pure consciousness." The poet's most poignant encounter with this dimension is then repeated and expanded in book eight, titled "Love of Nature Leading to Love of Man," whose progression appears to prefigure the integration of aesthetic form and organic collectivity. First nurtured by nature and awakened to the "glory" of the imagination, the poet goes on to invoke the possibility that this "glorious faculty" can be experienced as a force that universally binds humanity together as a shared sovereign unity.

As I will argue, however, the poet's reflection on the nature of poetic form at this moment not only calls political organicism into question, but demonstrates the limits of organizing the possibility of popular sovereignty according to the model of a shared humanity fashioned around the imagination's sublimity. Book eight is the crucial transition from the tutelage of nature to the poet's reimmersion in humanity, represented by the "throng" of London. The metropolitan and cosmopolitan space of London itself becomes a setting for the expansion of the imagination and a figure for a sense of imaginative sympathy with anonymous others—a sense of the collective that does not rely on personal or individual face-to-face relations. This is why my argument will pause to consider Wordsworth's encounter with a solitary figure whose singularity allows the poet to reflect on his own autonomy.[7] The episode of the "blind beggar" in book seven helps to define the *Prelude*'s movement from the poet's focus on nature to his direct encounter[8] with the other as a figure for the "dignity of Man." Another (missed) crossing in book eight attempts to universalize this encounter by foregrounding the anonymity of London and the need to discover an imaginative relation to it as a whole. This second missed crossing, however, uncovers a crucial impasse in the attempt to ground democratic sovereignty on an "inner" one, political sovereignty on a shared sense of Man's dignity instituted through the autonomy of the imagination. This impasse, I argue, remains a fundamental one for the construction of genuine democratic sovereignty today. What the poet goes on to develop in the sections on the French Revolution is the incommensurability between this overarching collective sense and its capacity to be projected into a single identifiable general will or sovereignty of the people.

Before turning to the poem itself, it is important to clarify what I mean by its "reflection on poetic form" to avoid a possible misunderstanding. Recent attention to the way that Wordsworth's poetry allegedly mystifies its own reflection on history, at the same time as it evades its own historical rootedness, emerged out of a legitimate reaction to earlier interpretations of the *Prelude* that understood it as a psychological poem, which is political only in terms of the idealized constructions it produces. Whether these constructions were conceived as the unification of the mind and nature or as a retreat into a fantasized past or future, these various evasions of history were viewed as projections of a utopia that was made possible by a purely imaginative apocalypse. Whenever Wordsworth focuses on the problems of poetic form, or the imagination, this is often read as *displacement* of history and the genuine political struggle of real producers and actors.

It is not enough, however, to accept this basic premise and to argue, for example, that the political dimension of Wordsworth's poetry must be located in his championing of rustic life or in the representation of the sublime within the mundane. To do so is to suggest that the politics of Wordsworth's poetry is reducible to his representation of particular themes, when in fact the more radical dimension of his work centers on the means by which the social represents itself. Far from the theme of the imagination being the point at which Wordsworth retreats into an idealized space, his poetic reflection on it constitutes his most acute form of political intervention, which he develops through his many images for the process of image-making itself. Wordsworth, with some help from Coleridge, returns to a classical understanding of poetry and the imagination as a form of *poesis*, which means "making" or "forming" in general. The notion of poetic form, for Wordsworth, is therefore inherently ambidextrous. It designates poetic devices and structures and everything that constitutes the formal dimensions of verse. But it also designates poetic form as a *formative power*, which governs and conditions appearances more generally.[9] If *poesis* and its formal genre, poetry, entail a kind of *production*, then, like its classical definition, one of its key functions is the production of the *polis*: the invention of, and method of identification for, the community or the nation. This production, however, requires a model. Unlike the productions of nature, no product of *poesis* contains within itself the ground of its own production. While both *poesis* and *physis* (later translated as nature) are modes of production, *poesis*, because it is not self-sufficient, attempts to model itself on natural production, which extends to the production of the community.[10] This concatenation of poetic form and nature leads to the ideology of the organic state or community.

On the surface, at least, the *Prelude* appears to follow something like this pattern. There could be no more tried and true theme in Wordsworth than the question of the imagination's relation to nature. His valorization of the "real language of men" and rustic life could be read as an attempt to naturalize the social dimension of the imagination, allowing its representation of collectivity to ground itself in instinctual forms, such as sympathy, fellow-feeling, or natural compassion. If the imagination did indeed produce community according to this model, it would constitute the epitome of ideology[11] because it would understand social relations as being analogous to natural productions, rather than as the products of historical contingency. Were this the case, Wordsworth's reflection on poetic form and the imagination would be in service of potentially violent homogenizing organic conceptions of community and collectivity. As I will argue, however, Wordsworth's reflections on this aspect of poetic form emphatically break with organic conceptions of community, even if his notion of the "Love of Nature leading to Love of Man" might suggest otherwise. I thus turn first to perhaps the most trenchant example of an imaginative projection in the face of personal and historical loss in the ode to the imagination that follows the crossing of the Alps in book six.

The Via Imaginatio Negativa

That the *Prelude*'s narrative of the poet's progress involves the education of his moral feelings out of a relationship to nature could hardly be disputed. What remains in dispute is the nature of the relationship between the imagination and nature that the poem establishes. Abrams early on depicted this relationship as a dialectical progression:

> *The Prelude*, correspondingly, is ordered in three stages. There is a process of mental development which, although at times suspended, remains a continuum; this process is violently broken by a crisis of apathy and despair; but the mind then recovers an integrity which, despite admitted losses, is represented as a level higher than the initial unity . . . .[12]

This reading of the *Prelude* long ago firmly established the recurring pattern that the poem plays out not only in its individual "spots of time," but in the larger temporal structure of the poem as a whole: a momentary loss is compensated for by a turn toward a power, the imagination, that projects the significance of this loss into a future that will recuperate it into a narrative of the development of the autonomous subject. Geoffrey Hartman's revision of this scheme essentially posits the relationship between the imagination and nature in Wordsworth as a break that involves no return to an original immediacy at a higher level:

> My purpose is to show . . . that Wordsworth came to realize that Nature itself led him beyond Nature; and how and when the realization was achieved. The poet's sense of a reality in Nature is kept alive by the very fact that Nature itself weans his mind, and especially his poetic mind, from its early dependence on immediate sensuous stimuli.[13]

Hartman's model effectively turns Abrams's circular return into a forward progress that negates the initial immediacy of the external world (hence the name Hartman gives for this process: the "*via naturaliter negativa*"). Though the emergence of the imagination ends up leaving nature behind, the process itself is, for Hartman, clearly dialectical.[14] The negation of nature puts the poet in touch with "a *personal* agent" that "replaces . . . Nature."[15] This substitution reveals the creative capacity of the imagination, which, though it endeavors to mirror the productive capacities of nature, can only do so by arbitrarily installing itself in nature's place. The poet progresses only by effacing nature, thereby ensuring that the narrative of his progress is a thoroughly *un*natural one, even as it uses nature as a necessary springboard for its own process.

Paul de Man further radicalized Hartman's argument by insisting that the key relationship in Wordsworth is not between the imagination and the external world, but an internal one that reveals an interiority more external than any natural object. Declaring in "Time and History in Wordsworth" that "an understanding of Wordsworth lies in the relationship between imagination and time, not in the relationship between imagination and nature,"[16] de Man argues that, in Wordsworth, the imagination cuts itself off radically from nature and the "temptation of permanence" that accompanies its attempt to identify with something external. Turned back upon itself, it encounters a temporal space that de Man describes as a "condition of falling that has never ceased to prevail"[17] a "truth" about the self that arises in the process of self-discovery:

> A truth about a self is best described, not in terms of accuracy, but in terms of authenticity; true knowledge of a self is knowledge that understands the self as it really is. And since the self never exists in isolation, but always in relation to entities, since it is not a thing but the common center of a system of relationships or intents, an authentic understanding of a self means first of all a description of the entities towards which it relates, and of the order of priority that exists among these entities. For Wordsworth, the relationships toward time have a priority over relationships toward nature; one finds in his work, a persistent deepening of self-insight represented as a movement that begins in a contact with nature, then grows beyond nature to become a contact with time.[18]

The break with nature, in de Man's reading, is far stranger than in Hartman. No longer even a negative content, nature becomes radically displaced and the focus of imaginative possibility shifts to an entirely different set of relationships. Though de Man is still here using Heidegger's phenomenological language of authenticity and the idea of a relation to time that precedes the constitution of the isolated self, it will become clear that the "system of relationships and intents" de Man has in mind is coextensive with the notion of a "tropological system" that he will later go on to develop.

My own reading of Wordsworth lies somewhere between Hartman's dialectical analysis of the supplanting of nature by the imagination, which leads to a purely individual or personal self, and de Man's insistence that the imagination's contact with time (figured famously in his analysis of the *Winander Boy* as a relationship to the death of someone else)[19] entails a relation to a *linguistic* death that can only be figured as what it is not. What my reading shares with them is their claim that Wordsworth moves beyond a conception of the imagination that treats it as a transcendent capacity that achieves ontological stability through its relation to nature.[20] For Wordsworth the imagination can neither be collapsed into a subjective faculty nor reduced to a system fundamentally cut off from any relationship to externality whatsoever. De Man's claim that the imagination's primary relationship is to time rather than to nature does suggest an emphasis on an internal division similar to Coleridge's conception of the relationship between primary and secondary imaginations that I discussed in the previous chapter. Although Coleridge will insist that Wordsworth treats the imagination as another mode of memory,[21] what matters for Wordsworth is *what* the imagination remembers. Wordsworth's attempt to distinguish Fancy from the Imagination in the second *Preface* (1815) defines the difference, partially, in terms of the nature of the associations each of them produces. Whereas the Fancy introduces "capricious" or purely accidental relations between impressions or memories, the Imagination reproduces "inherent" laws of their relationships to each other: "When the imagination frames a comparison, if it does not strike on the first presentation, a sense of the truth of the likeness, from the moment that it is perceived, grows—and continues to grow—upon the mind; the resemblance depending less upon outline of form and feature, than upon expression and effect; less upon casual and outstanding, than upon inherent and internal, properties."[22] The imagination's temporal structure involves a process that works by degrees to establish the truth of the comparisons it creates, which "grow" on the mind as if the connections it establishes between things had to be recalled, but from an anteriority that is not entirely conscious. For Wordsworth, the imagination does not simply remember a prior moment that had initially been present. Rather, it rediscovers an inherent law of association that *precedes* the comparison that it generates.

The growth of the effect of this rediscovery on the mind could be said to describe the entire *Prelude*, whose restoration of the significance of different Wordsworthian "spots of time" organizes its very structure. Wordsworth's intimation of the imagination entails something that begins with an encounter with what appears to be a natural object, something external to the imagination. The significance of this encounter, then, abruptly shifts away from an exteriority toward an *an*teriority (as opposed to a simple interiority) that has never been fully present to consciousness. This anteriority introduces a law of associations—of feelings, impressions, memories, etc.—that cannot be named except retrospectively and is not subject to any purely voluntary recombination. It also remains irreducible to the various recombinations that it makes possible. For Wordsworth, Nature *prompts* the imagination to the rediscovery of its own laws, but those laws are in no way natural. What happens instead is a subtle shift from a representation of the anteriority of a natural object (i.e., something external that precedes consciousness and that exists prior to it) to the intimation of an anteriority that is specific to the imagination itself, but which is not experienced as a formerly present object that can be reconstituted. Thus, Wordsworth's fundamentally *retrospective* conception of the imagination necessarily entails a proleptic moment that projects the reconstitution of the imagination's anteriority to itself into a future restoration or recovery. If this anteriority fundamentally eludes the subject in the present, the intimation of its "dark invisible workmanship"[23] suggests the possibility of its full repossession in the future.

This simultaneously retrospective and proleptic pattern is perhaps nowhere better exemplified than in what remains perhaps the most discussed passage in all of the *Prelude*: Wordsworth's recounting of his passage across the Alps. It is worth briefly recounting here if only to clarify in what way the relationship to nature leads to a "love of Man" in book eight, and to show furthermore how the *Prelude* already inscribes the loss of a particular kind of historical and political project directly into its own narrative of the "poet's progress." Coming immediately on the heels of Wordsworth's focus on the role of books in his development, and on the task of his poetry to find "shrines" for the imagination that are a little less frail, the recounting of the walking tour and the crossing of the Alps constitutes the first adult contact with a form of nature that can move the poet out of the "self-created sustenance of a mind / Debarred from Nature's living images / Compelled to be a life unto itself" (6:312–14). It is also what spurs the first great ode to the imagination, which is explicitly contextualized by the sublime and emblematic quality of the climb itself. The crossing of the Alps, as more than one commentator has insisted, represents at one and the same time the sublimity of nature, the sublimity of the human mind, and the sublimity of the social and political project that still motivates the poet's "irregular hopes":

> But Nature then was sovereign in my heart
> And mighty forms seizing a youthful Fancy
> Had given a charter to irregular hopes.
> In any age, without an impulse sent
> From work of Nations and their goings-on,
> I should have been possessed by like desire;
> But 'twas a time when Europe was rejoiced,
> France standing on the top of golden hours,
> And human nature seeming born again. (6:346–54)

The passage, famously, concatenates nature and human nature, the sublimity of the Alps with the historical project of the French Revolution.[24] The language of this concatenation is one of power: as nature is sovereign of the heart, so it gives rise to the "charter," the authority or sanction, of the "irregular hopes" that channel the poet's desire for the rebirth of *human* nature. The crossing of the Alps thus emblematizes, and through analogy *naturalizes*, the sublime interconnection between Nature, the Imagination, and the political.

What actually happens in the crossing, however, continues to be a matter of some debate.[25] The passage across, and the subsequent ode to the Imagination, operates according to something like the pattern established in Kant's mathematical sublime[26] where an initial failure of representation is converted into the presentation of something unrepresentable. The crossing only takes place through a retrospective turn toward something that cannot, at least initially, be integrated into the narrative of a developing self-consciousness. Making their way, the travelers cross the Alps without knowing it. Lost, they meet a peasant who informs them that they have, in fact, already passed the zenith and that the path now is downward from the summit. The realization that they have in fact *missed* the experience of crossing the Alps is then followed by a retrospective turn of the imagination that penetrates to the significance of the crossing:

> Imagination! lifting up itself
> Before the eye and progress of my Song
> Like an unfathered vapour; here that Power,
> In all the might of its endowments, came
> Athwart me; I was lost as in a cloud,
> Halted without a struggle to break through,
> And now recovering to my Soul I say
> I recognise thy glory. (6:525–32)

The famous "ode to the imagination," emerging seemingly without precedent (like an "unfathered vapour") interrupts the "progress" of the song and takes the poet off guard. The initial feeling of being "halted" or arrested in a narrative of progress is compensated for by making the interruption itself a figure for a "break through" that retrospectively makes the interruption significant, reading it as a figure for the "glory" and sublimity of the imagination itself, which substitutes this sense for the nonexperience of the crossing.[27] An odd temporality ensues: having missed the summit, the narrative moves from the retrospective to the proleptic. If the imagination is fundamentally unlike any object in nature, such as a summit, its absence can nonetheless be transformed into the projection of a future that remains, like a Kantian or Coleridgean regulative principle, "something evermore about to be" (6:542). The "visitings/of awful promise" (6:533–34) and the intimation of the "infinitude" that constitutes a "hope that can never die" (6:540), however, emerge out of a retrospective turn toward an anteriority that is not immediately available and that cannot be directly reconciled to a narrative of the autonomous subject. As we will see, the projection of this anteriority becomes the figure not of a sovereignty of nature or a symbol of Rousseau's "natural compassion" as the basis for the social,[28] but of a division internal to the imagination that calls into question how it becomes the basis for a more generalized "love of Man." This anteriority in the end opens up the autonomy of the subject to a temporal gap that structures the imagination and that cannot be integrated into the story of its development. This in turn complicates the project of basing political freedom on the subject's alleged autonomy. In short, the story of the development of the imagination, for Wordsworth, does not end in a retreat into a radical interiority or the championing of the bourgeois individual subject, but in the collapse of the analogy between imaginative autonomy and political freedom.

"Beyond Common Indications": The Passage into London

Book seven of the *Prelude*, which follows the apparent apotheosis of the imagination in the "missed crossing" of the Alps, begins the turn toward a sense of the common that much of the rest of the poem concerns itself with. Having experienced the imagination's "glory" in the turn away from nature toward an anteriority that was never present to consciousness, the return to London acts as preparation for the extrapolation of the imagination's sublimity into a common measure, the condition for a universal fraternity that unites Man through a shared sublimity. What most commentators have remarked about Wordsworth's turn back to the urban landscape from the lonesome heights of the Alps is the contrast that the poet, who claimed to write in the "real language of men," draws between rural man and his urban counterpart. The city assaults the poet's senses, contrasting the kinds of stimulation the *Preface to Lyrical Ballads* explicitly argues against and that the turn to the simplicity of rural life is supposed to counter. Stephen Gill, for instance, posits that "Wordsworth repeatedly presents the city as a threat to Imagination, and so ultimately a threat to the poet's identity. . . ."[29] R. F. Storch insists that the imagination's vocation is fundamentally "civic" and that the focus on the city in his reading of the *Prelude* concentrates on the question of whether "it is possible to live surrounded by human suffering without atrophying the love of mankind, fellow-feeling, etc., which is the crux of the imagination."[30] More recently, Anne Janowitz has sought to distinguish Wordsworth's interest in the "natural sublime" from a specifically "urban sublime," suggesting that the gap between self and non-self that conditions the former leaves the self intact, whereas in the urban sublime: "the lyric speaker is menaced by the incoherence of all the things and buildings that people have made, and so imagines that the stones and bricks of it are antithetical to the human, rather than constituted by it."[31] Alberto Gabriele, in turn, has argued that Wordsworth's description of the city prefigures a form of cinematic montage that overwhelms the spectator.[32] Commentary, in other words, has tended to focus on the sensory assault that the speaker undergoes and the threat to Wordsworth's conception of the imagination, or to his very sense of individuality that results. While there is little question that the civic dimension of the imagination that Storch highlights is under threat by certain forces associated with urban life, the poem's focus on the nature of this threat has to do with more than just the endless spectacle of false stimulation that book seven recounts.

In fact, Wordsworth's focus is less on the city's sensory assault on his individuality than on the *form* of commonality in which the endless spectacle enjoins its inhabitants to participate. Far from establishing an opposition between his own self and the mass or common that is the city, Wordsworth describes an experience of the city as a radical fragmentation into individual lives cut off from each other: "Above all, one thought / Baffled my understanding, how men lived / Even next-door neighbours, as we say, yet still / Strangers, and knowing not each other's names" (7:117–20). Though the city certainly contrasts with the country in the sense that the community depicted in a poem such as "Home at Grasmere" is formed around neighbors who, though distant, are at least familiar with each other, Wordsworth's interest in the *Prelude* is in fact in the possibility of solidarity with the stranger. The metropolitan and cosmopolitan space of London acts as a setting for the imagination and a figure for a sense of imaginative sympathy with specifically anonymous others. Wordsworth's description of the city, however, emphasizes the merely associative types of collectivity that the city enables, from the spectacles that appear to be assembled by the fancy's entirely capricious forms of connection to the purely commercialized relations between humans brought to its logical conclusion in the "outward form" of humanity become commodity, as represented in Wordsworth's encounter with a prostitute (7:413–35).[33] The sheer associative form of the lines that describes the Bartholomew Fair, or the apposition of the endless stream of faces and symbols of the city, belies a desire for an anterior, *inherent* commonality that the city can only simulate:

> Here, there, and everywhere, a weary Throng!
> The Comers and the Goers, face to face,
> Face after face; the string of dazzling Wares,
> Shop after shop, with Symbols, blazon'd Names,
> And all the Tradesman's honours overhead;
> Here, fronts of houses, like a title-page,
> With letters huge inscribed from top to toe;
> Stationed above the door like guardian Saints,
> There, allegoric shapes, female or male;
> Or physiognomies of real men. (7:171–80)

The "throng" of the city provides a certain illusion of proximity between individuals, as the "comers" and "goers" appear to meet "face to face." But this proximity is made possible by what Simon Jarvis identifies as the sheer "illimitability"[34] of the city, which moves the spectator from a position of encounter to the spectacle or pageant of serial "face *after* face." This associative community is linked to the extension of purely commercial relations through the juxtaposition between lines that identify this seriality not just with the city's inhabitants, but with the city's endless offering of advertisement ("shop after shop").

This endless seriality should not be mistaken, however, for a cosmopolitanism or an infinite plurality that threatens the poet's attempt to universalize his own subject position. David Simpson's claim about the nature of Wordsworth's depiction of various encounters with disaffected others needs also to be applied as well to Wordsworth's description of the city. The sights and sounds of London are continuously defined by an "inclusive logic that governs both the object of encounter, and the subject encountering it."[35] The poet, in short, attempts to locate a sympathetic universality that could bind the various constituents of the city together into a common fraternity, whether of shared dispossession, as is the case with many of the poems about rural life, or otherwise. The "inclusive logic" of the city, however, is not of the poet's, or the imagination's, own making. Organized more by the capricious associations of the fancy, the city is presented not just as the proliferation of illimitable possibilities, but as palimpsest, something "all jumbled up together" (7:691) into a parody of the wholeness that the poet tries to locate within its teeming endlessness. This purely associative wholeness hides the fact that London is intensely fractured, organized more by the sheer aggregation of humanity within its borders, or the vicissitudes of commercial relations, than any genuine fraternity. If the fair is in some ways meant to stand in for the city as a whole, Wordsworth's concluding description suggests that the form of wholeness that it offers constitutes a false universality: "Tents and Booths / Meanwhile, as if the whole were one vast Mill / Are vomiting, receiving, on all sides, / Men, Women, three-years Children, Babes in arms" (7:692–95). The "whole" here is described as something like a Blakean mechanical "Mill," a form of clockwork that links the various parts of the city together but without any intrinsic cohesion. This "perpetual flow" of people and objects becomes "melted and reduced / To one identity, by differences / That have no law, no meaning, and no end;" (7:703–5). Far from articulating a vast diversity, the many "differences" that the city offers actually establish the monolithic nature of the metropolis, the "one identity" that Simon Jarvis calls its "lived ideality of unchanging self-sameness."[36] The city presents a false generality, an appearance and a sense of time and space that is homogeneous, one and the same for all.

This is why Wordsworth once again invokes nature toward the end of book seven: not because he wants to escape the metropolis, or return to an agrarian sense of community that pre-dates modernity, or enter into relation with an externality less threatening than London's urban landscape. Rather, he invokes nature as a way of returning to a sense of integrality absent from the city, since it is in nature that he first encounters a "feeling of the whole" (7:713) that arises only through specific attention to the particular as the means of access to that whole. The difference between nature and the city is a difference between two different "feelings of the whole": one that is entirely *abstract*—the "one identity" Wordsworth mentions in his description of the fair—and another "feeling of the whole" the poet has encountered so far in nature only, by tarrying with the particularity that manifests it. As Wordsworth puts it toward the end of book seven: "In steadiness, who hath among least things / An under sense of greatest; sees the parts / As parts, but with a feeling of the whole" (7:711–13). This other sense of the whole, found in the "countenances" of the "ancient hills" (7:728–29), allows one not just to see the "parts as parts" in their particularity, but to understand them as intimating a unity that actually does have a "law, a meaning and an end."

The distinction between these two forms of unity, and the fact that nature helps to define an integral wholeness rather than one that is merely associative or commercial, leads to the possibility that Wordsworth is attempting to contrast mechanical unity with a wholly organic one. There is, no doubt, something to this claim insofar as the movement that follows Wordsworth's panoramic description of the city in book seven appears to establish a continuity between "love of nature" and "love of man," as if one necessarily implied the other. In fact, two competing conceptions of the universal are at stake. Since the city first offers a problematic and abstract sense of the whole—a false universal that could hardly be called community, much less an entrance into the "love of Man"—Wordsworth will seek to locate an alternative universalism there in an attempt to open up a shared sense of the greatness of the anteriority of the imagination that he encountered in the Alps. In the urban landscape of London, however, there is no recourse to any analogy with nature. And since the vast spectacle of the city offers nothing but an abstract and alienated sense of being-in-common, one that makes each individual both anonymous and infinitely substitutable, Wordsworth's gambit is to attempt to locate commonality in an encounter with the singular, either the singularity of the development of his own poetic imagination (as emblem for its realization), or in the singularity of the various figures of the solitary and the dispossessed that populate the *Prelude*. This is why the figure of the blind beggar in book seven is such an important one: like many of the other figures of dispossession in Wordsworth, he establishes the insistent claim in the *Prelude* that genuine universality is possible, if at all, only by first being understood in terms of the individual or idiosyncratic.

The *Prelude* prepares the way for this encounter early on in book three, when the poet, referring to himself, begins the process of extrapolating on his own imaginative development by explicitly generalizing it as an exploration of the nature of Man. As a prelude to the figure of the recluse, the other solitary figures in Wordsworth are explicitly catalysts for a meditation on Man, starting points for the possibility of a genuine collectivity or fraternity, as opposed to an end point that retreats into isolated individualism. In fact, it is only once the poet's own solitude is given direct attention that the conditions for universal brotherhood become possible. It is through an encounter first with nature and then with other solitary figures that the poet comes to understand the anteriority of the imagination as the condition of human solidarity. As Wordsworth explains in book three: “Points have we all of us within our souls / Where all stand single; this I feel, and make / Breathings for incommunicable powers” (3:186–88). This “point” within the soul cannot easily be reduced to abstract individuality, not just because it is implicitly shared (we *all* “stand single,” and we *all* “have” it), but because Wordsworth makes it clear that this “point” has yet to be encountered, it is not immediately available to the judging subject. As the line that follows makes clear, “each man is a memory to himself” (3:189), suggesting that the pattern of loss and recovery that governs the *Prelude* more generally also captures a fundamental prehistory of the imagination that is irreducible to the narrative it constructs of itself. If much of the early part of the *Prelude* involves an attempt to locate the point of singularity within the poet himself, it is only in order to facilitate the conditions in which this incommunicable power can be universalized. The turn toward the anteriority of the imagination is thus not just particular to the poet, but is from the beginning a condition of possibility for any genuine sense of collectivity.

What is so striking, then, about the sudden emergence of the blind beggar out of the terrifying anonymity of London is Wordsworth’s focus on his *emblematic* nature. Amid the semiotic spectacle of the city, the beggar stands out as explicitly a sign for something else: he stands propped against a wall, with a “written paper” affixed to his chest, explaining “the story of the Man, and who he was” (7:615). A number of commentators have noticed Wordsworth’s description of the beggar as an emblem,[37] but have tended to understand this in terms of an attempt to evade his individuality, or the social conditions that have dispossessed him. James Heffernan claims that the beggar serves only to restore the essentially “imperial” task of the *Prelude* itself: “The beggar thus launches Wordsworth on an ego trip. He silently authorizes the poet to recoil from the sights of the city, to secede from a crowd that had threatened to engulf him, and to contemplate himself as universal man.”[38] Framing the *Prelude* entirely as the tale of an “exemplary individual” (Wordsworth) whose exemplarity is under threat of being “engulfed” by the crowd, the beggar becomes, in this argument, a mere catalyst, a return to the inner world of the poem’s chief protagonist. The attempt to reduce the vast heterogeneity of the city to the homogeneity of the poet's perception is cast as a defense of the poet's individuality that the beggar catalyzes, framed by the poetic perspective of the panorama, which, invoking a viewpoint "above the crowd" is deemed "imperial."[39] Paul Hamilton suggests that Wordsworth's treatment of the beggar empties him of any individuality: "the label on the beggar's chest allows him to be transported into a poetic realm of 'emblem' and 'story' in which he already exists by reason of his need to beg."[40] In his reading, the beggar is nothing *but* his story, which exists presumably to enlist the mercy of others, serving the function of admonishing passersby for their custom.

What these readings neglect, however, is the fact that the beggar appears within the explicitly symbolic environment of the city, and that Wordsworth's reflection on him is not a turn toward himself, but toward a contrast between the beggar and the abstract universality, the anonymity of "face after face," represented by the city. In this context, the beggar is explicitly part of the environment of abstract individualism that surrounds the poet, and yet there is something else that "admonishes" (7:623) him in the beggar's appearance. In book six, Wordsworth had described the encounter with the Alps in terms of a scene of reading.[41] It is out of the "book of nature," in this case Mont Blanc in particular, that an intimation of something beyond the natural world becomes possible:

> By simple strains
> Of feeling, the pure breath of real life,
> We were not left untouch'd. With such a book
> Before our eyes, we could not chuse but read
> A frequent lesson of sound tenderness,
> The universal reason of mankind,
> The truth of Young and Old. (6:471–77)

Nature is here figured as a "book" that must be read, and the meaning and "truth" that it offers is necessarily universal: the "reason of mankind" and the "truth of Young and Old." This basic analogy is carried over into the city, which likewise calls for a scene of reading.[42] But the text of the city initially provides only an endless set of loose associations, a spectacle without any plot. Nature, at least, promises a feeling of the whole that is *like* the workings of one mind, even if this sense of commonality remains essentially only an analogy because it requires an externality (an object of nature) to legitimate it.

And yet, it is not nature, in the end, that is sovereign for Wordsworth. Having first awakened a sense of the imagination through an analogy with the prior externality of nature, the imagination must go on to relate to *itself* as an *a priori* that it rediscovers and that acts as the condition of its own sovereignty. In the context of a cityscape where social and political meaning must be deciphered, the blind beggar becomes something other than an analogy for the poet's interiority or a mere catalyst for the reassertion of poetic mastery over the heterogeneity of the metropolis. He becomes a figure that interrupts its endless, purely associative spectacle to offer access to a different sense of the common. The sense of this commonality is certainly one that is first intimated by nature, but in order for this sense to be more than just an analogy, it must be articulated out of the sights and sounds of the city. It is the beggar who plays this role; the poet's encounter with him is framed by an explicit contrast with the anonymity of the city:

> O Friend! one feeling was there which belong'd
> To this great City, by exclusive right:
> How often in the overflowing Streets,
> Have I gone forward with the Crowd, and said
> Unto myself, the face of every one
> That passes by me is a mystery!
> Thus have I look'd, nor ceas'd to look, oppress'd
> By thoughts of what, and whither, when and how,
> Until the shapes before my eyes became
> A second-sight procession, such as glides
> Over still mountains, or appears in dreams;
> And all the ballast of familiar life,
> The present, and the past; hope; fear; all stays,
> All laws of acting, thinking, speaking man
> Went from me, neither knowing me, nor known. (7:593–607)

The passage starts with a reiteration of the concern that guides the opening of book seven: the face of "every one" that passes by is a mystery. This anonymity is transformed into the "second-sight procession" of the city as an endless spectacle that is already familiar from Wordsworth's description of the fair. The feeling of anonymity that belongs to the city "by exclusive right" casts its shadow over everything, which eventually comes to appear as if it were a dream. What Paul Hamilton claims Wordsworth strips from the beggar, his "what, and whither, when and how," is precisely what has already been stripped from him by the feeling of anonymity that turns "the face of every one" into mere "shapes." This assault causes not just a complete loss of familiarity, but an epistemological crisis for the poet. As Wordsworth put its, "all laws of acting, thinking, speaking man" begin to elude him in two senses: they are neither known *by* him as one who observes and explores the nature of Man, nor do these laws "know" *him*, since the shock experience[43] of the city is one that threatens the very circumstances of his own subjectivity.

What breaks the trance of this "second-sight procession" is the view of the beggar propped against the wall. Wordsworth describes this encounter as a chance meeting that causes his head to spin, his mind to "turn round," and establishes, like the missed crossing of the Alps, a reflection on the loss of his bearings and a retrospective turn toward something that still cannot quite be named. The reflection is centered not just on himself, but on the potential loss of a certain promised universalism in the face of the nameless abstract individualism of London:

> And once, far-travell'd in such mood, beyond
> The reach of common indications, lost
> Amid the moving pageant, 'twas my chance
> Abruptly to be smitten with the view
> Of a blind Beggar, who, with upright face,
> Stood propp'd against a Wall; upon his Chest
> Wearing a written paper, to explain
> The Story of the Man, and who he was;
> My mind did at this spectacle turn round
> As with the might of waters, and it seem'd
> To me that in this Label was a type,
> Or emblem, of the utmost that we know,
> Both of ourselves and of the universe;
> And on the shape of the unmoving Man,
> His fixed face and sightless eyes, I look'd
> As if admonish'd from another world. (7:608–23)

The encounter with the beggar emerges "beyond the reach of common indications," suggesting not just a turn toward the unfamiliar but a break with the commonality represented by the "moving pageant" of shapes in front of the poet. The beggar's abrupt appearance, however, is not a radical break with this sense of the common. As David Simpson has suggested, "Wordsworth here recognizes the power of the metropolis in rearranging the mental dispositions of those who come to reside within it; those who are born there have even less chance of experiencing or understanding an alternative."[44] This is partly why the beggar is such a crucial figure for Wordsworth's project, since he suggests the possibility that an alternative could emerge from *within* the purely associative world of the city. If the kind of universality Wordsworth attempted to read out of the urban landscape were confined to rural life, the task of generating alternative conceptions of community would be futile, since the commercial forces arrayed against it were quickly rendering these conceptions obsolete. The point, rather, is to read an alternative commonality out of a very different landscape, one that signifies differently from the natural one. This is why the poet's view of the beggar is described in terms that mirror the general spectacle of the "second-sight procession" that determines the poet's (and presumably the other inhabitants') perceptions of city. Wordsworth's emphasis on the "written paper" affixed to the beggar's chest, in fact, makes him as anonymous as any of the other "shapes" or "faces" that Wordsworth encounters previously.

There is a difference, however, in the way that the beggar addresses the poet. In contrast to the seriality of the crowd, the view of the beggar focuses on the legibility of the scene of reading that his figurality makes central. His emergence out of the crowd makes visible the question of *how* it is possible to intimate the sovereignty of an imagination that is no longer dependent on an analogy with the natural world. Is there, in other words, something within the false abstract universality of the city that opens up a path toward a genuine relation to another form of the universal? Unlike the "book of nature," the scene of reading that the beggar institutes is about the legibility of the text itself. If the "soulless image on the eye" that characterizes Mont Blanc in book six can be retrospectively transformed into a source for contemplating the "universal reason of mankind," this is because it does not focus on the fact that the book it is attempting to read is explicitly framed in terms of something external to itself that allows it to analogize its anteriority with it. A missed crossing or "soulless image" can only be transposed into the "unfathered vapour" of the imagination through the negation of nature that Hartman argues is the condition for the emergence of the imagination.[45] But the attempt to *universalize* this anteriority, once cut off from the natural world and the ontological stability of the natural object, nevertheless requires a similar act of reading to affirm its legitimacy and to install it as the central principle of a new form of sociality. Wordsworth's city is, as Thomas Pfau has argued, an environment in which "authentic spiritual meanings have become permanently inaccessible to any traditional model of direct poetic naming, since what is seen, read and heard is only the symptom of a totalizing economic structure devoid of any definitive center, a capitalist and aesthetic mode of production reproducing forever the invariant 'sensation' of profit and pleasure."[46] To locate an alternative form of sovereignty, one that has a "meaning and an end" other than this, is to engage in a reflection on the process of reading itself. Once "direct poetic naming" is no longer possible, one must be able to discern from within the book of the city the possibility of a text that signifies something else, and it is here that the beggar provides the first opening toward another possibility.

This passage's reflection on the process of reading is generated out of its explicit focus on the "written paper" that is affixed to the beggar's chest, and its status as a "Label," "type," and "emblem, for the utmost that we know / Both of ourselves and of the universe" (7:618–20). The beggar's text is perfectly readable, since it "explains the Story of the Man, and who he was" (7:615), becoming perhaps a reference to the narrative of the *Prelude* itself. What makes the beggar an "emblem" of the limits of the knowledge of Man is his blindness. Since the beggar is not deaf or mute, and presumably could tell his own story, the written paper is not just another advertisement or form of address within the bustle of the city. Were he a figure of self-consciousness, this story would be available to him, but his own blindness turns his own story into an anteriority that remains fundamentally illegible to him since he himself is unable to read the explanation of "who he was." As Frances Ferguson has argued, "the wall which supports him and the written paper on his chest are so clearly not his own that he offers a rebuke to the fiction of an exclusively internal strength."[47]

More than a figure of mankind's limited knowledge of itself, the blind beggar also represents the ambiguity of this limit. In the case of the missed crossing of the Alps, what is not available to consciousness (the summit or apogee itself) is retrospectively projected forward into a moment in which it could be reintegrated into a narrative of the (poet's) progress. Its "unreadability" is only temporary, a "negative" moment that opens up a sense of the "dark invisible workmanship" (1:352) of the imagination. In the case of the missed crossing of the Alps, an absence is transposed into the potentiality of a presence, or rather, a becoming, "something ever more about to be." In the case of the blind beggar, what is at stake is not just a scene of reading, but a reflection *on* that scene of reading and the conditions in which an "invisible" anteriority is transposed either into an object to be contemplated or a condition for making a universal claim. If the blind beggar is a figure for the illegibility of Man to himself, this is so only because the poet is capable of providing the beggar with the eyes he needs to see this illegibility, or, rather, to read it. If the blind man's eyes cannot read his own story, Wordsworth's universalizing claim, that this represents the basic state of mankind, can be made only by rendering this unreadability itself legible and by making the beggar its symbol. This is where the ambiguity of the meaning of the beggar lies: between two different models of reading. Does one read the "written paper" that tells the story of Man as the poet does, by representing it as an illegibility or unreadability of mankind that can be seen and thus transposed into a limit that can be passed beyond? Is the anteriority of the imagination, in short, an invisibility that can be made visible, even as an absence? In this case, the alternative sense of the whole that the beggar puts on display is found in a shared supersensuous faculty, an anteriority whose unfolding remains to be accomplished. Or, alternatively, does one read the limit as the beggar does: blindly, and without any knowledge of the limit itself, since the beggar is unable to read or see his own blindness? In the latter case, the alternative sense of the whole or the universal that the beggar puts on display is a far stranger one, since what is in common is not a shared supersensuous faculty, but a fundamental blindness, a shared limit that becomes an emblem or type only through a secondary operation that transposes blindness into sight.

As I will suggest, this ambiguity returns when Wordsworth attempts to read the possibility of a shared sense of the common in a reflection on his passage into the city itself. Because the beggar represents an attempt to offer a figure for Man's shared inability to know himself, and for a different mode of being-in-common than the city's purely associative collectivity, Wordsworth will return to the motif of the city as a whole in order to ground this sense in something more than a chance encounter. The beggar, in short, signifies the possibility of a different collectivity read through the particularity of his solitary blindness. The poet, however, will attempt to universalize this encounter and sense of commonality through a renewed relation to the city as a whole. But it is in his attempt to universalize the beggar's admonishment as a figure for the limits to self-consciousness that the difficulties of Wordsworth's task (to develop a collective "love of man" out of nature's awakening of the imagination) comes into sharpest relief. Is the beggar's blindness something that can be shared, an as yet unconscious sense of the ideal capacities of the imagination, or a more radical blindness that cannot be so easily transposed into a shared sense of being-in-common? In fact, the subsequent encounter with the imagination in book eight, read through the city, reveals an anteriority that is irreducible to the supersensuous and is in fact its condition of possibility. What results is not just a conception of the imagination that can not be integrated into a narrative of self-consciousness, but a notion of the common and of sovereignty that is fundamentally divided from itself.

The Second Missed Crossing: "Love of Nature Leading to Love of Man"

Book eight's subtitle ("Love of Nature Leading to Love of Man") appears to announce something similar to the fiction of the organic state conceived as the mimesis and completion of nature. The progression from love of nature to love of Man appears to naturalize the social dimension of the imagination, to make its representation of collectivity ground itself in an instinctual sympathy or fellow-feeling. The poet's earlier encounter with the blind beggar in book seven, however, makes clear that the turn back toward the *polis* cannot, at least initially, ground itself as a natural production. What matters is a relation to an anteriority that can only be approached through an "outward form," whether of nature or of another kind of text. If the imagination acts *analogously* with nature, then the political or social dimension of the imagination in Wordsworth would quickly become a source of ideology because it would understand social relations as analogous to natural productions.

Yet, Wordsworth's insistent reflections on the conditions of the act of reading that makes a sense of being-in-common conceivable become the site of a turn away from nature and toward the "temporal predicament" of a relationship to an anterior text or form of articulation that precedes the subject, but remains fundamentally illegible to it. The blind beggar constitutes an exemplary case in Wordsworth's initial description of the metropolis as the site where "love of Man" could emerge and sets the stage for the poet's return to the metropolis armed with the non-knowledge that the beggar instantiates. The key passage from book eight repeats the pattern of imaginative projection in the face of a lost or missing experience that the crossing of the Alps develops. It involves Wordsworth's entrance into London and the traversal of another kind of threshold that results in a further projection of the future anterior of the imagination that marks a new stage in its development. In describing his passage into London, Wordsworth links the crossing of the threshold of the city with the intimation of a sense of universal humanity that is projected onto this scene and that moves from its temporary intuition to its projection of a principle of the whole that provides an alternative sense of the common to the merely associative one described in book seven. In fact, the pattern of these two moments (the crossing of the Alps and the crossing of the threshold of London) are so intertwined that manuscript copies show that its original location in the *Prelude* was in fact between the sequence leading to the crossing of the Alps and the ode to the imagination that follows. Similar poetic diction describes both crossings, but unlike the negative relation between the imagination and nature that characterizes the crossing of the Alps, the crossing of the threshold of London is framed explicitly in terms of its social significance. Wordsworth pinpoints the exact moment when he enters the city itself, having passed through the suburbs into its very center:

> Never shall I forget the hour
> The moment rather say, when having thridded
> The labyrinth of suburban Villages,

At length I did unto myself first seem
To enter the great City. On the Roof
Of an itinerant Vehicle I sate
With vulgar men about me, vulgar forms
Of houses, pavement, streets, of men and things,
Mean shapes on every side: but at the time
When to myself it might be said
The very moment that I seemed to know,
The threshold now is overpast,—Great God!
That aught external to the living mind
Should have such mighty sway! yet so it was—
A weight of Ages did at once descend
Upon my heart, no thought embodied, no
Distinct remembrances; but weight and power,
Power, growing with weight: alas! I feel
That I am trifling: 'twas a moment's pause,
All that took place within me, came and went
As in a moment, and I only now
Remember that it was a thing divine. (8:689–710)

The temporality of this passage is complex. The crossing of the threshold is marked by one of the most vexed of poetic gestures: a reference to the "now."[48] The "now" is fundamentally polyvalent: Does the "now" refer to the writing of the poem or the "now" of its reading? The passage is complicated by the fact that there are in fact *three* poetic "nows." The first is the moment of the crossing of the threshold ("the threshold *now* is overpast"), which, like the crossing of the Alps, is retrospective *from the very beginning.* The first "now" marks the moment when the threshold has already been crossed and is therefore a *past*, a moment whose significance must be restored. This restoration arrives through the second "now" of the passage ("I only now / Remember that it was a thing divine"), which appears to refer to the time of the writing of the *Prelude*. Both implicitly contain a third extra-diegetic "now" of the moment of reading. If the second "now" makes the first durational, continuous, capable of extending itself across time, the third extra-diegetic "now" *amplifies* this effect, so that the moment of the crossing of the threshold is extended from the past into the present and out into the future.

In short, we are thrust in this passage into a "temporal predicament," to borrow Paul de Man's term, that has already taken us quite far from the Wordsworthian motif of the imagination's relation to nature. We are once again dealing with a scene of reading, but one that attempts to project an anteriority (the first "now" that is already past) onto the homogeneous empty time[49] of a continuity that can transform this anteriority into something shareable. The passage first distinguishes between the kind of experience that Wordsworth describes in book seven, the endless association of "vulgar forms" represented in the apposition of "houses, pavement, streets, of men and things / Mean shapes on every side," and the moment of the crossing of the threshold of the city. These things are explicitly contrasted through the caesura in line 697, which distinguishes between them and suggests that the sublime moment that the rest of the passage articulates in fact occupies the same time and space as these vulgar forms, even if it is irreducible to them, since the moment that follows does so by interrupting their procession. This interruption occurs through the articulation of a discordant temporality: once the threshold of the city is crossed, the "now" of its crossing is initially, like the missed crossing of the Alps, retrospective, lying in an anteriority that must be recovered. The passage, in fact, describes this moment as a kind of half-knowledge (the poet only "seems to know" that he has crossed it), which like the "unremembered pleasure" of *Tintern Abbey*, is only partially reconstituted. Though the city is conceived here as something "external to the mind" that "holds sway" over it (like the beggar's written paper), its power derives not from its sheer externality, as in the mind's relationship to nature, but from the temporal discordance between the two "nows" of the passage. The first is constituted by the sheer power of its effect, a force without law, as it were: "no thought embodied, no / Distinct remembrances; but weight and power." This sense of "weight and power" is then sustained by the second "now," which projects this initial sense out of the past into the future: "I only now / Remember that it was a thing divine."

The question, however, is what status this second "now" has and how it helps to generate the political or communal import of the sense of power, the feeling of the divine, that Wordsworth develops out of this moment. If the second "now" is merely a projected future, then it assumes a temporality that is homogenous with the first "now," allowing the feeling of "weight and power" that it produces to be emblematized or universalized. It is important, then, to keep in view the political implications of this particular moment or crossing. Unlike the sublimity of the missed crossing of the Alps, the missed crossing into London entails a properly *collective* or universal sense of "something ever more about to be." One need only skip ahead forty-five lines to find Wordsworth spelling out at least one of its forms in explicitly global, perhaps even imperial, overtones. Projecting the significance of the sense of "weight and power," he later finds himself moved "in presence of that vast metropolis/The fountain of my country's destiny/And of the destiny of earth itself" (8:746–48). The sense of human nature that he participates in opens out from the *moment* of this initial "punctual Presence" into a "Spirit" that is "far diffused" (8:763–64) and produces less a feeling of nationalism than a sense of forgotten history and suffering, "a sense/Of what had been here done, and suffer'd here/Through ages, and was doing, suffering still" (8:782–84). The point, of course, is that the "thing divine" that the poet remembers as the crossing of the threshold is a figure for a sense of cohesion through time, a "weight of ages." Wordsworth here describes this feeling explicitly as a continuity that links past and present, suggesting that a temporality continuous with itself is the basis for the presentation of collectivity or community.

However, if the second "now" is something more like the time of the writing of the *Prelude* itself, then there exists a potential disjunction between them that separates the anteriority of this power from its realization in the present or the future. In fact, the temporal continuity between the two "nows" is broken at the moment when the poem reflects on the projection of a future restoration of the previous "now's" anteriority. This reflection takes place through a simile that attempts to become an image for the pattern itself (which distinguishes this passage from the other moments of loss and recuperation one can see at work throughout the *Prelude*):

> As when a traveller hath from open day
> With torches pass'd into some Vault of Earth,
> The Grotto of Antiparos, or the Den
> Of Yordas among Craven's mountain tracts;
> He looks and sees the Cavern spread and grow,
> Widening itself on all sides, sees, or thinks
> He sees, erelong, the roof above his head,

Which instantly unsettles and recedes
Substance and shadow, light and darkness, all
Commingled, making up a Canopy
Of Shapes, and Forms, and Tendencies to Shape,
That shift and vanish, change and interchange
Like Specters, ferment quiet and sublime;
Which, after a short space, works less and less
Till every effort, every motion gone,
The scene before him lies in perfect view,
Exposed and lifeless as a written book. (8:711–27)

This passage breaks off from the poetic narrative and the specific remembrances of the poet. Instead of advancing the poetic plot, it reflects on the *form* that this plot takes and provides an image meant to stand in for the process of loss and recuperation in evidence throughout the *Prelude*. The moment of the previous section of the passage is reinterpreted here in spatial terms. Crossing the threshold between the exterior and the interior of the cave, the imagined "traveler" is met with the optical illusion of a receding cave wall. This widening and expansion initially appears to mirror the development of the sense of the divine that captures Wordsworth as he crosses the threshold of London. However, the "Shapes, and Forms, and Tendencies to Shape" that emerge, move, and change against the backdrop of the cave roof are exposed as *spectral* and therefore "lifeless as a written book." Instead of an ideal unity of feeling, meaning, or sense underpinning the movement of these unnatural (and seemingly inhuman "forms" and "Tendencies to Shape"), the section ends with something more like the empty tomb of the imagination described in book five, where books are interpreted by the poet as frail shrines of the imagination that threaten the lasting influence of poetry on the world. The second half of the passage, however, will complete the image for the temporal structure of the *Prelude* and recover a meaning and signification for the lifelessness of the "written book," but not before it repeats the split between the two "nows" of the missed crossing into London.

The simile continues by marking the division between the spirit and the letter, "the thing divine" and the "written book":

But let him pause a while, and look again
And a new quickening shall succeed, at first

Beginning timidly, then creeping fast
Through all which he beholds: the senseless mass,
In its projections, wrinkles, cavities,
Through all its surface, with all colours streaming,
Like a magician's airy pageant, parts,
Unites, embodying every where some pressure
Or image, recognis'd or new, some type
Or picture of the world; forests and lakes,
Ships, rivers, towers, the Warrior clad in Mail,
The prancing Steed, the Pilgrim with his Staff,
The mitred Bishop and the thronèd King—
A Spectacle to which there is no end. (8:738–41)

The passage takes us from a scene of reading to a spectacle, from writing to an image, picture or type that makes the "senseless mass" of the surface of the cave into a particular formation, whether natural or historical (there are "forests and lakes," as well as "the mitred Bishop and the thronèd King"). The "pause" or break that this section opens with suggests once again a temporal disunity between the "forms and tendencies to shape" and the "picture of the world" that arrives in the second half of this passage. Just like the "moment's pause" that characterizes the crossing of the threshold of London, the "pause" that leads to the "new quickening" and the "projection" of meaning onto the cave's surface is divided between the figure of imprinting which "embod[ies] every where some pressure" and the "image" or "type" that emerges as a result. In fact, this vast simile for the poet's relationship to the feeling of the divine that emerges in the passage into London is split between two different moments. The first moment is an encounter with the city as a dead letter, which lies exposed and "lifeless," but which is nonetheless before him, "in perfect view," prior to the act of subsequent "quickening" that will give meaning and sense to the exposed cave wall. The simile, in effect, repeats the pattern of loss and recovery that much of the rest of the *Prelude* is built on: an encounter with a "blank desertion," an inherent blindness not unlike the beggar's, that is subsequently converted into sight.

And yet the simile repeats this pattern with a crucial difference: as an extra-diegetic moment it promises an unmasking, a way of accounting for the sense of the divine as something other than a fiction or a projection.

The simile, however, is careful not to oppose the reality of the cave wall to the fiction of a "Spectacle to which there is no end." This is not Plato's cave, a world of shadows that can be dismissed by stepping outside of its confines. What it figures, rather, is the internal temporal gap between the turn toward the conditions of appearance (the "Shapes, and Forms, and Tendencies to Shape" that characterize the first part of the simile) and the "picture of the world" that emerges out of these conditions to posit a unity, a sense of the whole that the poet wants to emblematize through his encounter with the city. As Simon Jarvis has pointed out, this particular passage should be read as an "unmasking of an unmasking in the sense that it does not take us from illusion to reality, but from appearance to appearance"[50] in a return to the city as a "Spectacle to which there is no end." While this passage does not take us to reality, it does nonetheless take us to the preconditions for the spectacle's return at the end. What takes place, in fact, is a turn toward the conditions in which this spectacle is possible and in which the initial blindness or blankness that characterizes these conditions can be retrospectively transformed into a shared unity.

What unites it into a whole is the process of emblematization itself: the surface of the cave is imprinted, embodying "some pressure," which in the next line is converted from a figure of printing into the visual "image," "type," or "picture of the world." The prior articulation of the "senseless mass," and the movement from the lifeless written book to the "picture of the world" takes place only through a repetition and forgetting of the temporal "pause" ("But let him pause awhile, and look again") that divides the prior differentiations that characterize the imagination ("Shapes, and Forms, and Tendencies to Shape") and the sense of commonality or unity that they make possible. The imagination is figured here less as a capacity that produces images than as a forming power that unites the "senseless mass" into a way of seeing that is at once historical and political. The "pressure" of the imagination, its impression or imprint, is legible in the "projections, wrinkles and cavities" that form the backdrop against which the picture of the world emerges and which we must read not just in the everyday sense of a representation of the world, but in Heidegger's sense of a "world-picture"[51] (*Weltbild*), a projecting ground-plan that maintains a reference to a gap or outline that is irreducible to what it makes appear. The "spectacle to which there is no end" emerges against the backdrop of the temporal gap between the

"Shapes, and Forms, and Tendencies to Shape" and the imaging or *embodiment* of particular appearances.

So what, then, does this imply for Wordsworth's attempt to construct a sense of the whole through a relation to the anteriority of the imagination? What book eight presents is not just a chain of figures for the imaginative positing of wholeness or the means by which self-"blindness" can be overcome. It puts on display, fundamentally, the conditions in which *any* sense of the whole can be posited, whether the false merely associative sense that is the primary focus of Wordsworth's early exploration of the city or the desire for an alternative conception of commonality that is the focus of book eight. The missed crossing into the city and the vast simile that describes it reveal that these conditions are anything but natural. The sense of a "thing divine" that can be shared as the imprint of a common humanity, and the possibility of a form of political cohesion that would result from it, is in fact produced through a transition from non-natural "Shapes, and Forms" to the *work* that the image and the imagination performs: the "pressure" and forming power of the image. In short, the transition into a community is not a *natural* progression for Wordsworth; it is instead *made* or *poetized*. The passage into London, and the simile that describes the nature of this passage, does not give access to any organic sense of community organized around an analogy between nature and the imagination.

The imagination fundamentally denaturalizes this transition, producing a picture of the world retrospectively, imprinting its images upon a "senseless mass." More important, however, the production of a community or collectivity happens only in reference to a fundamental *division* between its presentation or image and the material and temporally determined conditions that allow it to present itself. This temporal division is not merely the space between a "then" and a "now" recuperated in a future that remains continuous or homogeneous with the present. Rather, it entails a relation to an anteriority integral to the forming power of the imagination that can only be made the object of a shared sense by figuring it as continuous with the picture of the world that it makes possible. Wordsworth's passage into the city reveals that the "blank desertion" he encounters in the Alps, and the blindness he confronts in the beggar, and the half-knowledge of "weight and power" he encounters in the passage into the city are merely the *after*-effects of a power that cannot be located in the individual or be generalized into a political structure. In order to conceive of the unity of the sense of community as continuous with itself, one would have to *forget* or *efface* the division that is so vividly figured by the *specter* of the "lifeless book" and the "pause" that produces the "*Spectacle* without end." As Wordsworth's extended simile makes clear, we move from specters to the specular only by forgetting this gap. It is this temporal gap, furthermore, that distinguishes a form of being-in-common that must be constantly reinvented from a totalized synthetic or natural unity, suggesting that collective bonds do not emerge out of an image of unity or a belonging to nature, but out of the recognition of a shared temporal finitude.

"A Spirit Far Diffused": Wordsworth and the Ambivalence of Sovereignty

The problem, of course, is that the forgetting of this temporal gap happens throughout the *Prelude*, almost inevitably, and not only by the French Revolutionaries Wordsworth will take to task for having failed to stage the revolution on its proper ground, as a revolution organized around "love of Man." As Forest Pyle has persuasively argued, it is the imagination's failure to achieve an "identity of spirit and matter, self and society"[52] that constitutes its most productive moment, since it "leaves an image of the 'nontotalizability' of the social." The imagination in its most productive aspect would thus perpetually appear as the sign that "'something's missing.'"[53] Perhaps another way to formulate this in the context of Wordsworth's *Prelude* is to say that the temporal gap that lies between the conditions for the production of an image of the social and the sense of the whole that it produces begins to call into question the very project of grounding a new form of sovereignty in the "capacities" of Man.[54] It is not entirely clear, first of all, that the imagination should be understood as a "capacity."[55] Certainly, Wordsworth will call it repeatedly a "power," but it is one that he does not yet have and that can only be retrospectively encountered as a blank desertion, a missed crossing, or a text that cannot be read. Though it "lies far hidden beyond the reach of words" (3:185), this is precisely what threatens to make it illegible, a text that cannot be read, something that emerges only in the procession of a "second-sight" that animates it, and then only as a shadow or specter. And though Wordsworth will not immediately abandon his project of conceiving of a love of Man that could emerge out of a shared sense of this power, the temporal gap that emerges in book eight makes it difficult to discern the difference between extrinsic social relations and intrinsic ones, that is, ones that emerge out of essential structures within Man himself, as opposed to ones that do not. If book seven focuses on social relations governed by non-essential forces (commerce, the accumulation of people in cities), it is not clear that book eight provides a clear antidote, a way of resituating the social around the sovereign imagination so that it can be seen as the prior condition or power that makes another social world visible to itself.

In a sense, the indiscernibility between extrinsic and intrinsic forms of social relations becomes the focus for the rest of the *Prelude*, drawing in questions about why the French Revolution "failed" so spectacularly to whether Wordsworth's project can restore itself through a more complex return to nature. Wordsworth recognizes, in other words, the fact that the imagination is not only temporally determined, but itself a form of the "unimaginable touch of time,"[56] something fundamentally divided from itself, either always already past or always-not-yet arrived. This provokes a certain ambivalence: Wordsworth recognizes that his "political crisis" takes place much earlier than the French Revolution, in a recognition that the power of the imagination is not a form of sovereignty in any traditional sense of the term. As Simon Jarvis has argued, the many different definitions of the imagination in Wordsworth suggests that "what the imagination describes is not even a kind of capacity for experience but a kind of experience"[57] that does not relate to what one can "*decide* to imagine or not to imagine."[58] What imagination names, in other words, is an encounter with something that takes one by surprise, that cannot be immediately transposed into a capacity of the subject, and that disrupts the sovereignty of the self. It also disrupts the transposition of this sovereignty into a political project that tries to reground political sovereignty by aligning individual autonomy with a general will.

This does not prevent Wordsworth from hoping that his poetry can continue to "interest mankind permanently"[59] by situating the imagination at the heart of a renewed conception of Man, with the result being a refounding of the political by means other than revolution.[60] After the simile of the cave, Wordsworth explicitly addresses the "blank sense of greatness pass'd away" (8:744) that continues to affect him and puts him in pursuit of a power implied by this sense: "I sought not then / Knowledge; but craved for power, and power I found / In all things" (8:754–56). This "power," however, is explicitly described as temporal rather than eternal or transcendent:

> The Human-nature unto which I felt
> That I belong'd, and which I lov'd and reverenced,
> Was not a punctual Presence, but a Spirit
> Living in time and space, and far diffused. (8:761–64)

Here the imagination exceeds the poet's individual "punctual Presence" and is "diffused" through time and space, eventually creating a community between the living and the dead,[61] which gives shape to the sense of intrinsic connection to others that is the focus of book eight:

> I had been used to owe
> The pleasure which I found in place or thing
> To extrinsic, transitory accidents,
> To records or traditions: but a sense
> Of what had been here done, and suffer'd here
> Through ages, and was doing, suffering still
> Weigh'd with me, could support the test of thought,
> Was like the enduring majesty and power
> Of independent nature; . . . (8:778–86)

What David Simpson has called Wordsworth's "poetry of social concern"[62] is evident here with the focus on human suffering as the tie that binds the past to the present. Wordsworth focuses on the analogy with nature because this sense and its "enduring majesty and power" are *prior* to the poet as an individual and sovereign in the sense of something independent of him that is differentiated and temporal, yet also the precondition for his sense of belonging.

This sense of belonging, however, is often reconfigured in the *Prelude* as something more akin to a shared human nature that is closer to a timeless or eternal capacity of Man than the seemingly more diffused sense of belonging depicted in the passage above:

> Add also, that among the multitudes
> Of that great City, oftentimes was seen
> Affectingly set forth, more than elsewhere
> Is possible, the unity of man,
> One spirit over ignorance and vice
> Predominant, in good and evil hearts
> One sense for moral judgments, as one eye
> For the sun's light. (8:824–31)

The singular image that follows to exemplify the feeling "set forth" in this passage of a man with a "sickly" babe in his arms who looks upon it with "unutterable love" (8:859) belies what is ultimately an insistence on the sense of the "unity of man" that the passage emphasizes. Wordsworth makes clear that this "one spirit" is not just found in the kind-hearted (the man and his babe). It acts as a transcendental signified, figured here by the sun,[63] that governs all morality ("one sense for moral judgments") and all perception ("as one eye/For the sun's light"). There is, in short, a fundamental ambivalence in Wordsworth's articulation of the anteriority of the imagination: it either undoes any stable referent since it is differentiated, "far diffused" through time and space, which challenges a sense of belonging based on identification, or it becomes a unified spirit, transformed back into a unity and identity that can be shared, exchanged, and experienced. The *Prelude* continuously vacillates between these two possibilities.

Wordsworth's interpretation of the French Revolution must be situated in relation to this ambivalence. Books nine and ten of the *Prelude*, which deal with the Revolution and its aftermath, involve an attempt to *translate* the imagination's anteriority into a renewed principle of political sovereignty: love of nature, leading to love of Man, leading to love of the Republic. The motif of love for the stranger that opens book nine, for example, revisits the anonymity of London as a more general affect whose new task is to form the new body politic itself, a force that binds together the new Republic:

> Even files of Strangers merely, seen but once
> And for a moment, men from far with sound
> Of music, martial tunes, and banners spread,
> Entering the City, here and there a face

> Or person singled out among the rest,
> Yet still a stranger, and beloved as such—(9:281–86)

Here the anonymity of the "stranger" is recast: in London the inscrutability of the other is organized around "laws that have no meaning, and no end," laws of extrinsic association. Wordsworth here attempts to identify the cause of the Revolution with the sense of the common that he discovers in the passage into London, transporting the temporal gap that characterizes the imagination to France and into the political realm in the form of the beloved stranger. Once again it is a question of the universal sense of the whole that is conjured up through this figure, which Wordsworth frames in terms of the spontaneous emergence of a form of popular sovereignty:

> How quickly Nations have been form'd
> From least beginnings, how, together lock'd
> By new opinions, scatter'd tribes have made
> One body, spreading wide as clouds in heaven.
> To aspirations then of our own minds
> Did we appeal; and finally, beheld
> A living confirmation of the whole
> Before us in a People risen up
> Fresh, as the morning star. (9:384–92)

The "living confirmation of the whole" that he initially locates in the crowd is the beginning of an attempt to account for the origins of this power and for how it ties together the nation into "one body," a republic that moves from the "least beginnings" to a larger unit. The reference to "aspirations then of our own minds" reflects not just an attempt to read the Revolution according to the romance of "honorable deeds/Of ancient story" (9:372–73), but also reflects the more general project that sees political liberty generated out of an analogy between the autonomous individual and a sovereign body politic, where "social life" is "As just in regulation, and as pure/As individual in the wise and good" (9:370–71). The analogy between individual life and social life makes clear that Wordsworth's initial interest is in witnessing how the anteriority of the imagination comes to be manifested outwardly, nurtured first by nature and then realized in the revolution.

Yet the ambivalence that we read in book eight concerning whether the "whole" that this anteriority intimates should be read as a shared human nature returns with a vengeance in the question of whether this sense is capable of constituting a new form of sovereignty. What Wordsworth ends up exploring is the result of two conflicting, but barely differentiated, attempts to implement the universal through the unfolding of Man's faculties. What he keeps confronting in the sections on the French Revolution is the shadow of his own project as a pernicious doubling of the attempt to found a new form of community around the anteriority of the imagination.[64]

Wordsworth first couches the desire for this project in almost religious language.[65] In his description of the crowd as a "sect" motivated by truth, Wordsworth introduces the figure of Michel Beaupuy, who embodies the "deep sense" of the whole "in action" (9:408–9). Wordsworth describes Beaupuy's "creed" almost as though he were divinely inspired:

> Then doubt is not, and truth is more than truth,
> A hope it is and a desire, a creed
> Of zeal by an authority divine . . . (9:411–13)

This divinity within Man, emblematized by Beaupuy, allows Wordsworth to articulate the project of the Revolution with his conception of the imagination, locating both in a moment prior to the Terror and turning Beaupuy into a figure for the path the Revolution *could* have taken, but did not. Beaupuy's universal "love of Man" is presented as a form of faith rather than of *noblesse oblige*, a "tie invisible" that joins him to others not through any similarity or identity, but through an "oath" or promise that is not fully realized:

> By birth he rank'd
> With the most noble, but unto the poor
> Among mankind he was in service bound
> As by some tie invisible, oaths profess'd
> To a religious Order. Man he lov'd
> As man; . . . (9:309–14)

Wordsworth returns here to the moment of the crossed threshold in book eight and invests its significance in Beaupuy as its realization. The "tie invisible" that binds Beaupuy to mankind incarnates a universalism that maintains a relation to the singular, that does not surrender to the abstraction of the "face after face," but insists on the face *to* face: "Man he loved as man." This emphasis on the "face to face" is represented in Beaupuy's response to the encounter with the "hunger bitten girl" along the roadway. He states simply: "'Tis against that/Which we are fighting'" (9:519–20). The determiner "that," like "this" in Hegel's discussion of sense-certainty,[66] intends the particular but is also the most abstract or universal term possible. In the same way, it is not entirely clear what "that" refers to in Beaupuy's statement: the girl herself, the fact that she has been reduced to the status of an animal, or the poverty that she represents. The inability to tell these apart constitutes the force of Beaupuy's statement. The "face to face" encounter with the girl is the very basis of Beaupuy's universal love of Man, which would attempt to see her poverty and suffering abolished. Rather than abstracted individuals endowed with rights, or the faceless anonymity Wordsworth locates in the throng of humanity of London, Beaupuy represents a perfect harmonization of universal and particular, a love of Man that can only be realized in the here and now in a face to face encounter with what Wordsworth later calls "the dignity of individual Man/Of Man, no composition of the thought/Abstraction, shadow, image, but the man/Of whom we read, the man whom we behold/With our own eyes" (12:83–87). As Simon Jarvis has suggested, the figure of Beaupuy serves to differentiate this form of the love of Man from the "principled apriorism which came to dominate revolutionary *raison d'état*."[67]

Yet, the example of Beaupuy plays another role in Wordsworth's poetic narrative. Since Beaupuy's magnanimity is generated out of a certain apriorism of its own (the "sense of the whole" articulated in book eight), what he represents is also an alternative relationship to an anterior power that authorizes the formation of the body politic.[68] As in the section on the city, there is always more than one sense of the whole at stake and more than one way of understanding how it is generated and articulated; here, it is a question of how this sense comes to be articulated as an assertion of sovereign power. Yet, what comes more and more to the fore in the sections of the *Prelude* focusing on the French Revolution is a fundamental dilemma: once the anteriority of the imagination is transformed into a political principle, it becomes harder to tell the difference between an anteriority of the imagination determined by the temporal disjunction Wordsworth discovers in book eight, and this disjunction's subsequent erasure once it becomes a figure for the autonomy of the subject. In these sections Wordsworth plays an uncertain game, at some points criticizing the Revolution for having failed to ground itself on the former conception of the imagination, while at other times, especially in his later revisions of the poem, falling himself into the latter's identification of the imagination with a figure of atemporal autonomous subjectivity.

Wordsworth's ambivalence is perhaps no more apparent than in his presentation of the figure meant to stand in for the lost possibility of the Revolution. Beaupuy represents a sense of the whole that remains to some extent temporally determined, organized around a determiner: "'tis against *that*/Which we are fighting," suggesting a love of Man that loves "that" man, rather than Man as such. When Wordsworth begins to entertain the question of how the revolution could begin with love of Man only to end in the Terror, he invokes first of all the notion that "tyranny" (whether democratic or monarchical in origin) consists primarily in the absence of the "faith" and "love" evidenced in Beaupuy's character and actions, a truth he claims to be a "commonplace" which understands that:

> tyrannic Power is weak
> Hath neither gratitude, nor faith, nor love,
> Nor the support of good or evil men
> To trust in, that the Godhead which is ours
> Can never utterly be charm'd or still'd,
> That nothing hath a natural right to last
> But equity and reason. (10:167–73)

It is not so much that tyrants act without faith or love, but that their power is not sustained by it. A people ruled by fear are only temporary subjects; a people ruled by love or faith invest in their subjection and will act (as Beaupuy does) in its name. Wordsworth's phrase "the Godhead which is ours" references the source of Beaupuy's magnanimity and suggests that it cannot be "utterly" charmed by power.

Yet, this passage, while insisting on the inviolability and permanence of this "Godhead," nevertheless also suggests that it is subject to a certain *fasci-*

nation with power. Though it cannot "utterly be charmed," it can, Wordsworth suggests, be put to the service of ends that are not its own. This is perhaps why, in his addition of a passage that immediately precedes this reference to the Godhead in the 1850 version of the *Prelude*, Wordsworth emphasizes the Godhead's inviolability:

> A sovereign voice subsists within the soul
> Arbiter undisturb'd of right and wrong
> Of life and death, in majesty severe
> Enjoining, as may best promote the aims
> Of truth and justice, either sacrifice
> From whatsoever region our cares
> Or our infirm affections Nature pleads,
> Earnest and blind, against the stern decree. (1850, 10:183–90)

Wordsworth's revision turns the Godhead into something more akin to a Kantian voice of Reason.[69] This "sovereign voice" remains "undisturbed" in its "majesty severe," an unconditional source of judgment as arbiter of right and wrong. Its radical *apriority* allows it to "sacrifice" what Kant calls our "pathological interests" (and Wordsworth calls our "cares" and our "infirm affections") to its "stern decree," which promotes only "the aims of truth and justice." Thus, in the 1850 version of the *Prelude*, Wordsworth converts the Godhead into a form of radical autonomy that is "undisturbed," exempted from the threat of its corruption by the everyday temporal or material interests of our nature. In 1805, however, the same "sovereign voice" determines, through the figure of Beaupuy, the chief difference between Wordsworthian and revolutionary versions of the "apriorism" of the imagination. The latter is invested in an atemporal transcendent anteriority that must be realized or materialized in the world. The former, always already marked by time, begins only in the contingency of the "here and now," with "man as man," "not in Utopia" but in "the world which is the world of all of us" (10:725–26).

The ambivalence Wordsworth displays about the relation between the sovereign Godhead within and the structures it authorizes without constitutes the real crisis in his relation to the French Revolution. In a situation in which the Revolution produces tyrants "ten times stronger" (10:310) than before, and in which revolutionaries "throned/The human understanding paramount/And made of that their God" (10:317–18), it becomes more and more difficult to discern the difference between the sense of the whole intimated in the crossing into London and its simulacrum, parody, or shadow in the new version of despotism that the Revolution produces. As the Revolution slowly devolves into the Terror, Wordsworth pointedly remarks that its crimes are carried out under the banner of a newfound liberty: "all beneath/Her innocent authority was wrought/Nor could have been, without her blessed name" (10:349–51). Like the spectacle of the city, which enjoins a sense of the whole that has "no meaning and no end,"[70] Wordsworth focuses on the way in which the revolution converts the sense of the whole back into spectacle and in doing so elevates it into an imitation of transcendence. This liberty in name only, an even more radical despotism presenting itself as liberty, is represented ironically by Wordsworth in his remembrance of his walking tour of Arras:

> was I impelled to think
> Of the glad time when first I traversed France
> A youthful pilgrim, above all remember'd
> That day, when through an Arch that spann'd the Street,
> A rainbow made of garish ornaments,
> Triumphant pomp for Liberty confirm'd. (10:448–53)

In the "glad time" of 1790, while travelling with his friend Robert Jones, Wordsworth implies that he greeted the symbol of the rainbow as a straightforward manifestation of "Liberty confirmed." The rainbow, of course, signifies at once God's promise after the flood, but also the passage of a celestial element (light) through an earthly one (water). As such, it suggests a figure for the materialization of the "thing divine" intimated in the passage into the city.

In the context of 1794, however, this experience takes on a different aspect, one that mocks the poet. Remembering the moment ironically as the place that gave birth to Robespierre, Wordsworth avers: "I could almost/Have quarrel'd with that blameless spectacle/For being yet an image in my mind/To mock me under such a strange reverse" (10:462–65). Though he calls the moment a "blameless spectacle," the initial description of the rainbow emphasizes its *ornamental status.* It is man-made, "garish," a form of "pomp" that links its ostentatiousness with the false "pageant" and spectacle identified earlier with London. It is an image that "mocks" in two senses: it mocks the poet in the sense that it tortures him with a figure for his betrayed ideals. But it also mocks in the sense of being a "mock-up," an imposter whose artifice garishly presents itself as the realization of a new form of sovereignty grounded on the "dignity of man," on reason, or the imagination as "reason in her most exalted mood" (13:170). Part of the trauma stems from what Wordsworth discovers in book eight: this sense of a "thing divine," of the Godhead within, is no natural production, but relies on an imagination that is divided from itself, dependent on a form of prior articulation that allows it to present itself to itself. Thus, no natural production, including the symbol of the rainbow, could act as sufficient confirmation of its existence. In fact, since it is created rather than discovered, the "garish" rainbow is as good a confirmation as any.[71]

This problem of a false conception of the temporal structure of the imagination provokes different responses in Wordsworth. One of them involves an attempt to distinguish the thing divine once again from its imposter through a return to the conditions in which the imagination acts in the world otherwise than through the realization or instantiation of transcendence. An example of this can be found in his break with Godwin and the attempt to "build social freedom on its only basis: / the freedom of the individual mind" (10:824–25), a project that results in a work of "false imagination, placed beyond / The limits of experience and truth" (10:847–48). One could argue that Wordsworth's own project of the *Recluse* (of which the *Prelude* was meant to be merely preparatory) is precisely an attempt to do just that, but without *abstraction*. Hence, it is first of all autobiographical, in the hopes that what can be gleaned about the dignity of Man in the individual progress of a particular poet can later be universalized into an ameliorating social force. Wordsworth's retreat from the political is rather directly stated in book twelve when he reaffirms his desire "to seek in Man, and in the frame of life / Social and individual, what there is / Desirable, affecting, good or fair, / Of kindred permanence, the gifts divine / And universal" (12:39–42). The problem with the Revolution, for Wordsworth, is not that it confronts the poet with actuality or that it disappoints because it fails to integrate ideal goals with practical political realities. The problem, for Wordsworth, is exactly the opposite—the Revolution's implementation of the universal is far too abstract:

> seeing little worthy or sublime
> In what we blazon with the pompous names
> Of power and action, early tutor'd me
> To look with feelings of fraternal love
> Upon those unassuming things, that hold
> A silent station in this beauteous world. (12:47–52)

Claiming that notions such as "power" and "action" are mere "pompous names" implies that there are other ways to understand these terms.[72] Wordsworth's retreat from the political is thus a temporary one, an attempt to *particularize* Man's universal gifts enough to ward off the threat that they may be usurped by a politics capable of "mocking" them.

The other meanings of the terms "power" and "action" can be generated, Wordsworth thinks, through an encounter with "unassuming things" and persons, who offer a version of a "gentle shock of mild surprise" (5:406) by being the interpolation through which such terms might be rethought. The problem with "modern Statists" (12:78) and revolutionaries is that they ground these terms in abstractions. Wordsworth is:

> prepared to find
> Ambition, folly, madness in the men
> Who thrust themselves upon this passive world
> As Rulers of the world, to see in these,
> Even when the public welfare is their aim,
> Plans without thought, or bottomed on false thought
> And false philosophy. (12:70–76)

The view of Man as a pure abstraction (in the philosophy of Godwin, for example) is interpreted here as the very aim of the Revolution. Even with good intentions, the "new man" the revolutionaries attempt to empower as sovereign in the end becomes just another self-legitimating tyrant "bottomed" or grounded not on the "touch of time," but on the "false philosophy" of Man as "abstraction, shadow, image," rather than "the man whom we behold with our own eyes" (12:85–87). It is only from the singular and the discrete that one can approach a genuine, self-differentiated common—a true universalism, rather than the false pretense evident in the Revolution.

This, in effect, returns Wordsworth back to the question of approaching the universal through the particular that we found in the passage on the blind beggar. Wordsworth reinvigorates this question in book twelve by asking why "the dignity of individual Man" (12:83) becomes so difficult to locate: "What one is,/Why may not many be? What bars are thrown/By Nature in the way of such a hope?" (12:91–93). Entertaining the possibility that it is our "animal wants and the necessities/They impose" (12:94–95)[73] that may be the obstacle, Wordsworth goes on to consider those who struggle under the injustice of bodily labor "far exceeding their due portion" (12:101–2) as exemplars not of "natural Man"[74] so much as Man fully consumed by survival or the appetites of others. In a state like the blind beggar's, a condition of bare subsistence, can one still find the intimation of a fraternity, a "common" that does not originate in identity? In all of the various figures abandoned by the political, from beggars to discharged soldiers, Wordsworth will attempt to restore a relation to those whom every politics abandons, who become emblems of another revolution yet to come. A revolution no longer based on a shared abstraction, but on an imagination whose "prime and vital principle" (13:194) remains withdrawn from the "reach of any outward fellowship" (13:196) and yet nevertheless "comes into the heart/With awe and diffusive sentiment" (13:163–64), drawing together a community of the singular plural,[75] or as Jacques Rancière has argued, "the living hope of seeing injustice and error vanish and the dispersed populations unite in one body: not a Leviathan submitted to an imperious head and regulated interplay of organs, but a supple and harmonious form of the multiple."[76] An anti-sovereignty, in other words, breaking with the false universalism of community organized around a shared homogeneity and grounding the sovereign on a radical form of dispossession.

Wordsworth's other response to the Revolution's ability to artificially produce a false sense of the whole is to oppose this auto-*poeisis* or self-legitimation to a natural, *non*-created capacity that can preserve a genuine sense of Man "as he is." In book nine, Wordsworth considers the progress of the revolution as "nothing out of nature's certain course" (9:253). After his crisis of faith and the threat to his project of wedding the imagination to a new sense of collectivity caused by its false imitation in the Revolution, Wordsworth takes refuge in something akin to a natural right of the imagination:

What then remain'd in such eclipse? what light
To guide or chear? The laws of things which lie
Beyond the reach of human will or power;
The life of nature, by the God of love
Inspired—celestial presence ever pure—(11:96–100)

The attempt to restore the imagination and its social vocation, Wordsworth suggests, requires a return to "a genuine Counterpart / And Brother of the glorious faculty / Which higher minds bear with them as their own" (13:88–90). Nature acts as this counterpart because it is its "express resemblance" (13:86–87), a *visible* confirmation of its reality, which lends it a certain kind of transcendence modeled on something "beyond the reach of human will or power." The fact that both Nature and God are mentioned in the same breath emphasizes what is at stake: in the absence of divine legitimation, nature comes to take its place and the liberal compromise of natural right restores a foundationalism to the attempt to reground sovereignty on the faculties of Man. Wordsworth's loss of faith generates a need for an authenticating principle for the imagination's role in the founding of a new political sovereignty. Yet Wordsworth's return to nature, and its role in providing a model for imagination, ends up *forgetting* the self-division or temporal gap Wordsworth points to in book eight.

At the end of the 1805 version of the *Prelude*, Wordsworth will remain caught in a constitutive ambivalence regarding these two responses: a conception of the imagination that refuses the lure of authority based on transcendence and one that falls prey to it, making the imagination a source of sovereignty only by reference to something that "lies beyond the reach of human will or power." Nonetheless, the former tendency involves an attempt to think what the political vocation of the imagination might mean in the absence of any transcendent ground of authority, and in the process Wordsworth uncovers a conception of the imagination that remains inherently temporally determined. The attempt to ground a new form of sovereignty through the imagination would thus entail a founding moment that must include within itself a reference to the *finite* moment of its self-institution. The result is a turn toward the paradox of a sovereignty that is no longer grounded in any straightforward autonomous individualism. The sovereign subject and the republic for which it stands are no longer self-determined, but temporally determined, no longer homogenous with themselves, but always retrospective and thus insistently proleptic. Wordsworth's later tendency to bypass disappointment in the Revolution's false hopes by returning to the transcendence of nature, and by grounding the imagination's authority on a form of natural right, falls into the very trap that Schmitt's analysis outlines in *Political Romanticism*.[77] It represents precisely the liberal compromise with inherited structures of political sovereignty; by substituting nature for God, natural right for divine right, it keeps these structures in place even as it claims to overturn them.

Yet even Wordsworth's most emphatic statements about the role of nature at the end of the *Prelude* betray an ambivalence regarding this impasse within liberalism and within conceptions of the political founded on natural right. The imagination's mimetic relation to nature allows "native selves" to create "like transformation" (13:93–94) in the world and to create for themselves "a *like* existence" (13:95–96, emphasis mine). In the intimation that these transformations in the world and in the self occur *as if* they were natural, Wordsworth seems to recognize that they only take place through an analogy, one that mimes natural creation but cannot afford itself the same status. This miming of nature, in fact, betrays the sovereignty of the imagination insofar as it grounds its authority on an anteriority and externality not its own. Understood as a principle of natural right, the very "dignity of Man" said to make him sovereign ends by dispossessing him of sovereignty insofar as his dignity assumes the ontological status of something already given, already formed, already established. The imagination's "own" anteriority, paradoxically, opens Man to a sovereignty he must first create, to a form of establishing that offers no surety or fixity, only a process that exposes him to the irreducible finitude inherent in the production of every image of community. The *Prelude*'s focus on the political dimension of Wordsworth's conception of the imagination underscores the *aporia* of attempting to structure political sovereignty on a "sovereignty within" (13:114): either it already exists and its transcendence must be articulated, or it must be brought into existence and with it all this implies about the temporality of sovereignty itself. Perhaps, as Jacques Rancière has suggested, Wordsworth early on recognized the impotence of his own gesture of renaturalizing the imagination as a response to political failure, acknowledging that in the end, "Nature bears witness to no avenger; its spectacles symbolize no future for the community."[78] Perhaps. What is clear is that Wordsworth, in a poetics devoted consistently to the dignity of Man, at least temporarily opened another path and situated it at the heart of the rise of democratic sovereignty and the autonomous individual.

FOUR

Shelley's Metaleptic Imagination and the Future of Modern Sovereignty

Like Coleridge, Percy Shelley authored a number of longer political treatises and participated in what today might be called "direct actions," lending his writing talents to campaigns for Catholic emancipation and the repeal of the 1801 Act of Union in Ireland. One would expect that such attention to the direct mobilizing power of the word might translate into a politics of confrontation that privileges the efficacy of interventions meant to have force in the here and now. Yet, recent work has gradually come to the conclusion that Shelley's politics privileges the *future* and the promise of radical change.[1] Shelley clearly had specific democratic political reforms in mind in many of his later political treatises,[2] and he developed arguments that demonstrate that the past was often more attuned to the creative power of poetry and the imagination than the present. It is difficult, therefore, to attribute a simple theory of historical progress to Shelley, even if for him poets always contemplate a futurity that already exists in the present. A central motif in his work is the question of a relation between the present and the past that is not, strictly speaking, linear. If the notion of futurity to which his poetics is dedicated is to be anything other than a utopian hope for something better, it must account for how revolutions in thought, in art, and in politics have hitherto been conceived and enacted.

Much of Shelley's early poetry involves an attempt to discover a language that can account for the temporal dimension of genuine, radical social change while being mindful that what looks like revolution may in fact turn out to be a regression to something far more troubling than what preceded it. His poem "Queen Mab," for example, is told from the perspective of a "Fairy" who keeps "The secrets of the immeasurable past" in order to demonstrate "the future, from the causes which arise/In each event."[3] Though this early poem contains a faith in natural law and a form of progress that leads inevitably to the destruction of the present order, the poem's teleological conclusion, and Shelley's early allegiance to doctrines of "necessity,"[4] threaten to negate the very motor of transformation that the poem wants to prophesize. If change is inevitable, or part of the natural order, then its *possibility* is curtailed in advance. What reason would anyone have to risk imprisonment or death for a political cause if nature itself already dictates that a particular change will take place? This problem in Shelley's early political philosophy and poetry leads to his attempt to understand a sovereign act of founding or refounding as something whose effects cannot be foreseen, even by the actors in question. Each founding act thereby remains open to the uncontrollable risk of a future that offers no guarantee that the change, or revolution, it brings about will necessarily produce a positive outcome.

This prompts Shelley to reconsider the nature of the poetic act as an inaugural break with the context that enables it, thereby instituting a fundamental difference between past and present. It is this impetus that Shelley will give to poetry, and it is why he will insist, famously, that poets are the "unacknowledged legislators of the world." Since many commentators have taken this well-known phrase to be the central slogan of Shelley's work, it is important to understand in what sense poetry constitutes sovereign "legislation." It is not, as I will argue, that poets create new laws—aesthetic or political—in place of old ones. It is rather that they touch upon the conditions in which new laws come into being at all. These conditions highlight a past that is radically discontinuous with the present and that therefore has the potential to produce unforeseen effects in the future.

Shelley has many different definitions of "the imagination" in the *Defence of Poetry*, but a crucial one is linked explicitly with the rhetorical figure of metalepsis, or the substitution of cause for effect. The imagination, apart from being a creative capacity, a faculty for instituting the new and the unprecedented, also addresses the past by reconfiguring the relationship between a "before" and an "after," an anteriority and what this anteriority makes possible or forecloses. The result is that the imagination becomes a cipher for a force that is capable of founding a new regime or structure (whether political or aesthetic), but which itself remains irreducible to the structure it founds. By remaining irreducible, it continues to be the source of ever-changing future alterations. Whereas Wordsworth, as we saw in the previous chapter, sought to recover the anteriority of the imagination as a new ground of community, and the shaping force of a new secular sovereignty, Shelley pushes the link between the imagination and sovereignty to its limit, turning it into a principle of radical inauguration that takes its cue from prior originating acts in order to address itself to the future. Focusing directly on one of the most fundamental *aporias* of modern sovereignty—how does a sovereign institute new laws without recourse to an already determined ground of authority—Shelley locates the imagination at the heart of his answer to this question. Through his theory of the imagination, he attempts to account for a purely secular form of legislation that breaks fundamentally with all notions of sovereignty founded on the repetition of an *arche*, or absolute ground of authority.

This is why the imagination has an explicitly political valence for Shelley: the "founders" he has in mind in the *Defence of Poetry* are inaugurators of *any* kind, including founders of states and governments. It is also why Shelley links the deterioration of the political situation of a particular era with a concomitant deterioration of the arts. Both forms of regression entail a curtailing or redirection of the imagination's renovating powers into a form of stasis that arrests the process of metalepsis and insists instead on the *necessary* and unidirectional relation between cause and effect. The sovereignty, the inaugural radicalism, of the imagination's creative act becomes reduced to the repetition of the same through a valorization of the anteriority and identity of cause over effect. What Shelley calls "tyranny" involves, in part, a refusal to interpret this anteriority or past as itself subject to endless alteration,[5] making it instead into an eternal and absolute first cause.

Poetry thus becomes not just a representation of, or an address to, a given political situation. For Shelley, it instigates an attempt to set in motion a kind of counter-sovereignty, a reaffirmation of a radically inaugural force that is at work in the present, but which cannot be reduced to the political or aesthetic institutions that govern it. Typically, this force is represented by a particular figure in Shelley's poetry and is present in both Shelley's more popular political poems, such as the *Mask of Anarchy*, and in his epic quasi-mythological poems such as *Prometheus Unbound*. This chapter begins by unfolding Shelley's metaleptic conception of the imagination as he presents it in the *Defence of Poetry*. It then turns to the *Mask of Anarchy* and his more esoteric *Prometheus Unbound* in order to explore the way Shelley incorporates what he identifies as the metaleptic structure of the imagination into his political project: the attempt to construct an alternative to the hegemonic form of sovereignty emerging in post-Waterloo Europe. This counter-sovereignty not only breaks with the absolutism Shelley identifies with a tyranny grounded on a particular conception of the theological-political, but also attempts to imagine what it would mean to formulate political resistance around an anachronism, an *exception*, that does not appear to be represented in the political realm in any typical fashion. His conception of resistance to absolutism usually takes at least two different forms, involving either an attempt to seize the machinery of the state and replace the "false" sovereign with a "genuine" sovereignty of the people, or to oppose tyranny through other means (non-violence, for example). Though these forms of political opposition can certainly be the *result* of the counter-sovereignty that Shelley proposes, his formulation, as I will argue, also involves a radical gesture that challenges any form of sovereignty predicated on the logic of a first cause.

In order to understand this gesture, it is important to first situate Shelley's theory of the imagination in terms of the way it metaleptically articulates a relation between cause and effect. Recent studies that have focused on the enigmatic relationship between Shelley's poetry and his politics[6] have done much to clarify a sense that his poetics is organized around a future that promises radical change. What remains unresolved, however, is the link between Shelley's conception of the political vocation of poetry and his notion of the relation between the present and the *past*. Shelley asserts in the *Defence of Poetry* that any genuine poet "beholds the future in the present" (DP 513), a secular ability that wonders how the present came to be in the first place and in what relationship it stands to the past given that Shelley never conceives the past as unified or whole. Jerrold Hogle, in his seminal work *Shelley's Process*, argued that figural displacement is the key to understanding how Shelley's poetics achieves a renovating motility designed to prevent prior modes of thought and forms of association from coalescing into monolithic absolutes. By abandoning an idealist understanding of Shelley that reads him as attempting to return to a creative "center-at-one-with-itself,"[7] Hogle perceives language and metaphoric transposition as central to Shelley's ideas of poetic inspiration, social renovation, and history. An account of any relationship to a past moment in Shelley, therefore, must recognize that the past is no longer a simple cause of a later moment, but always already a projection into the past by transformations in the present that appear to be its result. Paul de Man argued that such transformations in Shelley are the effects of arbitrary performative shifts between figures. *The Triumph of Life*, he suggests, warns us that deeds, words, thoughts, and texts are only "random event[s] whose power, like the power of death, is due to the randomness of its occurrence."[8] Similarly, Joel Faflak has focused on *The Triumph of Life*'s non-teleological conception of life as analogous to psychoanalytic accounts of the desire for a return to a primal scene of trauma,[9] a desire that is constantly postponed by the poem's inability to separate the primal scene of the past from its reproduction. Thus, the poem develops a "ceaselessly revisionary practice, in which everything in the text becomes at once the product and source of a deeply inaccessible process."[10] These readings importantly draw our attention to a process that *precedes* specific figures in a causal way, but proves to be only arbitrarily related to them. As in Wordsworth, Shelley's conception of the imagination always involves a relation to an anteriority that the imagination relies on to institute the new. Exactly what relationship this anteriority has to the present and the future Shelley spells out most clearly in the *Defence of Poetry*.

The Metaleptic Imagination

Shelley's *Defence* registers this anteriority in a famous image for poetic creation:

> For the mind in creation is as a fading coal which some invisible influence, like an inconstant wind, awakens to transitory brightness: this power arises from within, like the colour of a flower which fades and changes as it is developed, and the conscious portions of our natures are unprophetic either of its approach or its departure. Could this influence be durable in its original purity and force, it is impossible to predict the greatness of the results: but when composition begins, inspiration is already on the decline. . . . (DP 531)

Received interpretations of the "fading coal" fall roughly into two groups: those who see it as a figure for an undifferentiated unity of mind that is lost or degraded through the process of poetic composition, and those that highlight the changing causality of the mind in creation.[11] Hogle, for instance, focuses on the transition between the "fading coal" and the "transitory brightness" not in terms of a movement away *from* an original purity, but rather as a ceaseless evolution *toward* a different condition, which entails the realization that the previous state is irrecoverable. Both of these interpretations leave intact a relation to a past the unity of which can either be recovered, remains permanently lost, or whose variability constantly displaces the unity of its point of departure. This passage's figural logic, however, focuses neither on a definite origin nor on a process that emphasizes the motility of a transformation yet to be realized. It addresses instead the temporal coexistence of the fading coal with the transitory brightness by articulating a complex suspension of the relation of cause and effect between them. The fading coal is not prior to its reawakened transitory brightness, but is rather contemporary with it; both elements are part of the same temporally indeterminate image. The coal's fading and its reawakening take place at the same time, as it were. Its transitory brightness is not marked as qualitatively different from its fading, nor is it clear this would be closer to a previous state. That a transition has taken place is clear, but it is one that is characterized by a lateral movement in which it is difficult to tell which element in the image is prior or which is privileged.

Shelley stresses that this ambivalence is internal to the image itself, since the invisible power of the imagination that it figures arises "from within" (though it is unclear whether Shelley means that it arises within the mind of the poet or within a particular act of creation). If neither the fading coal nor the transitory brightness are closer to this power, it is because Shelley insists on their contiguity, rather than their continuity; they are simultaneous but nevertheless *opposed* ways of viewing the same displaced origin from within a single representation of it. Their connection to each other is therefore organized by a figural transposition that is characterized not only by a process of semantic proximity or transfer, but also by a substitution that *suspends* cause and effect, making it impossible to tell antecedent from consequent. The image of the fading coal, which is already a partial indicator for a creative act that is on the decline, is recast metonymically by another partial indicator that exists in a purely adjacent relationship with it. The fading memory and its revival form two sides of a single image, which privileges not just the decentering power of an imagination that dethrones any unified origin, but a state in which even the transition from one partial indicator to the next is contingent and subject to figural disarticulation.

What is required, then, is a more precise understanding of the mode of figural transport that substitutes the fading coal for a transitory brightness without privileging one over the other. Shelley does not elevate this figural transposition to the status of the truth of a process of differentiation, but focuses instead on the way it contests the results of any transition: from what standpoint does one view succeeding moments as having been inaugurated by previous ones, and how does our understanding of their succession change once their causal connection has been problematized, especially since the present is *part* of that succession? Attention to figures other than metaphor that Shelley explicitly utilizes helps to characterize his conception of the historical and political task of the imagination[12] and reveals that its renovating powers are not inherently revolutionary or critical. One of Shelley's most important insights is the realization that the transformations that his poetics strives for involve both the chance for radical renovation and the threat of relapse or regression. Shelley's focus on the role of metalepsis reveals how figural transformation and the present that would reflect on it are divided from themselves and structured by the displacement of cause and effect that defines them.

Metalepsis is a form of substitution first introduced by Quintilian[13] that is arguably found in figurative language more generally and consists "in the metonymical substitution of one word for another which is itself figurative."[14] In short, it involves a substitution for something that is already figurative, already itself a substitution. It therefore suspends any clear-cut cause and effect relationship between terms or images, grounding itself on the relation between an antecedent (a word "which is itself figurative") and a consequent (the metonymical substitution of this word). It is difficult to definitively locate metalepsis's meaning in the indeterminate relationship between the substitute and the substituted: is its significance located in the antecedent term, which it merely redoubles, or in the consequent term, which displaces it? What metalepsis introduces into the problem of figurative transposition, in short, is a "before" and an "after" that are difficult to tell apart.

Shelley develops his understanding of metalepsis in the *Defence* by describing the relationship between language and the imagination and by elaborating on the dislocating effects that this relationship has on our sense of the past and the future. If, as Joel Faflak has suggested, Shelley's poetics is exposed to a "visionary future without or beyond vision, a no-future that escapes our capacity to envision even its own possibility,"[15] then this opening hazards contact with something radically unforeseeable and unprecedented. Such a prospect also motivates the description of the imagination in the *Defence*, where language, imagination, and poetry are developed in relation to this "no-future." Shelley's articulation of the imagination in terms of metaleptic substitution makes its acts strictly non-teleological, producing a radical vertigo where one cannot tell which moment is *a priori* and which *a posteriori*. The metaleptic structure of the imagination does not make the future indeterminate or subject to endless deferral. Rather, it opens itself toward a future that is latent in the present by disclosing the difficult structural relationship between the present and the past and by introducing an act of the imagination that is not the self-present act of a subject.[16] Through metalepsis, Shelley invokes what might be called the "performative"[17] dimension of the imagination, which involves an act that informs the present but is not visible or locatable within it. It thus reveals that the present is never fully saturated or stable.[18]

To elaborate the performative dimension of the imagination, Shelley first defines it as something other than a subjective faculty. His initial definition of the imagination in the *Defence* treats it as a principle of rearrangement, rather than (as in Kant) a faculty of the sensible.[19] Shelley opens the *Defence* by distinguishing between the faculties of reason and the imagination. Reason, he asserts, is a passive faculty that connects to already existing relations of thought, whereas the imagination acts on thoughts and rearranges them:

> According to one mode of regarding those two classes of mental action, which are called reason and imagination, the former may be considered as mind contemplating the relations borne by one thought to another, however produced; and the latter, as mind acting upon those thoughts so as to colour them with its own light, and composing from them as from elements, other thoughts, each containing within itself the principle of its own integrity. (DP 510)

This initial explanation of the imagination suggests that it is productive only to the extent that it is capable of taking preexisting thoughts and rearranging them into a new order. Beyond adding novelty to what is already given, the imagination, according to Shelley, is also capable of judgment, that is, it is capable of evaluating the connections between things and determining their value: "Reason is the enumeration of quantities already known; Imagination the perception of the value of those quantities, both separately and as a whole" (DP 510). Shelley's initial definition of the imagination thus focuses on the qualitative difference between it and reason. While both deal with already known quantities, the imagination is distinguished from reason by its ability to synthesize the qualitative and the quantitative through an act of supplementation. The imagination's productive capacity consists in its being able to articulate or disarticulate a given (historical or mental) arrangement according to its judgment of the value of the connections it makes or unmakes.

Since this act of the imagination is not directly visible, the question becomes how it is possible to represent it. The burden of Shelley's demonstration lies in what one could call the tropological system of the *Defence*,[20] which is defined as the interrelated poetic images Shelley uses to represent the imagination and its disarticulating power. In the development of this tropological system, Shelley uses metalepsis in two senses: first, as a metonymical figure (like the fading coal) that tries to encapsulate the imagination's reorganizational power; and second, as the metaleptic relation *between* successive figures and images within the tropological system itself. While the first sense treats metonymical displacement in semantic terms, the second, structural sense develops the performative dimension of metalepsis, as well as the radical future that defines the politics of Shelley's poetics.

Shelley's first representation of the displacing power of the imagination in the *Defence* happens through a rewriting of Coleridge's figure of the Æolian lyre, which depicts the cause and effect transition from a transcendental *a priori* (such as nature or the imagination) to its effect in the phenomenal world. Shelley begins with a metaphor that links Man with the lyre: "Man is an instrument over which a series of external and internal impressions are driven, like the alternations of an ever-changing wind over an Æolian lyre, which move it by their motion to ever-changing melody" (DP 511). In this image, the wind that moves the strings is made analogous to the invisible influence of the imagination as cause. The problem, however, is that this analogy turns Man into a passive instrument (or effect) like the lyre. This is why Shelley goes on to metonymically displace this initial cause and effect relationship with a metaleptic reversal that maintains the initial meaning of the lyre-image while introducing an opposing figural interpretation. Because the lyre-image reinforces something closer to the instrumental cause and effect relationship that he attributes to reason, Shelley suggests that it is not adequate as a representation of the relationship between the imagination and its materials, since what it leaves out is the imagination's reorganization of cause and effect: "But there is a principle within the human being, and perhaps within all sentient beings, which acts otherwise than in the lyre, and produces not melody alone, but harmony, by an internal adjustment of the sounds or motions thus excited to the impressions which excite them" (DP 511). The lyre-image achieves what Shelley calls an "internal adjustment," something that displaces the unidirectional cause and effect relationship between the "wind" of the imagination and its effects on its instrument. The internal adjustment in the lyre takes place through a metonymical substitution of the initial "melody" with a "harmony" that leaves undetermined whether it is the wind or the lyre itself that produces the sound that follows. As Shelley insists, "it is as if the lyre could accommodate its chords to the motions of that which strikes them, in a determined proportion of sound; even as the musician can accommodate his voice to the sound of the lyre" (DP 511). There is, in other words, already underway in the lyre a modification of the effects of the wind, suggesting differences internal to the functioning of the lyre that are not identical with nature or the imagination. The metaleptic substitution of the "melody" with the "harmony" of an "internal adjustment" suspends the interior/exterior, cause/effect relationship that the lyre-image initiates, while nonetheless keeping it intact as a component of the image itself. Like the fading coal and its transitory brightness, the lyre-image remains suspended between two distinct possibilities, neither of which is fundamentally prior. This not only displaces the invisible wind as the cause of the melody that the lyre produces, but raises the question of how to differentiate between the wind's melody and the harmony that results from its internal adjustment. Both possibilities remain part of the structure of the image itself. It is this internal difference within the image that becomes the condition of its further repetition and displacement.

This internal difference within the tropological system of the *Defence* gives way to a structural metalepsis that emphasizes the way in which each subsequent figure incorporates but also dislocates the preceding one by reintroducing its internal division at a new level. Shelley, for instance, brings the lyre-image into contact with the metaphor of a child seeking through play and imitation to prolong its pleasurable impressions: "as the lyre trembles and sounds after the wind has died away, so the child seeks, by prolonging in its voice and motions the duration of the effect, to prolong also a consciousness of the cause" (DP 511). The image of the child redoubles the apparent cause and effect relationship of the lyre-image because the child is already at a remove from the melody that has been produced and seeks to reestablish contact with its source. By attempting to do so, however, the image of the child-at-play "forgets" or displaces the lyre-image's original ambivalence concerning the priority of causes to effects, redefining the lyre-image by actually *embedding* it within itself as its forgotten ground or basis. The link between the two images happens by way of a simile ("as the lyre trembles . . . so the child seeks . . .") that structurally embeds one figure for the imagination within the next. This process takes place through an analogy between the child's voice and gestures on the one hand, and the "sound" and "trembling" of the lyre that has died away in the absence of the invisible wind that produced it on the other. What makes the image of the child structurally metaleptic is the fact that it uses the lyre-image as its absent ground of articulation. It is only through a metonymical displacement of the lyre's sound with the voice of the child that one can read the now absent wind of the lyre-image as a retrospective catachresis[21] for the unnamed cause that the child seeks to prolong.

The creation of this metaleptic chain of images gives way in the *Defence* to a whole series of further displacements, each of which disarticulates the relationship between antecedent and consequent. The image of the child, for example, leads to the savage ("for the savage is to ages what the child is to years" [DP 511]), which in turn is surpassed by "man in society" (DP 511). What at first appears to be a developmental structure is in fact a repetition of the original suspension of cause and effect that began with the lyre-image. The result is a series of figures that can be read as both causes *and* effects of prior effects. Expressions of the imagination become "at once the representation and the medium, the pencil and the picture, the chisel and the statue, the chord and the harmony" (DP 511). Throughout the *Defence*, Shelley repeatedly emphasizes the mutual coexistence of cause and effect, antecedent and consequent, within a single image or present.

Imagination and the Future Anterior

How, then, does the future intervene in what to this point would appear to be a metaleptic pattern of displacing a *past* moment or image? The possibility of a radical "no-future" (to use Faflak's term) opens up at the moment when this pattern reflects back upon itself and attempts to capture, through an image, the figural structure that makes the image possible. This pattern is not dissimilar to what occurs in the (missed) crossing into London in book eight of Wordsworth's *Prelude*, which I analyzed in the previous chapter. Shelley's *Defence*, at a crucial moment, takes as its object not a prior image, but the structural form of metalepsis itself. At the beginning of the *Defence*, Shelley develops a theory of the imagination as a metaleptic power of reorganization. Once this more general pattern has been established, Shelley turns to a slightly different problem: "the manner in which the imagination is expressed upon its forms" (DP 511). Given that the *Defence* initially focuses on articulating the metaleptic *effects* of the imagination's power of reorganization, this question involves a turn toward the problem of identifying the imagination as a unified cause underlying those effects. Shelley's question could be put this way: from what perspective and through which medium can one observe this metaleptic chain as though it were part of the same process?

To answer this question, Shelley begins by defining poetry as something irreducible to written verse. He defines it instead according to the connections that the imagination enacts between its material and the act of reorganization that it produces in relation to that material. Shelley therefore separates two different registers of poetry: "poetry in the general sense" and "poetry in the restricted sense." "Poetry in the general sense" is a classical definition of poetry as Greek *poesis*, which means any kind of making in general.[22] It includes a number of works, deeds, and things that are not reducible to the specific literary form of written verse:

> But poets . . . are not only the authors of language and of music, of the dance and architecture and statuary and painting: they are the institutors of laws, and the founders of civil society and the inventors of the arts of life and the teachers, who draw into a certain propinquity with the beautiful and the true that partial apprehension of the agencies of the invisible world which is called religion. (DP 512)

Poetry in the general sense is any "making" that expresses some relationship to the invisible process of rearrangement that the imagination enjoins in its act of creation, just as each builder or maker (from architects to inventors of civil society) is a poet insofar as he or she expresses this power.

Poets "in the restricted sense," whose medium is written verse, thus designate only a subset of makers in general. What makes them poets is something true of all poets in the general sense: the way that the imagination operates through them by rearranging and renovating a particular domain (such as sculpture or politics). According to Shelley, poets in the restricted sense were once called either "legislators" or "prophets" because they "behold intensely the present as it is" as well as "the future in the present" (DP 513). The structural metalepsis that governs the *Defence* clarifies the kind of prophecy poets are capable of: they are not prophets in the "gross sense of the word" (DP 513) but are prophetic insofar as they are capable of apprehending the metaleptically divided structure of the present and thus a certain "future" that is latent within it. Unlike other poets, however, Shelley privileges poets of written verse insofar as they are uniquely prophetic in this sense because of the medium particular to them: language. Their distinctive political and historical role originates from the fact that they not only see "the future in the present" as part of the power of the imagination to displace preceding and succeeding moments within a metaleptic chain, but also because they are capable of reflecting on the perspective from which one would be able to understand this chain as part of the same process. For Shelley, language alone is capable of this because it is the only material of the imagination capable of reflecting on its own conditions of production. Language has a unique relationship to the imagination because of the specific connection it institutes between production and expression. While an architect might be said to be a poet insofar as he or she arranges materials that remain external to the imagination, poets "in the restricted sense" work with and on the very material of the imagination itself.

Shelley develops this claim by turning first to the question of how individual expressions of the imagination can be interpreted as examples of poetry "in the general sense": "Language, colour, form, and religious and civil habits of action are all the instruments and materials of poetry; they may be called poetry by that figure of speech which considers the effect as a synonime of the cause" (DP 513). Again, the link between the imagination and its visible works is produced by metalepsis (the "figure of speech which considers the effect as synonime of the cause"). Shelley's use of denotative locution ("they may be called") signals that there is no proper name for the relation between the imagination and its materials. Metalepsis is both the device that allows a passage between "poetry in the general sense" and "poetry in the restricted sense" and the device that articulates the way in which each expression is grounded in the imagination. Such grounding, however, disarticulates the antecedence of the imagination to at least one of its products: language. The result is an opening to an event within the text, a "no-future," that cannot be accounted for from within its tropological system.

This opening will also be essential to the politics of Shelley's poetry, since language becomes an indispensable model for the sovereign. If in the absence of the divine only language (and by extension the imagination) can be said to create *ex nihilo*, then it becomes a key, though highly unstable, site through which to think the self-authorizing or self-founding nature of contemporary political power. As we will see, poets (including statesmen) are legislators insofar as they metaleptically inaugurate the new. What Shelley's texts continuously point toward is an event that cannot be fully anticipated by the creator, but that is nonetheless essential to the act of creation. This aspect of legislation or creation is something that constitutes the act's very performativity and whose radical self-inauguration must be repeated. This self-inaugurating act does not happen once and for all, however. It is immediately opened to something that cannot be accounted for from within the act itself. It is this metaleptic dimension of seeing "the future in the present" that Shelley's *Defence* will return to again and again as a fundamental anachronism inherent to the creative act that allows it to live beyond its initial moment, giving it a future that even it cannot foresee.

This future is articulated in the *Defence* through an elaboration of Shelley's argument about language's difference from the other expressions of the imagination on account of its "more direct" connection to the imagination:

> But poetry in a more restricted sense expresses those arrangements of language, and especially metrical language which are created by that imperial faculty, whose throne is curtained within the invisible nature of man. And this springs from the nature itself of language, which is a *more direct* representation of the actions and passions of our internal being, and is susceptible of more various and delicate combinations, than colour, form or motion, and is more plastic and obedient to the controul of that faculty of which it is the creation. (DP 513, emphasis mine)

Language is a "more direct representation" of "our internal being" because of the specifically *arbitrary* relation it establishes between itself and the imagination: "For language is arbitrarily produced by the Imagination and has relation to thoughts alone; but all other materials, instruments and conditions of art have relations among each other, which limit and interpose between conception and expression" (DP 513). Shelley invokes a unique relation between language, its arbitrary production, and its direct connection to the imagination. All the other materials of poetry "in the general sense" are internally differentiated (they have "relations among each other, which limit and interpose between conception and expression") and therefore remain exterior to the imagination's metaleptic power; color, for instance, exists within a continuum of other colors. Language, on the other hand, *because* it is arbitrarily produced, has a direct relationship to its own production. Its arbitrariness is precisely what makes it a more direct expression, since nothing intervenes between its (arbitrary) instantiation and the act that produces it. It is the only expression capable of naming itself *as* an expression of the imagination through the "figure of speech which considers the effect as a synonime of the cause" (i.e., the metaleptic substitution of cause for effect). Thus, language not only becomes a model for a *creatio ex nihilo*, it becomes a paradigm of the imagination's very metaleptic structure, making unclear whether language is an effect of the imagination (which would be prior to it) or its cause. It also becomes a model for the way that the imagination produces political and historical effects by becoming the privileged exemplar of the way in which the imagination posits arbitrarily without any determined referent prior to this positing. It becomes a figure for the unprecedented by becoming an example of something that breaks with (and refounds) its own conditions of possibility.

What emerges in the *Defence*, then, is an act or event that opens itself to a future by exceeding a given horizon of meaning, such as the tropological system or metaleptic chain of images that produces it. This act is not the product of any volition, but a turn toward something that makes various figures of the imagination possible, without functioning as their transcendental cause. To call this a "performative" is to insist less on the illocutionary or perlocutionary force[23] of a given image or statement than on the arbitrary nature of an event that precedes an image or statement. In other words, it cannot be understood as a prior referent or semantic content, but instead as that which puts a context or structure of meaning in place initially, while remaining both conditioned by *and* disjoined from that context.[24] The *Defence* moves from a semantic, to a structural, and finally to a performative understanding of the imagination by invoking something—language—that breaks with its own structure of articulation. Likewise, when Shelley begins to account for the way that the imagination liberates an unforeseeable future, he does so by way of something unforeseen in the present that acts as its condition of possibility without being actually temporally or logically prior to it.

Metaleptic Imagination and History

This is why when Shelley more directly addresses the question of the effect of poetry on society and history in the *Defence* his first articulation of its influence remains "unacknowledged" in the present, even by its practitioners: "In the infancy of the world, neither poets themselves nor their auditors are fully aware of the excellency of poetry: for it acts in a divine and unapprehended manner, beyond and above consciousness; and it is reserved for future generations to contemplate and measure the mighty cause and effect in all the strength and splendour of their union" (DP 516). The reference to poetry's "unapprehended manner" is not meant to suggest a developmental model that moves from naïveté to consciousness of the imagination's inaugural powers. His later discussion of Dante, in fact, suggests a latency to his poetry that remains "unapprehended" even in the present.[25] Shelley's insistence that only a future generation will be capable of "contemplating the mighty cause and effect" of the original "interstice" that these authors represent suggests something other than a return to an original cause that has been restored. It suggests, rather, a repetition of something *originally* or *fundamentally* unapprehended in the past that remains so in the present and that shatters the notion that the present can be fully apprehended at all. It is this potentiality within the present that remains the driving force of renovation in Shelley.

From here, Shelley goes on to demonstrate the way that history itself takes place as the metaleptic substitution of one founder or poet for another in an endless non-teleological displacement. Turning to the development of Christian literature out of its relation to Greek literature, he introduces the maxim that "no nation or religion can supersede any other without incorporating into itself a portion of that which it supersedes" (DP 525). This sets the stage for an understanding of historical transformation that parallels the structural metalepsis developed earlier in the *Defence*. The nature of the incorporation of Greek by Christian literature involves more than an assimilation of specific structures of meaning such as the transition from a monotheistic God to polytheism. Shelley discusses Homer, Dante, and Milton in terms of their respective innovations within the genre of epic to represent this process, although it becomes clear that Dante is the central figure for Shelley since he is "the bridge thrown over the stream of time, which unites the modern and antient world" (DP 526). Shelley focuses on what remains unapprehended in each author and how this metaleptically determines their particular innovations. Milton's work, for example, "contains within itself a philosophical refutation of that system of which, by a strange and natural antithesis, it has been a chief popular support" (DP

526). Nonetheless, this initially unapprehended element by Milton about his own work is still conceived as the latent truth of his epic that a later moment could unveil. Yet, what Shelley emphasizes is the way in which the unapprehended element of truly great poetry continues to be redefined even after the historical moment in which it was composed. Like the semantic and structural forms of metalepsis earlier in the *Defence*, this continuous redefinition takes place both internally within a given *oeuvre* and structurally between great poets who incorporate and displace their predecessors.

The incorporation of a previous poet as a forgotten cause or origin is developed, for example, through Shelley's discussion of the way Dante becomes Homer's most important successor: "Homer was the first, and Dante the second epic poet: that is, the second poet the series of whose creations bore a defined and intelligible relation to the knowledge, and sentiment, and religion, and political conditions of the age in which he lived, and of the ages which followed it, developing itself in correspondence with their development" (DP 527). In other words, Homer's and Dante's poetry remains defined by their respective historical contexts (the "sentiment, and religion, and political conditions of the age"). At the same time, there is something within their work that continues to develop in relationship to the historical contexts that follow. Shelley sees no contradiction between something that is at once historically determined and able to redefine itself with regard to subsequent ages. This feature of a work is in fact what makes the poetry historical or unprecedented to begin with because it exceeds a particular context's structures of articulation. Homer, as the first epic poet, remains inimitable;[26] the unapprehended within his poetry is what remains unprecedented in him, his "eternity of genius" (DP 527). This "eternity," however, is not a stable content that is somehow outside of time or true for any context; it is instead a reference to the imagination's ongoing metaleptic power of reorganization that continues to develop a relationship between its inimitable acts and other subsequent contexts.

How then does Dante become the second great epic poet, and thus the "bridge between the antient and modern worlds," according to Shelley? Like Homer, Dante's poetry contains something unapprehended insofar as he imitates Homer's originality itself. He does this, however, by metaleptically shifting the relationship between Homer's religious context and the "distorted notions of invisible things which Dante and his rival Milton have idealized" (DP 526). These distorted notions "are merely the mask and the mantle in which these great poets walk through eternity enveloped and disguised" (DP 526). Homer's immersion in his particular historical context's conception of the invisible is thus displaced by Christianity's conception of the invisible.[27] What Shelley wants to make clear, however, is that one partial indicator (Greek religion) is merely being displaced or replaced by a different "mask" (Christian religion). What matters, then, is not the truth of Christian conceptions of the invisible so much as the substitution of one partial conception for another, which builds the bridge from the "antient to the modern" because it metaleptically incorporates Greek religion into itself as its forgotten ground. As Shelley insists, "Dante and Milton were both deeply penetrated with the antient religion of the civilized world; and its spirit exists in their poetry probably in the same proportion as its forms survived in the unreformed worship of modern Europe" (DP 527). Within two of the most important Christian poets of the Western canon, there is the vestige of a displaced origin in ancient Greece that they perhaps unknowingly reinscribe into a new context. This reinscription repeats what remains unapprehended in Homer's epics not by producing two different conceptions of the *same* invisible realm, but by repeating the partiality of Homer's conception in a context completely foreign to its original articulation.

An act of the imagination thus becomes historical for Shelley only by breaking with the conditions that produced it, just as language is seen to be arbitrarily produced by the imagination only by breaking with normal relations of cause and effect. Out of this process emerges a conception of the task of poetry that is fundamentally at odds with a theory of action predicated on a conscious subject that realizes his/her actions within a determined and verifiable context. What makes a literary work worthy of its place within Shelley's literary history is its ability to continue to produce effects beyond its initial context and the intentions of its author by articulating a metaleptic relation to its historical conditions of enunciation. Homer's greatness is defined by a continued development of what remains unapprehended in his work, which occurs through a repetition of his original untimeliness vis-à-vis his own historical context within other contexts that Homer could never have anticipated. Likewise, Dante's greatness emerges out of his metaleptic substitution of Homer's form of unapprehension with his own. Shelley's literary-historical account of the metaleptic structure of the imagination suggests that its effects are achieved in part through its inability to coincide with its own creative act, rather than by preceding and self-presently grounding an action according to its sovereign autonomy.

The most trenchant application of this structure for Shelley is in the question of how this conception of the imagination can be brought to bear on an attempt to rethink the nature of political power and resistance to it. If poets are "legislators" for Shelley because they inaugurate something unapprehended, unprecedented, and metaleptically related to what precedes them, then the imagination has a political dimension insofar as poets inaugurate a metalepsis of past *political* forms as well. In fact, what makes them legislators is precisely this power of metaleptic reversal. But it is a power that is very different from traditional sovereignty in that it does not install itself through a self-founding act. Insofar as modern sovereignty depends on an absolute decision, a self-conscious act of self-founding, and the appropriation of this inaugurality as the unique identity of the sovereign, the founding or legislation that the poet engages in, for Shelley, is much more aleatory, less autochthonous. If metalepsis challenges the notion of a stable anteriority, it also challenges any figure of the sovereign that would erect itself on the premise of a self-identical relation between figure and ground.

From Metalepsis to Act: The Mask of Anarchy

Shelley's political poetry, even its popular variety, usually involves a contretemps between a form of sovereignty that attempts to authorize itself through identification with a stable anteriority, and a poetic form of legislation that calls this sovereignty into question. Perhaps no better example of this exists than Shelley's posthumously celebrated poem *The Mask of Anarchy*, which has often been read as a kind of litmus test for the question of the nature of Shelley's politics. While most readings have concentrated on the specific content of the political vision that emerges in the later half of the poem, less attention has been paid to the question of the *form* that this vision takes and specifically what enables it.[28] While the poem may appear to advocate a relatively simple form of passive resistance, or a democratic alternative to the absolutism Shelley perceived in the English government, there is a more formal component to the poem. This component complicates what appears to be a poem straightforwardly about political resistance and turns its focus toward the seemingly more abstract question of the conditions under which a radical resistance could be mounted to the *form* of sovereignty that makes tyranny possible.

At stake is a conception of political sovereignty that no longer attempts to justify itself according to an absolute anteriority and that opens itself to the event of a founding that is metaleptic, and thus radically contingent, never fully established. In *The Mask of Anarchy*, a conflict between two *forms* of sovereignty materializes in the poem's apparent opposition between the "masque" of the first part of the poem, which details the authoritarianism and corruption of the government responsible for the massacre at Manchester,[29] and the figure of "Hope" that emerges to resist it. The nature of this opposition, however, has continued to be a source of disagreement. Recent criticism has tended to see the poem as attempting to confront a contradiction between Shelley's populism and his concerns about the dangers that might emerge from popular agitation. Richard Cronin, for example, interprets one of the poem's figures as a "mythopoetic version of the Whig aristocrat, authorized by his culture and moral refinement to act as the champion of the inarticulate masses."[30] The measure of the extent of Shelley's radicalism, in other words, forms a significant part of the body of criticism on the poem. What exactly does Shelley advocate in the poem? Does the poem's political program go beyond a general call for individual rights? Does it advocate violence only when the option of non-violence has been exhausted? And what is the relationship between the political content of the poem and its posthumous effects?

The poem remains notoriously ambivalent about its political aims, but it is clear that it involves an attempt to distinguish the illegitimate sovereignty of the British government from another relation to sovereignty that would produce a genuinely democratic alternative. If governmental power is represented in the poem as a form of Anarchy—the illegitimate self-production of authority—then one of the tasks of the poem is to imagine an alternative to the "mask" of legitimacy that the British government gives itself. It is here that the question of metalepsis returns, since one of the features that characterizes this difference is how each form of sovereignty relates to the anterior performative that sets it into place to begin with. Since metalepsis always displaces the origin that makes it possible, no sovereign worthy of the name could ever claim that his self-founding act, which he could only ever partially apprehend and on which his sovereignty depends, is produced of his own volition. And if the figure of metalepsis always entails an anteriority that is constantly in the process of becoming, then every act of founding, of legislation, or of creation remains always partial, destined for a posthumous existence that may resemble its initial emergence very little. What matters, then, is how the sovereign understands his relationship to this act of grounding, legislation, or self-creation. In the case of the tyrant, this act is seen as the product of his own will: absolute and identifiable. In the case of Shelley's counter-sovereignty, this act is much more open to the contingency of metalepsis, including the threat that it simply *repeats* the gesture of self-authorization that characterizes the tyranny of Anarchy. What will distinguish "Anarchy" from "Hope," then, is a subtle difference in the way that their anterior ground is materialized in specific social forms, institutions, and political gestures.

The Mask of Anarchy could be said to be divided into three main sections: the first twenty-one stanzas articulate a poetic critique of the "mask" of illegitimate power in the allegory of specific government representatives, as well as in the broader political and legal system that this government helped erect and maintain. The opening section is then followed by ten stanzas that articulate the conditions of the emergence of an alternative to the mask of power in the figure of Hope, along with a "Shape" that emerges coextensively and makes possible the defeat of Anarchy. The final, largest section of the poem, comprising sixty stanzas, articulates the full development of Hope, including an exhortation to the people of England to "Rise like lions" and establish a new democratic order grounded in material and intellectual freedom. The second section, therefore, constitutes the crucial hinge of the poem, articulating the difference between illegitimate sovereignty and a legitimate form that, nevertheless, has to negotiate the fact that both forms of sovereignty initially appear to have the same structure. How these forms of sovereignty are distinguished in the second section of the poem is therefore the most enigmatic and complex aspect of it, since it is where Shelley explicitly describes the metaleptic conditions that govern the presentation of the democratic alternative, in whatever form it might take.

The question of the mode of appearance of each respective form of political sovereignty is made explicit by the opening frame of the poem, which finds the speaker "asleep" in Italy when a voice greets him and bids him to "walk in the visions of Poesy." The first stanza clearly positions the action of the poem in terms of poetry's capacity to envision not only the violence and illegitimacy of the mask of power, but also its opposition. It is the failure of this opening frame to return in the poem that marks, for Susan Wolfson,[31] a "slumber" that conditions the poem's entirety, making it unable to effectuate anything other than a dream or aesthetic fantasy. If one considers the way in which the poem goes on to meditate on how the forces of Anarchy are grounded though symbol and are, in turn, satirized and unmasked by Shelley's allegory, then the status of the "visions of Poesy" that opens the poem is in fact more ambiguous. As Marc Redfield has suggested, Shelley's poetics is always faced with the possibility that it "repeats what it condemns."[32] Because illegitimate power erects itself in part by means of aesthetics, poetry always runs the risk of reinforcing its collusion with this power. However, poetry can also counter the relation between power and aesthetics, unmasking their collusion. It is this unmasking that constitutes the first part of the poem, while the second attempts to present an alternative that opens itself to an equally contingent and groundless form of self-assertion. Shelley's poem will attempt to account for the way in which this alternative also presents a different relation to the groundlessness of its own assertion.

As in Coleridge's conception of the unconditional that we explored in Chapter 2, Shelley's *Mask of Anarchy* is situated in the tenuous and ambiguous distinction between two relations to the paradox of modern sovereignty's foundation in its unconditionality. This is evidenced in the poem's unmasking of the self-grounding and therefore arbitrary rule of Anarchy in the first section of the poem and the address to the men of England made possible by the Shape that arises in the second. In the first part of the poem, the illegitimate figures of British power understand this unconditionality as an absolute ground of their authority. The satirical allegory of the masque of power works by revealing the abstractions that underpin these particular historical figures or institutions. Murder "has a mask like Castlereagh" (MA 6), Fraud has on "like Eldon, an ermined gown" (MA 14), and ecclesiastical authority is "clothed" (MA 22) in the Bible. In each case, the relationship between the mask, gown, or clothing is inverted so that the historical figures themselves become the mask for the abstraction, which acts as their ground or referent, an anterior source of power and prestige. It then reveals the arbitrary relation between this ground and the institution it makes possible. If the litany of allegorical figures of power can be unmasked, it is because they have appropriated the groundless anteriority that marks their condition of appearance as their own rightful property.[33] What the mask of Anarchy reveals is in fact quite the opposite of an-archy. Each figure acts as a representation of an abstract *archē* or anterior ground that gives it authority, casting it as necessary or natural, thereby masking the purely arbitrary (and violent) relation between each figure of power and the anteriority that legitimates it.

This arbitrary connection is made clearer when the poem develops the specific nature of Anarchy's power, which is associated with no particular historical figure but becomes a *form* that organizes the juridical, political, and economic systems that emerge through their reference to its repeated self-assertion: "I am God and King and Law!" (MA 37). This line, delivered first by Anarchy itself, and then repeated by the lawyers, priests, and soldiers who acquire their own authority by reference to it, constitutes the poem's first articulation of illegitimate sovereign assertion. The line enacts a self-identification that links Anarchy's declaration with an attempt to unite divine transcendence with its own political and juridical power. Though it mirrors a theological grounding of political power by mimicking an assertion of divine right, the poem makes clear, through the isolation of the phrase "I am God and King and Law!," that its sheer repetition is all that guarantees its efficacy. Anarchy's self-assertion, in turn, makes possible an entire system of power—juridical, military, and economic—that erects itself through this self-legitimation. First, the militia who perpetrated the violence of the massacre itself is implicated in the sovereign assertion of Anarchy: "For with pomp to meet him came / Clothed in arms like blood and flame, / The hired Murderers, who did sing / 'Thou art God, and Law, and King'" (MA 58–61). Next, the juridical system and ecclesiastical authority ratify Anarchy, as well as their own claim to authority, through the same assertion: "Lawyers and priests, a motley crowd / To the earth their pale brows bowed; / Like a bad prayer not over loud / Whispering—'Thou art Law and God'" (MA 66–69). This mutual recognition and ratification reaches its crescendo in the "one accord" that repeats the assertion "Thou art King, and God and Lord: Anarchy to Thee we bow. Be thy name made holy now!" (MA 70–73). Anarchy's repeated assertion becomes a felicitous speech act in Austin's sense[34] doing what it says by generating the "one accord" that metes out authority to lawyers, priests, soldiers, each of whom in turn ratify Anarchy's dominion. Anarchy's self-legitimation takes shape only in the repetition and iteration of this phrase in new contexts: legal, ecclesiastical, and military. The power of this self-assertion works by attempting to incorporate the groundlessness of Anarchy's legitimation into the juridical system it simultaneously erects. Anarchy's force and power, therefore, rely on the inclusion of something within the legal order that is radically exterior to law. Once this exteriority or anteriority becomes incorporated into the juridical order or system of power, Anarchy reclaims it as a self-evident, identical (though repeated) ground of legitimation that thenceforth becomes the source of all legal and political justification.

If the first section of the poem unmasks the groundless self-legitimation of Anarchy, the second section articulates the condition of the emergence of Hope in opposition to it. Like the pageant of power that opens the poem, Hope's first appearance also takes the form of a mask. She initially appears as despair, but separates herself from this appearance only through an act of self-naming: "And her name was Hope, she said / But she looked more like Despair" (MA 87–88). Her initial appearance brings about an almost hyperbolic passivity: her first act, after lamenting her many other appearances as failures, is to lay supplicant in front of the charging horses of Anarchy and its minions. This imagery, of course, is meant to identify the crowds of Peterloo, trampled and maimed by militia cavalry, with the figure of Hope. But it is also meant to contrast the violent self-assertion evidenced by Anarchy in the previous section of the poem. If both Anarchy and Hope are masks, emerging like something that they are not, what characterizes Hope differently from Anarchy is her specific relation to her own performative self-assertion, to the metaleptic act that gives her legitimacy. If Anarchy attempts to incorporate the moment of its own sheer imposition inside the juridical system that it founds, Hope's relation to its own self-naming is more obscure.

Unlike Anarchy, whose violent self-assertion is ratified by an entire juridical and legal structure, Hope's tentative power originates in an explicit relation to an image whose indeterminate "rising up" in the poem is described in almost unmotivated terms. Hope's subsequent defeat of Anarchy is made possible by a Shape that separates Hope from Anarchy: "When between her and her foes / A mist, a light, an image rose, / Small at first, and weak and frail / Like the vapour of a vale" (MA 102–5). The Shape merely rises to distinguish Hope from Anarchy, taking on first a natural and then a militant violence in its emergence, since the figure moves from the conventional link between revolution and lightning to an indeterminate "Shape" clad in armor:

Till as clouds grow on the blast
Like tower-crowned giants striding fast
And glare with lightnings as they fly,
And speak in thunder to the sky,
It grew—a Shape arrayed in mail
Brighter than the Viper's scale
And upborne on wings whose grain
Was the light of sunny rain. (MA 106–13)

The Shape's emergence, however, leads to no particular act of resistance or assertion. Instead, it merely arises "between" Hope and Anarchy, drawing a division between them, but one that remains unspecified. The action of the Shape, in fact, remains, throughout this entire section of the poem, rather ghostly and immaterial. After its sudden emergence, the Shape's significance hovers between action and passivity. Rather than the violent acts of trampling that "Anarchy" threatens, the Shape walks "with step as soft as wind" (MA 118) passing "o'er the heads of men" who can feel its presence, but who look and find only "empty air" (MA 121). Not just the action of the Shape but the agency that is behind it remain fundamentally indeterminate, a mere "vapour." If it is true, as Marc Redfield has argued in his reading of the poem that it "stages a drama of personification,"[35] then the introduction of the Shape as the ground of Hope's emergence, in fact, also adds a dimension of the impersonal to the personification of Hope since the former neither acts as a mask nor points to any specific power that is behind Hope or is that is articulated through her. Unlike the "mask" of Anarchy, which appropriates its own groundlessness as the source of its authority, Hope's grounding in the Shape is rooted in a wholly arbitrary and indeterminate relation between figure and ground that is never effaced or disguised by a mask of performative self-justification.

Just what the Shape might signify politically has been the topic of extensive debate. If early commentators identified the Shape with the personification of the Spirit of Liberty, more recent commentary has emphasized the multiplicity of references that might determine its significance. Stephen Jones, for example, has suggested that the Shape is "overdetermined" and may be a reference not only to Liberty, but to a "revolutionary appropriation of the traditional feminine figure of Britannia."[36] He goes on to suggest that the Shape may also be a modeled after a "transparency," "a popular device which involved a kind of print that exploited special effects of light . . . by unfolding to superimpose or overlay multiple images."[37] William Keach correctly identifies the Shape with the opening of Hope's call to arms for the Men of England, but finds its "deflection of a clear political agency" behind its manifestation the sign of a "strategically evasive mystification."[38] Susan Wolfson has recently argued that the Shape must be read as a figure of the feminine, "the repository of a myth of transformative revolution without violence."[39] It appears, in fact, to act not just as a repository of various myths of transformation, but as an undecidable reference that authorizes a number of readings. What these readings tend to do is interpret the Shape as yet another allegorical figure alongside Anarchy and Hope.

The Shape, however, is not an allegorical figure like the ones that emerge in the first section of the poem. Nor is it identical with the emergence of Hope in the second section, since Hope is explicitly defined as something that it is not: Despair. The Shape, I suggest, must be read here as de Man reads the "Shape all light" in *The Triumph of Life*: as a "figure for the figurality of all signification."[40] That is, rather than conflate it with other allegorical figures such as Hope and Anarchy, the Shape must be understood as the condition of possibility for allegory itself. As in *The Triumph of Life*, the Shape in the *Mask of Anarchy* is linked with light imagery and optics, the very conditions of appearance. It first arises "between" Hope and her foes as "a mist, a light, an image" (MA 103). The stanzas that describe the Shape emphasize not only its ephemerality, but its nature as a source of visibility: the Shape is "upborne on wings whose grain / Was as the light of sunny rain" (MA 112–13). The reference to Venus and Lucifer in line 115 reinforces the extent to which the Shape does not just coincide with a "new dawn," but actually becomes a Luciferean "bearer of light" by establishing the conditions in which Hope can appear. This is reinforced all the more by the extent to which it withdraws from the scene and from being a direct actor in the poem's development of the allegory of Hope itself. The men who "feel" the Shape's presence "look," but find only "empty air" (MA 121). The pause in the poetic line between the men looking and the vision itself suggests that the Shape is an image, although not in the sense of a symbol for a concealed referent or an original ground. Rather, it must be understood in the same way, as I argued in Chapter 2, that we should understand Coleridge's definition of the symbol: as an image in the Kantian sense[41] in that it *images* or makes possible that which is visible. The second "look" by the multitude at line 126, which repeats the same pause in the poetic line that conditions the first "look," returns us to the "poetic vision" of a triumphant Hope who has overthrown Anarchy. But this vision occurs only through the *visibility* of Hope and the relative *obscurity* of the Shape that makes Hope possible. The Shape is, thus, not the direct agent of change, but the anterior condition of that vision's emergence.

As the ground or condition for the possibility of Hope, the Shape also thereby enacts a metaleptic relation between the sovereignty of Hope over Anarchy. If the Shape inaugurates a vision of democratic reform and passive resistance that characterizes the third section of the poem, it does so by remaining fundamentally distinct from the vision it enables.[42] What separates the illegitimate sovereignty of Anarchy from the legitimate sovereignty of Hope is not an *erasure* of the arbitrariness that characterizes self-legitimation. Quite the opposite: the role of the Shape in the poem is similar to the role of language in the *Defence*—it emphasizes the absolutely arbitrary relation between figure and ground and calls into question the relation between cause and effect. Far from constituting an absolute starting point, the Shape constitutes both the radically inaugural and radically unapprehended quality of any truly revolutionary act that always proceeds without any guarantee that what it brings about will be an improvement over what it supersedes. The very inappropriability of the Shape as a resource for self-authorization is what gives rise to the possibility of an alternative form of sovereignty in Shelley's poem. If Anarchy attempts to make its own self-assertion the basis of its legitimation by effacing the difference between ground and figure, the Shape's production of Hope *insists* on this difference by manifesting the distinction between figure and ground *figuratively*, through the separation between Hope and the Shape that makes her possible. It is this anachronism that destines both for an uncertain future. As in any genuinely inaugural, creative, and thus poetic act in Shelley's sense, Hope's emergence necessitates a metaleptic displacement of the Shape, which becomes a figure of the future anterior, a precondition or cause that is also simultaneously an effect of what it makes possible. Its force, which remains not yet fully apprehended by those who sense its presence, opens up a vision of the future that constitutes the latter half of the poem, but gestures insistently toward an efficacy that has not yet arrived and toward a future fundamentally without guarantee.

Through the Shape, furthermore, the poem highlights the difference between Anarchy's relation to the unconditionality of its sovereign assertion and Hope's relation to the unconditionality of its emergence. The Shape and Hope are not simply identical, unlike Anarchy's attempt to incorporate its own groundlessness into its performative self-justification. Hope's emergence, on the other hand, is characterized by a very different relationship to its own unconditional ground. Its emergence through the Shape points toward a metaleptic anteriority that it attempts to mirror, but that remains fundamentally withdrawn from the particular act and speech it makes possible. Hope, therefore, gestures toward a different sense of sovereignty than the one personified by Anarchy, a sovereignty no longer identified with mastery, that remains fundamentally contingent, open to an unconditionality that it cannot identify entirely with its own power or will. It also makes clear that this emergence is at best tentative, always subject to the threat of its own dispersal, undoing, or metaleptic overturning, whether by a new act of inauguration or by its own collapse into what it opposes.

Hence, while Anarchy attempts to appropriate the anteriority that grounds it by retrospectively restoring it to the status of an original cause, Hope's development out of the Shape takes on the appearance of the dissemination that Shelley associates with the metaleptic imagination in the *Defence*, thus grounding its sovereignty on something irreducible to the (speech) act that initially set it in place or in power. At line 125 of the *Mask*, for example, the Shape "steps" over the heads of men in order to become a catalyst for new and unheard-of "thoughts" which "sprung where'er that step did fall."

These thoughts lead to the vision of Hope's triumph, but they also evoke the questions that Rousseau asks in *Triumph of Life* prior to encountering the "shape all light." The question of Rousseau's posthumous legacy is addressed when he asks whether the "sparks" of his thought have produced the "seeds of misery" (Napoleon) or whether there are yet other "beacons" that might emerge from these seeds to challenge that legacy. Asked the question of his origins by the narrator ("Whence camest thou and whither goest thou?" [TL 296]), Rousseau links his response to the encounter with the "Shape all light." Like the Shape in *Mask of Anarchy*, the steps of the "shape all light" induce not just a new vision but a forgetting:

> And still her feet, no less than the sweet tune
> To which they moved, seemed as they moved, to blot
> The thoughts of him who gazed on them, and soon
> All that was seemed as if it had been not—
> As if the gazer's mind was strewn beneath
> Her feet like embers, and she, thought by thought,
> Trampled its fires into the dust of death,
> As Day upon the threshold of the east
> Treads out the lamps of night. (TL 382–90)

Each seemingly absolute starting point in the *Triumph of Life* always points toward a receding anteriority that is metaleptically displaced by a succeeding one.[43] The image of the "shape all light" trampling Rousseau's mind like daybreak effacing the stars, for example, is barely discernible from the sunrise that opens the poem. The repetition of this metaleptic inauguration is always simultaneously radically initial and a reiteration, always the invocation of a new vision, and the displacement and forgetting of the old. This is perhaps why Rousseau later in the poem calls the shape somewhat enigmatically "the ghost of a forgotten form of sleep" (TL 428). This odd phrase best captures the way in which the "shape all light" constitutes a figure of anteriority without representing this anteriority as a fully realized transcendence. What is forgotten is itself still inaccessible to consciousness (it is a "form of sleep"), and the shape is merely its remnant or specter.

In the context of *The Mask of Anarchy*, the attempt to ground political resistance on the metaleptic displacement of the legislative or founding act of the imagination is in the end to relinquish any ultimate foundation or ground. The performative that enacts Hope can never be assured that it is felicitous in Austin's sense, nor does it produce a fully stable counter-sovereignty, since its own inaugural act is immediately subject to metaleptic displacement. Rather, what results in the third part of the poem is a list of not-yet felicitous performatives, each of which marks the distance between saying and doing, revealing the desire the poem has to turn words into deeds. Starting at line 262 ("Let a great Assembly be"), the poem develops a series of specific actions that the reform movement might take in response to government violence. Each of these take the form of the original performative of Genesis, God's "let there be light," though, of course, none of them have the immediate efficacy of a *fiat lux*. The accumulating phrases that begin with the admonishment to "let" something occur appear to culminate in Shelley's vision of a movement of passive resistance that will eventually sway the conscience of the military. Yet what "become[s] / Like oppression's thundered doom" (MA 364–65) is not this vision *per se*, but rather "these words" (MA 364), the words of the poem itself, which has so often been repeated in other contexts, in the midst of other political struggles:

> And these words shall then become
> Like oppression's thundered doom
> Ringing through each heart and brain,
> Heard again—again—again—
> Rise like lions after slumber
> In unvanquishable number—
> Shake your chains to earth like dew
> Which in sleep had fallen on you—
> Ye are many—they are few. (MA 364–72)

The last two stanzas of the poem emphasize less the content of a specific vision of the future than the fact of repetition, as the words are "Heard again—again—again—" (MA 367). Far from the assurance of a future moment in which Hope's sovereignty reigns supreme, the end of the poem gestures toward other future contexts in which these words, repeated, and "ringing through each heart and brain" (MA 366) might be able to do what they say. The poem in the end reflects on its own posthumous effectivity. If the series of performatives that culminate the poem do not provide any assurance of this, it is not because of the impotence of their gesture but because they are modeled on the emergence of the Shape, whose indeterminate rising up maintains a relationship to its own radical contingency. Thus, a truly creative act, for Shelley, an act that exceeds to a certain extent its own particular context, is always structured by a metaleptic anteriority that opens it to a future repetition. The creative or legislative act is always situated within the awareness of its own partiality, grounded not by a unvarying and self-same unconditionality, but by an unconditionality that is not quite its own and that it can only remember as a "forgotten form of sleep."

Prometheus Unbound: *Demogorgon and the Future of Political Sovereignty*

Though *The Mask of Anarchy* highlights the opposition between the absolutism of Anarchy and the contingency of Hope, Shelley's more "esoteric"[44] closet drama, *Prometheus Unbound*, extends this opposition into the realm of a critique of forms of thinking that sustain specific kinds of power. Exactly what the poem allegorizes is not clear, whether "operations of the human mind" or a more direct narrative of the movement from monarchy to a democratic alternative. Yet, the conflict that Shelley presents between Jupiter and Prometheus appears in many ways similar to the allegorized conflict between Anarchy and Hope. Jupiter, however, more clearly connects the concepts of monotheism and monarchy and thus represents an interlacing of forms of absolute authority and hegemony in a variety of domains: theological, political, and intellectual. He is both sacred and secular at the same time, a figure of monocentrism more generally.[45] Prometheus, as Jupiter's antagonist, is a figure of opposition to Jupiter's rule, though he often appears to reflect him in substantial ways, notably in his desire for revenge. Shelley's addition of the enigmatic figure of Demogorgon to his version of the Prometheus myth complicates what would otherwise appear to be the straightforward opposition in the poem between absolute rule and resistance to it. While some commentators have speculated that Demogorgon could be an allegory for "the people" in the transition to a democratic alternative to monarchy, it is not clear that he is yet another allegorical figure of resistance, like Prometheus, even though it is Demogorgon who brings about the fall of Jupiter. In fact, as I will suggest, Demogorgon appears to exist, initially, outside the conflict that characterizes most of the poem. Like the Shape in *The Mask of Anarchy*, he represents a kind of potentiality that is part of any genuine act of the metaleptic imagination and, as a result, begins to outline an alternative conception of the unconditional and its relation to the exercise of power that will essentially displace Jupiterian absolutism in all of its various forms.

In Act I of *Prometheus Unbound*, Demogorgon is first introduced in the context of an opposition between the visible world of "life" and the world of "death," which is inhabited by "The shadows of all forms that think and live" (PU I:198). This world, populated by the "Dreams, and the light imaginings of men / And all that faith creates, or love desires" (PU I:200–1), appears as the repository of the imaginary structures that give significance and form to the fictions Man creates and to the power he bestows upon them. "All the Gods / Are there, and all the powers of nameless worlds, / Vast sceptered Phantoms" (PU I:204–6), whose fictionality or simulation of "life" hardly alters their hold on it. These Phantoms include both "Demogorgon, a tremendous Gloom" (PU I:207) and "he, the Supreme Tyrant, on his throne / Of burning Gold" (PU I:208–9)—clearly a reference to Jupiter. The coexistence in this world of various "strange, sublime and beauteous shapes" (PU I:202), including the supreme tyrant and the instigator of his eventual downfall, implies that these "shapes" are merely potentialities; what makes them actual, part of the world of the living, is their being called forth as an image. Thus, when the "phantasm" of Jupiter greets Prometheus to recall the curse that will bring about Jupiter's fall, it is uttered as a challenge for Jupiter to unmask himself:

> And thou, and thy self-torturing solitude
> An awful Image of calm power
> Though now thou sittest, let the hour
> Come, when thou must appear to be
> That which thou art internally. (PU I:295–99)

The suggestion here is that the curse demands that Jupiter demonstrate he is in fact a "phantasm," merely an image whose non-necessity can be made apparent, but whose power nevertheless relies on a *false* image of inevitability. Like Anarchy, Jupiter presents the scaffolding that underpins his sovereignty as absolute, whereas the curse itself reveals the inherent groundlessness of his claim to authority.

Demogorgon's opposition to Jupiter, like the Shape in *The Mask of Anarchy*, does not take the form of a counter-sovereignty or the return to a stable foundation. Demogorgon is first introduced in Act II through Panthea's second dream, which is interpreted by Asia as another form of "forgotten sleep": "As you speak, your words / Fill, pause by pause, my own forgotten sleep / with shapes . . ." (PU II:i, 142–44). This recounting of the dream produces an echo that leads them to the cave of Demogorgon, whom Panthea and Asia encounter sitting on a throne. Panthea's original description of Demogorgon emphasizes his "shapelessness" and the fact that, were it not for the sense that he is a "living spirit," the "seat of power" that he occupies would appear empty:

> I see a mighty Darkness
> Filling the seat of power; and rays of gloom
> Dart round, as light from the meridian Sun,
> Ungazed upon and shapeless:—neither limb
> Nor form nor outline, yet we feel it is
> A living Spirit. (PU II:iv, 3–6)

Not only can Demogorgon not be seen directly (he is "ungazed" upon), but he offers not even the barest "outline" of a form. The only indication of his presence is in the oxymoron of the "rays of gloom" that emanate from the seat of power. As an obverse image of Jupiter, Demogorgon appears as the source of a power that has not yet taken shape, one that occupies the position of the sovereign without yet presenting a concrete image.[46]

When Asia asks Demogorgon a series of questions about the origin of the world and of the Earth, his answers at first appear straightforwardly theological, as he responds to her questions ("who made the living world" and "who made all that it contains") with "God," "God, Almighty God," and finally "merciful God" (PU II:iv, 8;12;19). When Asia follows these questions with the traditional theological one about how evil and terror could be created by the same God, Demogorgon replies enigmatically simply "He reigns" (PU II:iv, 28), an answer that he repeats even after he is explicitly asked by Asia to *name* who it is that holds this power. The third enigmatic response prompts Asia to enter a long narration that makes clear that both Prometheus and Jupiter are "enslaved," each in their respective ways. She thus poses once again the question of what force or power is capable of enslaving both the tyrant *and* the power that resists him. This question elicits a response from Demogorgon that transforms the meaning of his prior responses to all of Asia's questions: "All spirits are enslaved which serve things evil. / Thou knowest if Jupiter be such or no" (PU II:iv, 110–11). In the world of Aeschylus's play, Zeus constitutes the sovereign deity, an absolute seat of power over gods and mortals. In Shelley's revision, the apparently Christian notion of an absolute deity becomes a way of speaking, a form of rhetoric, that is not necessarily equivalent to belief in an absolute sovereign. When Demogorgon responds to Asia's question, "whom called'st thou God?" (PU II:iv, 112), Demogorgon emphasizes that his response has been translated for her: "I spoke but as ye speak—for Jove is the supreme of living things" (PU II:iv, 113). In other words, "God" is only a name, a placeholder, for something that Demogorgon will go on to make clear is entirely provisional.[47] Jupiter's "mastery" or his "enslavement" depends entirely on how one understands the nature of his absolute power as reinforced by such metaphysical terms as "God." Rather than answer Asia's questions affirmatively, Demogorgon turns them back on her and forces her to reflect on the nature of her questioning, which seeks out the cause of all causes, the "master" of both the sovereign (Jupiter) and that which calls his sovereignty into question (Prometheus). Demogorgon's enigmatic responses appear to reveal that a problematic conception of sovereignty is buried in the assumptions that guide Asia's questions and that perhaps different kinds of questions are in order, ones that will no longer assume the structure of an unconditional cause as a model for the sovereign.

Demogorgon's role as a figure separate from the struggle that characterizes Jupiter and Prometheus is made clearest, perhaps, when Asia repeats for the last time her desire for a kind of super-sovereignty: a master whose authority is anterior to both figures of slavery, Jupiter and Prometheus. Demogorgon's famous reply—"the deep truth is imageless" (PU II:iv, 116)—is less a claim that there is a deep truth not subject to representation than that this truth cannot be localized in a single absolute figure, whether the figure of a tyrant like Jupiter, a rebel like Prometheus, or a predetermined placeholder like God.[48] Demogorgon's response is less an attempt to respond to Asia's questions than an attempt to articulate a different way in which they might be posed. In response to Asia's question, he does not offer an absolute ground, or a monocentric anteriority prior to either Jupiter's or Prometheus's claims to sovereignty. Rather, he provides a response that appears to link his own indeterminacy with that very "imageless" truth:

> —If the Abysm
> Could vomit forth its secrets:—but a voice
> Is wanting, the deep truth is imageless;
> For what would it avail to bid thee gaze
> On the revolving world? what to bid speak
> Fate, Time, Occasion, Chance and Change?—To these
> All things are subject but eternal Love. (PU II:iv, 114–20)

One way to read Demogorgon's response is to understand the imagelessness of the truth that subtends Prometheus and Jupiter in terms of the opposition between the timelessness of eternity ("eternal Love") and the temporality of the world, which is subject to "Fate, Time, Occasion, Chance and Change." The deep truth, in this case, would be eternal because it would not be subject to finitude and decay. However, this passage occurs shortly after Demogorgon's initial description, cited previously, which emphasizes that he is "ungazed upon and shapeless," a "mighty Darkness." Like the "truth" of which he speaks, Demogorgon, unlike Prometheus, never coalesces into a particular figure of a counter-sovereign. He constitutes something closer to the voiceless "abysm" that remains without any perceptible corollary, but that is nonetheless capable of engulfing "in lasting night Heaven's kingless throne" (PU II:iv, 148–49). Demogorgon, in a sense, constitutes, as in Coleridge's understanding of the sovereignty of the imagination that we explored in Chapter 2, an empty place of power.[49] He constitutes this either by way of revealing that the current seat of power—Jupiter—is merely a temporally bound "image" that will soon pass away, or by opening up the threat of a *prior* moment of founding with which the sovereign cannot fully identify. This threat subverts the authority of the sovereign by calling into question his unconditionality. If there is a founding act prior to him that is not *produced* by him, this suggests that there is something more sovereign than he, even if that something never materializes into a specific figure or structure. Demogorgon thus constitutes not just a figure for the finitude of Jupiter's reign, but also the promise of a retrospective—and metaleptic—undoing of any claim to absolute foundation.

Thus, when at the beginning of Act III Demogorgon brings about Jupiter's downfall, he does not institute a new theocratic order but leaves open the question of what regime will succeed Jupiter. Jupiter's opening speech reiterates Asia's encounter with an "unbodied" (PU 3:1, 44) Demogorgon. Like Asia, Jupiter "feels" his presence, but is unable to identify him as a specific force or threat. When he calls out to Demogorgon to ask what he is, Demogorgon enigmatically replies:

> Eternity—demand no direr name.
> Descend and follow me down the abyss;
> I am thy child, as thou wert Saturn's child,
> Mightier than thee; and we must dwell together
> Henceforth in darkness.—Lift thy lightnings not.
> The tyranny of Heaven none may retain,
> Or reassume, or hold succeeding thee . . . . (PU III:i, 53–58)

Like his replies to Asia's questions, Demogorgon's response emphasizes that his identification as "eternity" is a mere "name," suggesting that he speaks here too as Jupiter would, but that this name is a placeholder for something else that reestablishes the *contingency* of Jupiter's reign.[50] Though the passage contains an allusion to Hesiod's version of the Zeus myth, where it becomes possible that Zeus will be overthrown by his progeny (Metis), Demogorgon makes clear that the challenge to Jupiter's sovereignty is foundational. Though Demogorgon is "mightier" than Jupiter, "none may retain" or "reassume" his particular form of sovereignty. Whatever comes after Jupiter must break with the very notion of an absolute foundation that his power rests upon.

Though the ending of Act III seems to suggest a triumphant utopia that leaves man "Scepterless, free, uncircumscribed" and "equal, unclassed, tribeless and nationless" (PU III:iv, 194–95), the text nonetheless hints at why the particular form of sovereignty that Jupiter represents cannot be so easily overcome. As the "Spirit of the hour" gives his triumphant speech, it becomes unclear why a fourth act is necessary, given that the main conflict of the play has apparently come to an end. Though Demogorgon has dragged Jupiter to the "abyss," it is the threat of his return that preoccupies the end of the play. The ending is also preoccupied with the question of what sorts of authority or social organization might be possible in the wake of the dissolution of a sovereignty predicated on the realization, through an "image" of the sovereign, of an absolute ground. The unfurling of "love" in Act IV appears to take the shape of a return to a Rousseau-like form of "natural compassion"[51] capable of organically reorganizing human community in the absence of the false image of a sovereign, whose solicitation of the affects of his subjects forms the community or nation around him. Yet the language that closes the play in Demogorgon's final speech reveals not only the possibility of Jupiter's return, but also the possibility that his return is already figured in the very language of triumphant "love" that the play closes with:

> Gentleness, Virtue, Wisdom and Endurance,—
> These are the seals of that most firm assurance
> Which bars the pit over Destruction's strength;
> And if, with infirm hand, Eternity,
> Mother of many acts and hours, should free
> The serpent that would clasp her with his length,—
> These are the spells by which to reassume
> An empire o'er the disentangled Doom. (PU IV, 562–69)

Though the description of the "rising up" of love in the wake of Jupiter's fall that precedes this passage gives way to abstractions ("Gentleness, Virtue, Wisdom and Endurance") that are supposed to prevent any return to despotism, Demogorgon's very language begins to blur the distinction between a pre- and post-Jupiterian world. He refers to Jupiter as a "serpent," which mirrors the language in Act II that describes Demogorgon himself as a "snake-like Doom coiled underneath [Jupiter's] throne," which is likewise "unloosed" by "Eternity" (PU II:iii, 95–98). Demogorgon also claims that the "infirm hand" of Eternity might "free the serpent that would clasp her with his length," suggesting not only that Jupiter's return would reappropriate a sense of timelessness and necessity to reinvigorate itself, but that this possibility is already intimated in the very act of Demogorgon's reversal of Jupiter, since this is the name he gives himself when dragging

Jupiter into the abyss. In short, although the play appears to imagine a future beyond the Jupiterian model of sovereignty, it is also keenly aware of the possibility that the very act that wants to overturn it may end up reconstituting it anew in ways not immediately obvious.

This is precisely why *Prometheus Unbound*, as well as *The Mask of Anarchy*, leave the future that they envision tentative, hinting at the possibility of its metaleptic reversal. Though each poem envisions a triumphant moment in which not only a particular despot but the structures that sustain him—mental, linguistic, economic, philosophical, poetic—are overcome, they each also suggest that such a break always runs the risk of reintroducing these same structures through the unconditionality of the act that overturns them. That is, they risk restoring a form of absolutism through the fact that they always break (metaleptically) with their particular context, and thus remain grounded on an anteriority that cannot be reconstituted except through the image of a unified or consummated unconditional: "God" in Demogorgon's language, or what Shelley had called in "Queen Mab" simply a "prototype of human misrule."[52] Shelley suggests that these acts, founded on a fundamental exigency as opposed to a monolithic absolute, are at risk of reconstituting this very foundation as a stable referent.

It is from within Shelley's metaleptic conception of the imagination, and its challenge to the hegemonic forms of sovereignty in Shelley's own time, that its political efficacy becomes clearer. To repeat, Shelley's famous declaration at the end of the *Defence of Poetry* that "poets are the unacknowledged legislators of the world"[53] must be read not just as a slogan attempting to link the performative aspects of poetry to political events or to notions of self-authorizing genius. It must also be read as a claim about the self-overcoming "sovereignty" of poetry more generally. That is, poets are "unacknowledged legislators" not just because their genius goes unrecognized by their contemporaries, but because the process by which the imagination reorganizes the present and breaks with its own structure of articulation also makes poets' creative acts incomprehensible even to themselves. The series of images that concludes the *Defence* emphasizes this disjunction between self-present intervention within an existing context and unapprehended effects in subsequent ones. This disjunction opens any genuinely creative act to the future:

> Poets are the hierophants of an unapprehended inspiration, the mirrors of the gigantic shadows which futurity casts on the present, the words which express what they understand not, the trumpets which sing to battle and feel not what they inspire: the influence which is moved not, but moves. (DP 535)

This passage suggests not only a futurity that remains latent in the present, but also one that lies beyond any predetermined horizon of meaning. Poets write words that "express what they understand not," the signification of which persists within ever-new contexts, without the promise of arrival at a determined destination. They likewise sound a battle call for a struggle they may not actually fight, all without any guarantee of its outcome. The trumpet that calls to battle but does not feel what it inspires, like the Shape in *The Mask of Anarchy* or Demogorgon in *Prometheus Unbound*, are figures of a creative act that is immediately political insofar as, like the figure of Orc in Blake's *America: A Prophecy* that we explored in Chapter 1, it attempts to bring about something unprecedented. For Shelley, however, this attempt always involves the chance that it may bring about the worst, even as it takes this risk in the name of something better. Most important, however, the very nature of this act, and its purely contingent relation to the anteriority that makes it possible, leaves it permanently open to the prospect of its own metaleptic reversal. In the context of the self-founding structure of modern sovereignty, this inherent contingency creates a form of sovereignty that gives up a certain kind of mastery. No longer able to identify its act with an absolute ground or foundation, it leaves itself open to an anteriority that cannot be integrated into any figure of the sovereign. This metaleptic anteriority delimits the sovereign act in advance and creates the possibility of a politics no longer founded on the realization of a fixed or definite nature.

Like the efforts of many of the Romantic poets before him, Shelley's attempt to rethink the sovereign subject and political sovereignty passes through the imagination as a site in which something new and unprecedented might emerge. For Shelley, the imagination is political not by fantasizing an indeterminate future that the imagination *opposes* to the present, but by touching on the possibility of a legislative or creative act that is already riven by a future at work within it. The metaleptic conception of the imagination and of politics that Shelley advances emphasizes not just the tension between the present and the past, but the risk of an unforeseeable future that this tension makes possible. In doing so, it enables political acts by understanding their effects as no longer determined solely by the particular context of their enunciation. His conception of the imagination names a linguistic effect at one with a conception of history and politics that opens itself toward a future without guarantee and gives an impossible name to the structural kernel of what, in any concrete political situation, exceeds itself and its given historical context. In short, it names a principle of rupture with the very thing that establishes its mode of appearance.[54] On the political level, it attempts to comprehend the notion of an act that would no longer be identical with the sovereign intention of a subject and a form of sovereignty that would no longer be indistinguishable from its own act of founding, since it is exposed to an exteriority that constitutes it. This exposure doesn't just change the way in which the sovereign becomes manifested or represented in the political realm. It also disarticulates the notion that a poetic or political revolution could found, once and for all, ultimately and finally, a sovereign who is fully identical with himself, emerging organically from the ground that authorizes him, without repeating the tyranny from which he sought to liberate himself.

Shelley was a "second-generation" Romantic who, even in his short life, brought to a logical conclusion many of the ideas in Romanticism that connected its attempt to rethink the limits and conditions of the political with its various conceptions of the imagination. Yet, he did so by radicalizing what it means to recognize that what Schmitt calls the "exception" is the very basis of modern forms of sovereignty.[55] Shelley, however, eschews anything like the "decisionism" that characterizes Schmitt's political philosophy. For Shelley, the sovereign is certainly bound up with the exception. But this ground of sovereignty cannot be made to correspond with a sovereign, self-conscious, decisive act. Shelley's creative or poetic act of legislation offers a figure for a conception of sovereignty that would no longer decide on the exception, but which would be, in a sense, decided *by* the exception, by an exposure to what remains unapprehended in every sovereign act and in every political or poetic founding. It is the contours of this other thinking of sovereignty that we have only begun to understand in all its implications. Shelley's theory of the imagination begins a poetic and philosophical meditation on the possibility of a truly modern form of sovereignty, divorced from any theological or quasi-theological foundation. And it is in his theory of the imagination that we find not just a principle of his poetics, but the contours of his most powerful political gambit: the figure of a future revolution the basis of which is already "here," if only we knew how to repeat its unapprehended inimitability.

Epilogue: "Upping the Ante"

In his commentary on Paul Celan's Meridian Address,[1] Jacques Derrida argues that a specific gesture or strategy is at work in Celan's attempt to distinguish the sovereignty of poetics from political sovereignty. This happens, according to Derrida, through Celan's claims about the "majesty" of poetry. Analyzing Georg Büchner's *Danton's Death*, Celan argues that Lucile's cry "Long live the King!" as she goes to her death on the scaffold in the course of the French Revolution constitutes, paradoxically, an "act of freedom" and an example of the "majesty" of poetry. As Derrida contends, in order to show that this cry is indeed a poetic act of sovereignty in the face of political repression, its significance must first be withdrawn from any political code that would read it as counter-revolutionary or as already determined by a specific understanding of the relation between the sovereignty of the king and the sovereignty of poetry (or speech). Celan's gesture, according to Derrida, "consists in placing one majesty above another, and thus upping the ante with respect to sovereignty. An upping that attempts to change the meaning of majesty or sovereignty, to make its meaning mutate, while keeping the old word and while claiming to give it back its most dignified meaning."[2] Such a gesture is always fraught, caught in a dilemma of least two conceptions of sovereignty that are nearly impossible to disentangle, especially since the gesture of "freedom" must still pass through what appears to be the most traditional sign of a recognition of absolute sovereignty.

In the absence of established grounds for articulating a properly modern form of sovereignty, the Romantics faced something similar to this dilemma. That they too sought to locate an alternative conception of sovereignty in the name of the majesty of poetry, or the establishment of the imagination as a new ground of authority, has been the principle argument of my readings of the political valence of the imagination in Romanticism. The gestures of "upping of the ante"[3] with respect to sovereignty that I have explored in the Romantics always involve the risk of repeating the absolutism from which they attempted to free themselves. However, this threat, along with the possibility of hyperbolizing the paradox of sovereignty by situating it on other foundations (or on the absence of them), is a structure proper to modern sovereignty itself. This structure becomes a metaphysical machine that, in the absence of an absolute foundation such as God, opens itself without reserve to an upping of the ante without reserve. Since there can be no politics without reference to some form of sovereignty, a gesture of upping the ante is inevitable, yet inherently ambivalent, especially for the Romantics.

Yet this hyperbolization of sovereignty was precisely the path taken by a number of key Romantic writers, in one way or another, with all of the accompanying risks and possible misunderstandings it entails. The attempt to up the ante by locating a more original conception of the infinite to the traditional Christian one at the heart of political authority allows Blake both to reconceive the relation between the political and the theological and to redefine the connection between a particular figure of the sovereign and his ground of legitimation. Coleridge, from the standpoint of a very different conception of the imagination, likewise ups the ante by rearticulating political theology around the question of an unconditional ground that is immediately exposed to its finite conditions of possibility. In both of these cases, the basic structures of traditional political theology are exposed to an internal excess that deracinates them from within, allowing them to give shape or voice to something else: another form of sovereignty whose reference to an unconditional ground gives way to an uncontrollable propagation of sovereign figures, none of whom can claim ownership over that which sanctions their authority.

My readings of Wordsworth and Shelley, on the other hand, constitute examples of Romantic attempts to up the ante in relation to modern sovereignty through the invention of new forms of popular sovereignty. Wordsworth's discovery of the temporal dimension of the imagination ends up calling into question aspects of the foundation of natural law and the autonomous subject that become the basis for the new liberal-democratic conception of the state. Likewise, Shelley's focus on the conditions that produce forms of popular sovereignty capable of contesting illegitimate absolutism reveals the fragility of any movement predicated on radical change, especially in relation to a form of power that offers the temptation of permanence. In each case, the shift toward a form of popular sovereignty reveals that there is no divine or natural law capable of providing a stable foundation, or a predetermined form, for social organization. As Shelley's work suggests, there is instead only the emergence of a contingent, temporal, power: a *poesis* that provides the means by which the social world becomes manifest to itself, even if its effects remain fundamentally unapprehended in the present. It thus produces itself not as a community or body politic that is necessary or natural, but as one that is in each case provisional and historical.

In the final analysis, Romanticism's ambivalence toward a gesture of upping the ante with respect to sovereignty—of proposing an alternative basis to social organization and political authority—results in the question of the nature and meaning of the sovereign's spectacle of power. Since traditional forms of sovereignty and Romantic challenges to those forms both make reference to the unconditional, what comes to the fore is a struggle over how the relation between the sovereign and the unconditional can be given the force of law, becoming instituted within the political domain. All four poets in this study attempt to account for the problem of the spectacle of power through the imagination, which they see as engaged in a process that is something other than the incarnation of a transcendent ground or principle. Hence, and this becomes the crucial inference of the readings presented here, one of the key legacies that the Romantics bequeath to the present is the question of what role aesthetics plays in the construction of a genuinely modern form of sovereignty. The sovereign cannot do without spectacle. Yet this spectacle no longer constitutes a sensuous presentation of a non-sensuous source of legitimation. Once it is no longer a question of the incarnation or representation of a preexisting ground, the aesthetic dimension of sovereignty begins to be understood as a necessary effect of something that accelerates the dissemination and proliferation of figures of the sovereign. This new role for aesthetics constitutes a second upping of the ante. Since the sovereign is related to a ground that eludes him, sovereignty becomes a matter of producing, fashioning, or "fictioning" an anteriority that is no longer foundational, and whose integration into the political is never assured. The legitimation of the sovereign that follows from this is owed to an anteriority that, though unconditional, eludes any attempt to appropriate it to a figure of absolute sovereignty. Aesthetics is thus involved in a deracination as much as a confirmation of traditional forms of sovereignty.

As in Schmitt's definition of the sovereign as "he who decides on the exception," the Romantics understand sovereignty as grounded on something other than a rule or norm. Unlike Schmitt, however, they insist on the role of *fiction* in the articulation of the sovereign and the exception, thus invoking an altogether different relation between the two. This question of how the sovereign's relation to the exception that grounds him is materialized in the political remains a crucial one for contemporary critiques of sovereignty. Agamben, for example, suggests that something must mediate or intercede between the sovereign's decision and the exception. Since the juridical or political order is always constructed on an a-legal "zone of anomie," something must materialize this relation within the legal order itself. This anomic space within the law, represented most clearly by the state of exception, acts as "something like a mystical element, or rather a *fictio* by means of which the law seeks to annex anomie itself."[4] The "annexation" of anomie by the law, its attempt to fictionalize or give shape to the exception that grounds it, is not a fiction in the sense of a ruse of power that appropriates something it has no right to. Rather, Agamben's focus on the necessity of *fictio* to draw the link between the sovereign and the exception constitutes, as for the Romantics, the precondition for *any* relation between the sovereign and the exception, regardless of the form it takes.

The consequences that follow from this newfound role of fiction in the critique of modern sovereignty, however, remain an open question. If our own age is witnessing yet another mutation in the concept and application of sovereignty, if it is only now that the possibility of what Jean-Luc Nancy calls a "non-sovereign politics"[5] becomes thinkable, then the elaboration of this possibility must take into account the role of fiction that the Romantics highlighted earlier on. This problem has been addressed in at least two ways in contemporary critiques of sovereignty. The first, exemplified by Agamben, seeks to unmask the fiction that binds the sovereign to a particular figuration of the exception within the political, which for Agamben is always the object of a sovereign ban. Unmasking the fiction of the relation between law and life, anomie and *nomos*, would thus involve an attempt to circumvent it by moving outside of the paradox of sovereignty altogether, toward "a politics freed from every ban."[6] The alternative approach, articulated most powerfully in Derrida's last seminars on the concept of sovereignty,[7] would remain *within* the paradox of sovereignty. From within this paradox, however, this approach would seek to locate an exit from the "machine of sovereignty" that identifies the sovereign with the exception as its exclusive right. It does so by rethinking the relation between the sovereign and the exception through closer attention to the proliferation of figures of exceptionality that emerge as a result of the *aporias* of sovereignty.

Romanticism, is seems to me, is closer to the latter of these trajectories. In their various attempts to redefine sovereignty through the imagination, sometimes even despite themselves, the Romantics articulate the possibility that it is the exception that decides, not the sovereign. The exceptional ground of sovereignty thus becomes multiplied into various figures, calling into question the sovereign's exclusive right over his own exceptional status. Within Romanticism there is thus an upping of the ante not just in relation to the figure of the sovereign, but in relation to the exception and the unconditionality that he relies on as well. If the exception can no longer be the object of a decision, if it fractures and multiplies into various figures that define the sovereign of modern politics—from "the people" to the dictator and beyond—then the Romantics constitute an early example of an attempt to think a different relation to the exception that might open the problem of sovereignty to forms other than state power. Even if their ambivalence toward the risks of disclosing another relation to the unconditional (or exceptional) ground of the sovereign forced the Romantics to retreat to positions that resembled the ones they initially criticized or sought to overturn, they nonetheless set the stage for thinking other ways that the unconditional might be related to the political. The *aporias* they encountered and multiplied to their limit remain, in fundamental ways, our own today. While the site of the imagination as understood by the Romantics might be said to have receded as a political problem, the question of the necessity of the role "fictioning" and *poesis* in the production of political power have only become more and more essential.

The readings I offer here are an attempt to revive an early approach to other ways of reconceiving the relation between sovereign power and the exception in order to recover a sense in which the relation of the sovereign to his ground of sovereignty has not yet crystallized, nor been dismissed as a hopelessly (or dangerously) metaphysical question. Romanticism opens up the problem of how the sovereign's relation to the exception might be expressed otherwise than as the history of the state of exception that has been accelerating since the beginning of the twentieth century. To that end, Romanticism offers the figure of a precursor to our own attempts to extricate ourselves from a "machine of sovereignty" that appears ready to produce figures of the most dangerous and murderous forms of exceptionality or unconditionality yet witnessed, including those that exceed state power. Although embedded in discourses and theologies that were resistant to breaks with the structures of authority upon which they relied, the Romantics nonetheless gave rise to a countertradition within the history of sovereignty. At once defining the limits to the conception of sovereignty in their own time and retreating before it, the Romantics pose the possibility of constructing a "non-sovereign politics." That is, they begin to think the figure of a form of sovereignty that, founded on nothing, tries to think what it would mean to make this nothing the very unconditional *factum* of "the people" itself, in all of its non-natural, non-foundational, non-transcendent, non-substantial "majesty."

NOTES

INTRODUCTION: TOWARD A NEW POLITICAL ROMANTICISM

1. See Harold Bloom, *Visionary Company* (Ithaca, NY: Cornell University Press, 1961).

2. Jerome McGann's seminal work begins the historicist turn in Romantic studies and sets the stage for a variety of approaches that attempt to unpack the ideology specific to Romanticism. See Jerome McGann, *The Romantic Ideology* (Chicago: University of Chicago Press, 1983).

3. A growing number of publications are addressing these questions and challenging more straightforward historicist interpretations of the role of the imagination in Romanticism. Marc Redfield, for example, has attempted to cast Romantic aesthetics as much more ambivalently related to its politics. See Marc Redfield, *The Politics of Aesthetics: Nationalism, Gender Romanticism* (Stanford, CA: Stanford University Press, 2003). Susan Wolfson, likewise, has emphasized the role of poetic form in the construction of Romantic politics. See, for example, Susan Wolfson, *Formal Charges: The Shaping of Poetry in British Romanticism* (Stanford, CA: Stanford University Press, 1997).

4. See Forest Pyle, *The Ideology of Imagination* (Stanford, CA: Stanford University Press, 1995).

5. Ibid., 10.

6. See McGann, *Romantic Ideology*. For other examples of this approach see Marjorie Levinson, ed., *Rethinking Historicism: Critical Readings in Romantic History* (Oxford: Oxford University Press, 1989). For a far more productive articulation of the relation between literary theory and literary history, see David Ferris, *Theory and the Evasion of History* (Baltimore, MD: The Johns Hopkins University Press, 1993). Ferris correctly argues that the evasion of history can also take the form of certain kinds of historical analysis, precisely because the central question of the relationship between an interpretation of a text and its history is a central feature of literary theory, which itself has a history marked by shifts and ruptures within particular interpretive paradigms.

7. William Wordsworth, *The Thirteen-Book "Prelude,"* ed. Mark L. Reed (Ithaca, NY: Cornell University Press, 1991), 1:317.

8. Simon Jarvis, *Wordsworth's Philosophic Song* (Cambridge: Cambridge University Press, 2007), 222.

9. For an excellent analysis of this problem see William Keach, *Arbitrary Power: Romanticism, Language, Politics* (Princeton, NJ: Princeton University Press, 2004).

10. Martin Heidegger, *Kant and the Problem of Metaphysics*, trans. Richard Taft (Bloomington: Indiana University Press, 1990), 88.

11. For the classic study of divine right, see Ernst Kantorowicz, *The King's Two Bodies: A Study in Medieval Political Theology* (Princeton, NJ: Princeton University Press, 1957).

12. One could say that this argument is ubiquitous in Foucault; see, for example, his "Truth and Power," in *Power/Knowledge*, ed. Colin Gordon (New York: Pantheon Books, 1977), 109–33.

13. Wordsworth, *The Thirteen-Book "Prelude,"* 138.

14. See Carl Schmitt, *Political Theology*, trans. George Schwab (Chicago: University of Chicago Press, 1985), 36.

15. Derrida discusses this term throughout both volumes of *Beast and the Sovereign*. Its first significant mention is in Jacques Derrida, *Beast and the Sovereign*, vol. 1, trans. Geoffrey Bennington (Chicago: University of Chicago Press, 2009), 47.

16. See Giorgio Agamben, *State of Exception*, trans. Kevin Attell (Chicago: University of Chicago Press, 2005).

17. Agamben unpacks this logic in the first part of *Homo Sacer*, insisting that the primary form of an exteriority to law that materializes inside the juridical order is what he calls "bare life." See *Homo Sacer: Sovereign Power and Bare Life*, trans. Daniel Heller-Roazen (Stanford, CA: Stanford University Press, 1998), 1–67.

18. See Agamben, *State of Exception*, 41–51.

19. See Percy Shelley, "The Defence of Poetry," in *Shelley's Poetry and Prose*, ed. Donald H. Reiman and Neil Fraistat (New York: W. W. Norton, 2002), 535.

20. Schmitt, *Political Theology*, 5.

21. The best-known example of occasionalism is the work of Nicolas Malebranche. See especially Nicolas Malebranche, "The Search after Truth," in *Philosophical Selections*, ed. Steven Nadler (Indianapolis, IN: Hackett Publishing, 1992), 3–144.

22. See Carl Schmitt, *Political Romanticism*, trans. Guy Oakes (Cambridge, MA: MIT Press, 1986), 6. For the German text, see Carl Schmitt, *Politische Romantik* (München: Verlag von Duncker & Humblot, 1925), 22.

23. Schmitt, *Political Romanticism*, 162, and *Politische Romantik*, 228.

24. Ibid.

25. Shelley, "The Defence of Poetry," 535.

26. Derrida, *Beast and the Sovereign*, vol. 1, 230. "Upping the ante" is a translation of the French *surenchére*, which entails the notion of a sort of hyperbolization: there is always something "more" sovereign than the sovereign.

27. Still the most profound meditation of the possibility of thinking sovereignty as something other than a form of mastery is to be found in the work of Georges Bataille. Though this problem is ubiquitous throughout his work, it receives its most systematic formulation in the third part of *The Accursed Share*. See Georges Bataille, "Sovereignty," in *The Accursed Share*, vols. 2 & 3, trans. Robert Hurley (New York: Zone Books, 1993), 197–361.

28. I take this term from Claude Lefort's remarkable work on the transition from political- theology to the basis of democracy. See Claude Lefort, "Permanence of the Theological-Political?," in *Democracy and Political Theory*, trans. David Macey (Minneapolis: University of Minnesota Press, 1988), 213–55.

29. Agamben has recently addressed this question through the topic of "glory" and the need for ritual and spectacle in the construction of sovereignty. See Giorgio Agamben, *The Kingdom and the Glory*, trans. Lorenzo Chiesa (Stanford, CA: Stanford University Press, 2011).

30. For a recent important analysis of the relation between aesthetics, technics, media, and the theological-political, see Jacques Derrida, "Faith and Knowledge: The Two Sources of 'Religion' within the Limits of Reason Alone," in *Acts of Religion*, ed. Gil Anidjar (New York: Routledge Press, 2002), 42–101.

31. This is one of the main claims that Antonio Negri and Michael Hardt make in their discussion of the notion of "empire" as a shift from a conception of sovereignty rooted in the nation state to a more mobile and versatile form of domination. See Michael Hardt and Antonio Negri, *Empire* (Cambridge, MA: Harvard University Press, 2000).

1. "HONEST INDIGNATION IS THE VOICE OF GOD": BLAKE AND POLITICAL THEOLOGY

1. For the most thorough study of this topic, see Jon Mee, *Dangerous Enthusiasm: William Blake and the Culture of Radicalism in the 1790s* (Oxford: Oxford University Press, 1992).

2. See Saree Makdisi, *William Blake and the Impossible History of the 1790s* (Chicago: University of Chicago Press, 2003).

3. William Blake, "The Divine Image," in *The Complete Poetry and Prose*, ed. David V. Erdman, rev. ed. (New York: Anchor Books, 1988), 13, line 15. All citations from the works of Blake are taken from this edition and will henceforth be

cited in text. Parenthetical references for the poetry will include plate number and line numbers where applicable. All references to Blake's prose works will be marked by the page numbers from the Erdman edition preceded by "E." The following abbreviations will be used in-text to indicate which work is being cited: AI (*Augeries of Innocence)*, AM (*America: A Prophecy*), ARO (*All Religions Are One*), DC (*Descriptive Catalogue*), J (*Jerusalem*), FR (*The French Revolution*), M (*Milton*), MHH (*Marriage of Heaven and Hell*), NNR (*There Is No Natural Religion*), BU (*The [First] Book of Urizen*).

4. Although the link between Blake and the sect known as the Muggletonians has largely been questioned, E. P. Thomson's book on Blake still convincingly places dissenting interpretations of the Bible (specific to a history of antinomianism that challenges the interests behind the codification of the Bible into law) at the heart of Blake's writing. See E. P. Thomson, *Witness against the Beast: William Blake and the Moral Law* (Cambridge: Cambridge University Press, 1993).

5. Makdisi, *William Blake and the Impossible History of the 1790s*, 7–8.

6. For a particularly coherent account of Urizen's performative self-instantiation, see Angela Esterhammer, "Calling into Existence: *The Book of Urizen*," in *Blake in the Nineties*, ed. Steve Clark and David Worrall, 114–32 (New York: St. Martin's Press, 1999). There she argues that Blake's reading of Genesis, and the paradigmatic case of the performative (God's "let there be light"), which she defines as a phenomenological performative (which calls things into existence), cannot be rigorously separated from a performative that constitutes the world of social and political relations. *The Book of Urizen*, in her account, ties creative power to "division, restriction and imposition" (115). For a more fleshed out version of her argument about the role of performative language in Blake more generally, see Angela Esterhammer, *Creating States: Studies in the Performative Language of John Milton and William Blake* (Toronto: University of Toronto Press, 1994). See also James Rovira's excellent reading of the ambiguities of creation in "Creation Anxiety and *The (First) Book of Urizen*," in *Blake and Kierkegaard: Creation and Anxiety* (New York: Continuum Press, 2010), 121–43.

7. Jon Mee, "Blake's Politics in History," in *Cambridge Companion to William Blake* (Cambridge: Cambridge University Press, 2003), 143.

8. Chapter four of *The Book of Urizen* moves from the development of Los's eyes to a focus on his ears, nostrils, throat, and eventually tongue, all of which bring about a repeated "state of dismal woe."

9. Saree Makdisi argues that Blake's conception of the imagination is less a faculty of the subject and more the expression of a materialist ontology: "For Blake's concept of the imagination unifies body and mind, thought and action, material and immaterial, not in the sense that it mediates between them, but in the sense that it marks the deployment of pure creative ontologi-

cal power on both a mental and material plane. It is, in other words, the expression of a materialist ontology." *William Blake and the Impossible History of the 1790s*, 266.

10. The central reading of Blake as an apocalyptic poet is Harold Bloom, *Blake's Apocalypse: A Study in Poetic Argument* (Ithaca, NY: Cornell University Press, 1963). Versions of this interpretation have persisted in other readings of Blake that are not so sympathetic to Bloom. For an example, see David Wageknecht, *Blake's Night: William Blake and the Idea of Pastoral* (Cambridge, MA: Harvard University Press, 1973). The reading of Blake as an apocalyptic thinker and poet has had an influence well beyond Blake studies. One could argue that Paul de Man's critique of what he views as Bloom's conflation of an "eccentric" Blake with all of Romanticism is central to many of his later critical insights about Wordsworth and Hölderlin as non-apocalyptic thinkers. See, for example, his review of Bloom's *Visionary Company* in Paul de Man, "A New Vitalism: Harold Bloom," in *Critical Writings: 1953–1978*, ed. Lindsay Waters (Minneapolis: University of Minnesota Press, 1989), 90–96.

11. Though Leopold Damrosch does not directly deal with the problem of poetic genius, he does claim that Blake's theory of the imagination entails Forms that are "unchanging and eternal" even if they are only perceived in this world as "imaginative images." Their reality, therefore, "*transcends* the realm of 'Vegetative & Generative Nature' where we ordinarily suppose that the objects of our perceptions are located" (13, emphasis mine). See Leopold Damrosch, "Vision and Perception," in *Symbol and Truth in Blake's Myth* (Princeton, NJ: Princeton University Press, 1980), 11–37.

12. See, for example, Damrosch's claim that Blake desires his readers to "see through" his images and symbols in "The Truth of Symbols," in *Symbol and Truth in Blake's Myth*, 38–62. Blake, in fact, attempts to interrupt the idea that his texts are directly referential, symbols of something transcendent.

13. *Oxford English Dictionary*, s.v. "vortex."

14. References to how Urizen's "void" of infinity becomes a globe are found throughout *The Book of Urizen* as well, from the "globe" that forms out of the caverns of Urizen's spine (11:1–4, E75) to the globe of blood, and then life, that emerges after Los attempts to cordon off Urizen's "abyss" (13:58–59, E77), to the final line of the poem that culminates in Urizen's victory: "And the salt ocean rolled englob'd" (28:23, E83). Of course Urizen's "globe" or void takes the place of all eternity, whereas Milton sees the vortex become a globe once he has passed through it and recognized its limitations.

15. Ronald Grimes, "Time and Space in Blake's Major Prophecies," in *Blake's Sublime Allegory*, ed. Stuart Curran and Joseph Wittreich Jr. (Madison: University of Wisconsin Press, 1973), 79.

16. James Swearingen argues that, rather than attempting to imagine an ideal republic or constitution, Blake "envisions a process of perpetual constituting

that needs no legitimating principle because it locates the origin of power in the pluralism of mental warfare." James E. Swearingen, "William Blake's Figural Politics," in *Blake, Politics, and History* (New York: Routledge, 1998), 82. This refusal of foundations, as it were, for the body politic is a key insight into Blake's figural politics. However, there is in Blake, I would argue, not just a pluralism but a marked partisanship on the side of envisioning the conditions in which social and political life could be radically reimagined. Just as it is not possible to tolerate, in the ideal of pluralism, a position that cannot tolerate other positions it is in dialogue with, so must Urizen's position be deconstructed, in order for the "pluralism of mental warfare" or the "perpetual constitution" of social and political life to be possible.

17. Blake's most extensive discussion of minute particulars outside of the poetic works occurs in his *Annotations to the Works of Sir Joshua Reynolds*. Blake's reaction against Reynolds's pseudo-idealist aesthetics tends to take the form throughout of a resistance to the notion that beauty is located in a generalized intellectual ideal, emphasizing instead the notion that true beauty can only be found in the singular and the particular. In response to Reynolds's assertion that ". . . art [must] get above all singular forms, local customs, particularities, and details of every kind," for example, Blake writes in the margins ". . . a Folly. Singular and Particular Detail is the Foundation of the Sublime" (E647).

18. On Blake's antinomianism see E. P. Thomson, *Witness against the Beast*. On the question of the rational dictates of the moral law, see Immanuel Kant, *Critique of Practical Reason*, trans. Lewis White Beck (New York: Macmillan Publishing, 1956).

19. A recent study by John Jones convincingly lays out the case that much of Blake's work is directed against the notion of a traditionally stable subject and toward a project of "self-annihilation." Using Bakhtin's dialogical model of discourse, Jones argues that Blake envisions the subject or the self as emerging only in relation to an other, in distinction from Urizenic solipsism, which is strictly monological, appropriating to itself the right to speak and flattening out the relational nature of subjectivity. Though Jones explores slightly different consequences to his claims, the notion of the imagination as a relational concept is certainly germane to my own argument here. See John H. Jones, *Blake on Language, Power, and Self-Annihilation* (Houndmills, UK: Palgrave Macmillan, 2010).

20. For a recent, close reading of Blake's critique of imperialism, see Saree Makdisi, "Blake and Romantic Imperialism," in *William Blake and the Impossible History of the 1790s*, 204–59.

21. See David V. Erdman, *Blake: Prophet against Empire* (Princeton, NJ: Princeton University Press, 1954), and Jon Mee, *Dangerous Enthusiasm*; and the recent essays in Jackie DiSalvo, G. A. Rosso, and Christopher Z. Hobson, eds., *Blake, Politics, and History* (New York: Garland Publishing, 1998).

22. See Mee, "Blake's Politics in History."

23. Ibid., 147.

24. See Nicholas Williams, *Ideology and Utopia in the Poetry of William Blake* (Cambridge: Cambridge University Press, 2006).

25. Williams, *Ideology and Utopia in the Poetry of William Blake*, 31.

26. For an excellent interpretation of Blake's specific conception of prophecy, see Ian Balfour, "The Mediated Vision: Blake, *Milton*, and the Lines of Prophetic Tradition," in *The Rhetoric of Romantic Prophecy* (Stanford, CA: Stanford University Press, 2002), 127–72.

27. Ibid.

28. Makdisi, *William Blake and the Impossible History of the 1790s*, 10.

29. For an excellent reading of the problem of difference and repetition at the formal level of Blake's poetics, see Susan Wolfson, "Blake's Language in Poetic Form," in *Cambridge Companion to William Blake* (Cambridge: Cambridge University Press, 2003), 63–84.

30. See S. Foster Damon, *A Blake Dictionary* (Hanover, NH: University Press of New England, 1988), 9–16.

31. See Erdman, *Blake: Prophet against Empire*, 587; and Northrop Frye, *Fearful Symmetry* (Princeton, NJ: Princeton University Press, 1947), 207–35.

32. Blake likely had in mind a reference to the "dragon and two beasts" that appear in Revelations 13:1, linked with the battle against Satan in heaven (who takes the form of a "dragon" or the snake) and his attempt to control and deceive earthly political powers. Through this deception, Satan is eventually is given power "over all kindreds, and tongues, and nations" (Rev. 13:7).

33. See Vincent De Luca, *Words of Eternity: Blake and the Poetics of the Sublime* (Princeton, NJ: Princeton University Press, 1991).

34. Angela Esterhammer has pioneered the question of the role of linguistic performatives in Blake and in Romanticism more generally. See Angela Esterhammer, *Creating States* and *The Romantic Performative: Language and Action in British and German Romanticism* (Stanford, CA: Stanford University Press, 2000). In *Creating States*, she problematizes the strictness of the distinction between what she calls "sociopolitical" and "phenomenological" performatives in Blake. The former are linguistic acts that attempt to intervene within the social, political, and institutional discourses of a particular historical context, while the latter are performatives that develop a constitutive or "visionary" language that, for Esterhammer, entails a reaffirmation of "faith in individual visionary consciousness" (xiv). What is missing from her analysis, however, is the notion of a *constitutive* performative, what Derrida in *Limited INC* calls a "performative without performative," which is prior to any particular speech act. Rather than articulate a particular context's understanding of what would make a performative "felicitous," in Austin's sense, a constitutive performative first sets in place the rules of legitimation through which it becomes

enunciated, without being reducible to a particular individual consciousness or creative vision. See Jacques Derrida, *Limited INC*, trans. Samuel Weber (Evanston, IL: Northwestern University Press, 1988).

35. Hegel, defining what will later be called the "bad infinity," argues that a version of it is found in abstract skepticism: "The skepticism that ends with the bare abstraction of nothingness or emptiness cannot get any further from there, but must wait to see whether something new comes along, and what it is, in order to throw it too into the empty abyss." G. W. F. Hegel, *The Phenomenology of Spirit*, trans. A. V. Miller (Oxford: Oxford University Press, 1977), 51.

36. Blake's *Milton* offers a similar understanding of a perspectival shift framed in the language of the end of times and focusing on the moment, the significance of which I explored in the section "Poetic Genius as Counter-Sovereignty" of this chapter: "Every Time less than a pulsation of the artery/Is equal in its period and value to Six Thousand Years" (M 28:63–64, E127). The fact that this moment of six thousand years is not an end point but rather a *starting point* is clarified in the next line: "For in this Period the Poets Work is Done: and all the Great events of Time start forth & are concievd in such a Period Within a Moment:" (M 29:1–2, E127). In other words, the finite world is not ended, just a particular *vision* of its finitude, which "starts forth" from the moment that inaugurates it.

37. John Milton, *Complete Poems and Major Prose*, ed. Merritt Hughes (Saddle River, NJ: Prentice Hall, 1957), 212.

38. Makdisi, *William Blake and the Impossible History of the 1790s*, 16–77.

39. A passage on plate fifteen of *America: A Prophecy* suggests the extent to which Orc's break with Urizenic law also entails an unleashing of desire: "The doors of marriage are open, and the Priests in rustling scales/Rush into reptile coverts, hiding from the fires of Orc,/That play around the golden roofs in wreaths of fierce desire/Leaving the females naked and glowing with the lusts of youth/For the female spirit of the dead pining in bonds of religion;/Run from their fetters reddening, & in long drawn arches sitting:/They feel the nerves of youth renew, and desires of ancient times,/Over their pale limbs as a vine when the tender grape appears" (AM 15:19–26, E57). Blake makes clear in this passage that the stamping of Urizen's "stony law" to dust brings about a radical unleashing of what that law had denied. For a careful reading of the relationship between Blake's conception of desire and his politics, see Andrew Lincoln, "Politics and Desire in Blake's *The French Revolution*," in *Blake, Politics and History*, ed. Jackie DiSalvo, G. A. Rosso, and Christopher Z. Hobson (New York: Routledge, 1998), 187–95.

40. Though Blake could not have known about Robespierre's speech before the National Convention of February 5, 1794, which posits a necessary relation between terror and moral virtue, Blake was not unaware of the justifications for the terror that linked it with the carrying out of moral law. See Maximilien

Robespierre, *Virtue and Terror*, trans. John Howe (London: Verso, 2007), 108–25.

41. This view of Blake's relation to the French Revolution is present throughout much of Erdman's classic study. See, for example, his *Blake: Prophet against Empire*, 370–76.

42. See Lincoln, "Politics and Desire in Blake's *The French Revolution*," 187.

43. This idea, of course, is central to Rousseau's conception of the social contract. See Jean-Jacques Rousseau, "On Social Contract," in *Political Writings*, trans. Julia Bondanella (New York: W. W. Norton, 1988), 84–173.

44. Blake's notion of the suspension of the law is different from Agamben's understanding of the contemporary "state of exception," where the law is suspended in exceptional circumstances but remains in force. For Blake, the suspension of the law is a return to a moment prior to that law's founding. See Giorgio Agamben, *State of Exception*.

45. In *The Marriage of Heaven and Hell*, Blake links this notion of fire with the "enjoyments of 'Genius'" (MHH 6, E35) and with the power of the imagination more generally.

46. I draw here, while changing slightly, Derrida's enigmatic phrase "Every other (one) is every (bit) other [*tout autre est tout autre*]," which is an attempt to think through the question of an ethical responsibility to the Other in general and the negotiation that must be made with every particular other, each of which is infinitely other. See Jacques Derrida, *The Gift of Death*, trans. David Wills (Chicago: University of Chicago Press, 1999), esp. 68–69.

47. For an extensive interpretation of Blake's relation to a wide variety of emancipatory political thought, see Nicholas Williams, *Ideology and Utopia in the Poetry of William Blake*.

48. One could argue that contemporary political theory tends to be divided between these two tendencies, pairing thinkers who are often quite close to each other but whose approach to the problem constitutes the difference between a critical and an ontological approach to the question of modern sovereignty. For example, a difference could be drawn in approaches between, on the one hand, Jacques Derrida's examination of the political category of friendship, which advances a deconstruction of a tradition for which the concept of friendship is particularly problematic (see Jacques Derrida, *The Politics of Friendship*, trans. George Collins [London: Verso Press, 1997]) and, on the other, Jean-Luc Nancy's attempt to construct a quasi-ontology of non-identitarian community (see Jean-Luc Nancy, "Being Singular Plural," in *Being Singular Plural*, trans. Robert D. Richardson and Anne E. O'Byrne [Stanford, CA: Stanford University Press, 2000], 1–99; and Jean-Luc Nancy, *The Inoperative Community*, trans. Peter Connor [Minneapolis: University of Minnesota Press, 1991]).

2. THE BLIND SPOT OF POWER: SOVEREIGNTY AND UNCONDITIONALITY IN COLERIDGE'S *BIOGRAPHIA LITERARIA* AND *THE FRIEND*

1. R. F. Storch, "The Politics of the Imagination," *Studies in Romanticism* 21 (Fall 1982): 448.

2. For a developed reading of the relationship between the high theory of the imagination and the resultant practical criticism, see J. R. de J. Jackson, *Method and Imagination in Coleridge's Criticism* (Cambridge, MA: Harvard University Press, 1969).

3. A notable exception to this rule is Nicholas Halmi's recent book on the history of the concept of the symbol. Engaging in a genealogical approach to the symbol, Halmi contends that its development by various Romantic authors involved an attempt to "foster a sense of the harmony of the human mind with nature, of the unity of seemingly disparate intellectual disciplines, and of the compatibility of individual freedom with a cohesive social structure—all for the sake of reducing anxiety about the place of the individual in bourgeois society (especially in the aftermath of the French Revolution and ensuing European wars) and about the increasing dominance of mechanistic science (which, by opposing mind to nature as subject to object, undermined the traditional basis on which the world's meaningfulness had been assumed)" (24). The problem of the symbol in Romanticism, in other words, is not strictly a literary-theoretical problem. See Nicholas Halmi, *The Genealogy of the Romantic Symbol* (Oxford: Oxford University Press, 2007).

4. For an extensive study of Coleridge's indebtedness to various idealist thinkers, including Kant, Fichte, and Schelling, see G. N. G. Orsini, *Coleridge and German Idealism* (Carbondale: Southern Illinois University Press, 1969). For a more recent study on the same topic, see Paul Hamilton, *Coleridge and German Philosophy* (New York: Continuum Press, 2007).

5. Coleridge, *The Friend*, ed. Barbara E. Rooke (Princeton, NJ: Princeton University Press, 1969), 197. All citations from Coleridge's *The Friend* are taken from this edition and will henceforth be cited in text as "FR" followed by the page number.

6. For a classic study that links Coleridge's aesthetics of the symbol with his theological concerns to propose a reading of the "scriptural imagination," see J. Robert Barth, *The Symbolic Imagination: Coleridge and the Romantic Tradition*, 2nd ed. (New York: Fordham University Press, 2001). See also David Jasper, *Coleridge as Poet and Religious Thinker* (London: Macmillan Press, 1985), and Anthony John Harding, *Coleridge and the Inspired Word* (Kingston, ON: McGill University Press, 1985).

7. For a good overview of the development of Coleridge's political ideas, see Peter J. Kitson, "Coleridge as Political Thinker," in *Cambridge Companion to*

Coleridge, ed. Lucy Newlyn, 156–69 (Cambridge: Cambridge University Press, 2002).

8. The first study to explore Coleridge as a conservative political thinker is John Stuart Mill's short essay on Coleridge and Bentham, *Mill on Bentham and Coleridge* (Cambridge: Cambridge University Press, 1980). More recent studies have explored Coleridge's late conservatism as a product of his changing perspective on property; see John Morrow, *Coleridge's Political Thought* (London: Macmillan Press, 1990). The most in-depth study of the relationship between Coleridge's theory of the imagination and his political philosophy is Nigel Leask, *The Politics of Imagination in Coleridge's Critical Thought* (London: Macmillan Press, 1988).

9. For a recent exploration of Coleridge's shifting allegiances to the Anglican Church, see Luke Savin Herrick Wright, *Samuel Taylor Coleridge and the Anglican Church* (Notre Dame, IN: University of Notre Dame Press, 2010). For a broader reading of Coleridge's understanding of Christian doctrine, see J. Robert Barth, *Coleridge and Christian Doctrine* (Cambridge, MA: Harvard University Press, 1969).

10. Of course, the classic and still most important study of this topic remains Thomas McFarland, *Coleridge and the Pantheist Tradition* (Oxford: Oxford University Press, 1969).

11. Halmi argues that the Romantics, Coleridge especially, treat the symbol as neither strictly theological nor aesthetic, but *sui generic*. See Halmi, "The Uses of Theology," in *The Genealogy of the Romantic Symbol*, 99–132.

12. S. T. Coleridge, "A Lay Sermon," in *Lay Sermons*, ed. R. J. White (Princeton, NJ: Princeton University Press, 1972), 202. All citations from "A Lay Sermon" and *The Statesman's Manual* are taken from this edition and will henceforth be cited in text as "LS" followed by the page number.

13. Leask, *The Politics of the Imagination in Coleridge's Critical Thought*, 33.

14. Ibid., 216.

15. Ibid., 33.

16. Recent work has sought to argue that Coleridge, in fact, turned away from more radical political implications of the imagination. See, for example, Alan Gregory, *Coleridge and the Conservative Imagination* (Macon, GA: Mercer University Press, 2003).

17. An example of this position can be found in John Morrow's claim that Coleridge's theory of the State in *The Friend* is "essentially Platonic in character." See Morrow, *Coleridge's Political Thought*, 81. More recently, Ian Balfour has carefully articulated the way in which Coleridge's ". . . politics, rhetoric and theory of language are all grounded in a theological metaphysics authorized by a certain ventriloquism of the divine word" that relies "on a system of tropes privileging the synecdoche that, while making a claim to universality and totality, enforces a regime of hierarchy and exclusion."

See Ian Balfour, "Allegories of the Symbol: Rhetoric, Politics, and Prophecy in Coleridge's *The Statesman's Manual*," in *The Rhetoric of Romantic Prophecy*, 283.

18. For Coleridge, the deduction of the imagination is fundamentally a question of the condition of possibility of the political itself. In the opening pages of *The Statesman's Manual*, for instance, he argues that historical change, including all the "*epoch-forming* Revolutions of the Christian world" have "coincided with the rise and fall of metaphysical systems" (LS 14). He adds: "So few are the minds that really govern the machine of society, and so incomparably more numerous and more important are the indirect consequences of things than their foreseen and direct effects" (LS 14). These claims make it clear that, for Coleridge, the political and the philosophical are inherently intertwined, even if they are not identical. In other words, the political emerges, for Coleridge, only in relation to the metaphysics that enables it, just as "epoch-forming" revolutions coincide with the collapse of the particular metaphysical moments that sustained them.

19. This term is not used by Coleridge in chapter thirteen, but as numerous commentators and editors have pointed out, his definition of the imagination takes the form of similar deductions in Kant, Fichte, and Schelling. See S. T. Coleridge, *Biographia Literaria*, 2 vols., ed. James Engell and W. Jackson Bate (Princeton, NJ: Princeton University Press, 1983), 299n1. Throughout the rest of this chapter I will use this term to define the process by which Coleridge does more than posit the *logical* necessity of the principle of the imagination, but instead attempts to define its *real* necessity. All citations from *Biographia Literaria* are taken from this edition and will henceforth be cited in text as "BL" followed by the volume and page number.

20. The full exposition of Coleridge's conception of the imagination never takes place because it is interrupted by a letter (which Coleridge wrote himself) whose content and effects will be analyzed in what follows. For an excellent reading of the "missing" deduction, see Nicholas Reid, "Coleridge and Schelling: The Missing Transcendental Deduction," *Studies in Romanticism* 33 (Fall 1994): 451–79.

21. As Coleridge avers in *The Friend*, the principle of Reason "must be impersonated" (FR 197) in order to "act on Man." Likewise, the fixed principles that articulate the political must be realized, impersonated, materialized by a particular figure of the sovereign.

22. The famous reference to truth as a "divine ventriloquist" (BL 164) in the *Biographia* is echoed in *The Friend* when Coleridge insists that Reason acts "like the voice of an external Ventriloquist, it is indifferent from whose lips it appears to come, if only it be audible" (FR 192).

23. Coleridge's investment in a critical stance, rather than a systematic exposition of principles, may account for some readings of *The Friend* that see it

as fundamentally contradictory or equivocal. See, for example, the first three chapters of Deirdre Coleman's careful and patient study of the periodical edition of *The Friend* (1810): Deirdre Coleman, *Coleridge and the Friend (1809–1810)* (Oxford: Oxford University Press, 1988), 1–62.

24. For a careful reading of this desire and the relation between writing and truth in *The Friend*, see Jerome Christensen, "The Method of *The Friend*," in *Coleridge's Blessed Machine of Language* (Ithaca, NY: Cornell University Press, 1981), 186–269.

25. For an extensive exploration of the philosophical and theological background to Coleridge's understanding of Reason, see Richard Berkeley, *Coleridge and the Crisis of Reason* (Houndmills, UK: Palgrave Macmillan, 2007).

26. As Thomas McFarland has argued, Coleridge's definition of Reason, in its distinction from the Understanding, involves a redefinition of the mantra of the French Enlightenment against it. Though he overemphasizes Jacobi's influence, he argues convincingly that Reason "resumed the threat of 17th-century theologizing to become a guarantor of Christianity." See his "Aspect of Coleridge's Distinction between Reason and Understanding," in *Coleridge's Visionary Languages*, ed. Tim Fulford and Morton Paley (Cambridge: D. S. Brewer, 1993), 172. For an in-depth discussion of Coleridge's indebtedness to Kant's distinction between Reason and Understanding, see G. N. G. Orsini, *Coleridge and German Idealism*, 57–97.

27. For a developed reading of the motif of ventriloquy in Coleridge's and Wordsworth's poetics, see Susan Eilenberg, *Strange Power of Speech: Wordsworth, Coleridge, and Literary Possession* (Oxford: Oxford University Press, 1992).

28. Like Coleridge, Hegel's conception of Reason could be likewise deemed theological or, better, onto-theological. In the *Introduction to the Philosophy of History*, Hegel writes: "The insight to which philosophy ought to lead, therefore . . . is that the real world is as it ought to be, that the truly good, the universal divine Reason is also the power capable of actualizing itself. This good, this Reason—in its most concrete representation—is God. God governs the world: the content of His governance, the fulfillment of His plan, is world history" (39). Hegel goes on to articulate how this universal plan is articulated through the particular passions of individuals: "The particular interest linked to passion is thus inseparable from the actualization of the universal principle; for the universal is the outcome of the particular and determinate, and form its negation. . . . This may be called the Cunning of Reason, that it allows the passions to work for it, while what it brings into existence suffers loss and injury" (35). See G. W. F. Hegel, *Introduction to the Philosophy of History*, trans. Leo Rausch (Indianapolis, IN: Hackett Publishing, 1988).

29. Paul Hamilton outlines Coleridge's definition and practice of "desynonymy," which involves "increasing the vocabulary of a language by showing how words which were thought to be synonymous in fact mean different things" (65). Hamilton goes on to elaborate very carefully how this concept models the working of the Understanding itself in *Coleridge's Poetics* (Oxford: Blackwell Publishing, 1983), 58–96.

30. Nicholas Reid has challenged the reading of Coleridge that argues that he traces the imagination (and by extension the symbol) back to an original unity of subject and object. Reid claims that, for Coleridge, a plurality (specifically the Trinity) constitutes this origin. Reid relies on a notion of incarnation in order to explain the unity of this division. See his *Coleridge, Form and Symbol: Or the Ascertaining Vision* (Burlington, VT: Ashgate Publishing, 2006).

31. This term is one that Coleridge likely derived from the scholastics, Duns Scotus in particular. In Scotus, an "*ens logicum*" is a pure *factum*, an "it is." Everything thinkable is encompassed by it and it applies to both finite and infinite being.

32. I borrow this description of the non-oppositional nature of the relation between subject and object in Coleridge's *Biographia Literaria* from David Ferris's perceptive and convincing analysis. See his "Coleridge's Ventriloquy: The Abduction from the *Biographia*," *Studies in Romanticism* 24 (Spring 1985): 41–84.

33. Immanuel Kant, *Critique of Practical Reason*, trans. Lewis White Beck (New York: Macmillan Publishing, 1956), 58.

34. Ibid., 49.

35. Ibid., 49.

36. Ibid., 49.

37. Still the best discussion of the eighteenth-century precursors to Coleridge's theory of the imagination is James Engell, *The Creative Imagination* (Cambridge, MA: Harvard University Press, 1981).

38. This distinction is perhaps the most crucial one that Coleridge borrows from Kant, since it defines the very possibility of the critical project that seeks to determine the limits of knowledge. Coleridge's clearest paraphrase, in fact, comes in Coleridge's *Logic*:

> Transcendental knowledge is that by which we endeavor to climb above our experience into its sources by an analysis of our intellectual faculties, still, however, standing as it were on the shoulders of our experience in order to reach at truths which are above experience, while transcendent philosophy would consist in the attempt to master a knowledge that is beyond our faculties, an attempt to grasp at objects beyond the reach of eye and hand, of objects therefore the existence of which, if they did exist, the human mind has no means of ascertaining, and therefore has not even the power of imagining

or conceiving; that which the pretended sages pass off for such objects being merely images from the senses variously disjoined and recomposed, or mere words expressing classes of these images and by addition of other words associated with obscure feelings. (S. T. Coleridge, *Logic*, ed. J. R. de J. Jackson [Princeton, NJ: Princeton University Press, 1981], 147)

39. Fichte, like Coleridge, attempts to ground his entire philosophical system on the unconditional. However, the pure "act" of the "I Am" is not the first moment in Fichte's system. The apodictic certainty that inaugurates *The Science of Knowledge* is the proposition A=A, which in turn gives way to the formalization of the proposition in the "I am I." See J. G. Fichte, *The Science of Knowledge*, trans. Peter Heath and John Lachs (Cambridge: Cambridge University Press, 1970), 93–119.

40. Fichte, *The Science of Knowledge*, 93.

41. Ibid.

42. Kathleen Wheeler makes a convincing case that, for Coleridge, "polarity is a term which acts as a focal point around which a number of relations revolve, such as the distinction between imagination/fancy, part/whole, symbol/allegory, organic/mechanical and opposition/contrariety" (56). See her *Sources, Processes and Methods in Coleridge's* Biographia Literaria (Cambridge: Cambridge University Press, 1980).

43. This is also a crucial difference from Fichte, since for him the "I am I" is not the "first principle" but emerges only after a reflection on the tautological proposition A=A, where the "I am I" emerges as the copula of the original identity. See Fichte, *The Science of Knowledge*, 93–96.

44. See McFarland, *Coleridge and the Pantheist Tradition*.

45. Jacques Derrida has analyzed the way in which Reason and Religion develop in tandem by drawing on a common notion of the "unscathed" (*Heilig* or *l'indemne*), the untouched, that which has not suffered harm. See Jacques Derrida, "Faith and Knowledge: The Two Sources of 'Religion' as the Limits of Reason Alone."

46. Ferris, "Coleridge's Ventriloquy," 60.

47. Schelling asks: "How . . . can it be established beyond doubt, that such an intuition does not rest upon a purely subjective deception, if it possesses no objectivity that is universal and acknowledged by all men? This universally acknowledged and altogether incontestable objectivity of intellectual intuition is art itself." See F. W. J. Schelling, *System of Transcendental Idealism*, trans. Peter Heath (Charlottesville: University Press of Virginia, 1993), 229.

48. For a recent in-depth study of the conflict between Reason and faith in Coleridge, see Richard Berkeley, *Coleridge and the Crisis of Reason*. See also Orsini's careful exegesis of this question as a philosophical problem: Orsini, *Coleridge and German Idealism*, 207–9.

49. For a brief, but provocative reading of the links between Coleridge's linguistic and his theology, see Robert N. Essick, "Coleridge and the Language of Adam," in *Coleridge's* Biographia Literaria, ed. Frederick Burwick (Columbus: Ohio University Press, 1989), 62–74.

50. Balfour, "Allegories of the Symbol," in *The Rhetoric of Romantic Prophecy*, 283.

51. For a careful exploration of the relation in Coleridge between unity and division, see Seamus Perry, "Coleridge and Division," in *Coleridge and the Uses of Division* (Oxford: Oxford University Press, 1999), 7–34.

52. For an elaboration of this concept, see Claude Lefort, "The Permanence of the Theological-Political?," in *Democracy and Political Theory*, 213–55.

53. Still the clearest and most convincing exposition of what is at stake in the interruption of the letter is found in David Ferris, "Coleridge's Ventriloquy." For an astute psychoanalytic analysis of the letter, see Gayatri Spivak, "The Letter as Cutting Edge," *Yale French Studies* 55/56 (1977): 206–26. Kathleen Wheeler reads the interruption of the letter as a description of the design of the *Biographia* as a whole, enlisting the participation of the reader to complete the argument and providing a model for what she reads as the reflective structure of the text as a whole; see Kathleen Wheeler, *Sources, Processes and Methods in Coleridge's* Biographia Literaria, 100–33. For an in-depth exploration of the philosophical context of the letter's interruption, see Nicholas Reid, "Coleridge and Schelling."

54. It is certainly important to note that Coleridge continued to develop the argument for the deduction of the imagination. The promissory note in the *Biographia* and the friend's mention of a prospectus for a longer philosophical work on the topic was never written. An argument could be made that he continued the work of the deduction in *Logic*, but the focus there remains on the logic of its necessity (i.e., the notional thesis). See S. T. Coleridge, *Logic*.

55. S. T. Coleridge, *Poetical Works I*, ed. J. C. C. Mays (Princeton, NJ: Princeton University Press, 2001), 511. Hereafter cited in text by line numbers.

56. This oft-cited phrase is found in Lecture 31 of Freud's *New Introductory Lectures on Psychoanalysis* and is usually translated as "Where Id was, there Ego shall be." See Sigmund Freud, "Dissection of the Psychical Personality," in *New Introductory Lectures on Psychoanalysis*, trans. James Strachey (New York: Penguin, 1983), 88–112.

57. I draw here on Lacoue-Labarthe's understanding of the "fictioning of the political" that he outlines in *Fiction du Politique*, which entails the idea that the political is a form of *techne* or "plastic art" involving the mimesis of an original *physis* that it reveals or accomplishes. See Phillipe Lacoue-Labarthe,

Heidegger, Art and Politics, trans. Chris Turner (Cambridge, MA: Blackwell Publishing, 1990).

58. Immanuel Kant, *Critique of Pure Reason*, trans. Paul Guyer (Cambridge: Cambridge University Press, 1998), A644/B672.

59. S. T. Coleridge, *On the Constitution of Church and State*, ed. John Colmer (Princeton, NJ: Princeton University Press, 1976), 20.

60. David Aram Kaiser has suggested that Coleridge, like Schiller, has a conception of the symbol that "purports to reconcile the opposition between individual subjectivity and the objective political state." Coleridge's understanding of *how* this takes place is what separates them, however. See David Aram Kaiser, *Romanticism, Aesthetics, Nationalism* (Cambridge: Cambridge University Press, 1999), 3.

61. For Coleridge, there is nothing accidental in this development. More than just accounting for the genealogy of his own political investments, Coleridge is also addressing the possibility that this legacy could take on another shape in the present, specifically in the growing reform movement in England: ". . . though the French code of revolutionary principles is now generally rejected as a *system*, yet everywhere in the speeches and writings of the English reformers, nay, not seldom in those of their opponents, I find certain maxims asserted or appealed to, which are not tenable, except as constituent parts of that system" (FR 184).

62. Edmund Burke, "Note on a Motion Relative to the Speech from the Throne," cited in S.T. Coleridge, *The Friend*, 193.

63. Paul de Man claims that both symbol and allegory "have a common origin beyond the world of matter," which is no doubt true. His subsequent claim, that "the reference, in both cases, to a transcendental source, is now more important than the kind of relationship that exists between the reflection and its source," however, is not as clear. See Paul de Man, "The Rhetoric of Temporality," in *Blindness and Insight* (Minneapolis: University of Minnesota Press, 1983), 192.

64. Nicholas Halmi argues convincingly that Coleridge was torn between "two concepts of the symbol that are virtually identical, but mutually exclusive." The first insists on the copresence of the infinite and the finite. The second, in the context of a corrective to the doctrine of consubstantiation, claims that the "Eucharist cannot be consubstantial with the body and blood of Christ *because* it is symbolic of them." See Nicholas Halmi, *Genealogy of the Romantic Symbol*, 130.

65. While the distinction between symbol and allegory has received extensive critical commentary, one of the clearest expositions remains John Hodgson's careful discussion of the difficulties Coleridge has actually distinguishing between symbol and allegory. See John A. Hodgson, "Transcendental Tropes: Coleridge's Rhetoric of Allegory and Symbol," in *Allegory, Myth and Symbol*,

ed. Morton W. Bloomfield (Cambridge, MA: Harvard University Press, 1981), 273–92.

66. Though Kant details the transcendental schematism in the first chapter of the "Analytic of Principles" titled "On the Schematism of the Pure Concepts of Understanding," the schema also appears in the section on the "Architectonic of Pure Reason." See Immanuel Kant, *Critique of Pure Reason*, A133/ B172–A147/ B187, and A832/B860–A851/B879. For a careful reading of Kant's conception of the schematism and the schema-image as a "quasi-transcendental" see Geoffrey Bennington, "X," in *Interrupting Derrida* (London: Routledge Press, 2000), 76–92. Heidegger makes his reading of the transcendental schematism the starting point for his claim that Kant understands the imagination as an essential determination of time. See Heidegger, *Kant and the Problem of Metaphysics*.

67. Immanuel Kant, *Critique of Pure Reason*, A253.

68. Ibid., A251.

69. Ibid., A140/ B179.

70. Ibid., A142/B181.

71. See, for example, Thomas McFarland, "Involute and Symbol in the Romantic Imagination," in *Coleridge, Keats and the Imagination*, ed. J. Robert Barth, S. J. and John L. Mahoney (Columbia: University of Missouri Press, 1990).

72. Balfour, "Allegories of the Symbol," in *The Rhetoric of Romantic Prophecy*, 283.

73. This may partly have to do with the fact that the symbol is not entirely a visual or aesthetic figure, but a linguistic or rhetorical one. For an excellent reading of the relation between Coleridge's rhetoric and the symbol, see Frances Ferguson, "Coleridge on Language and Delusion," *Genre* 2 (Summer 1978): 191–207. See also Tim Fulford, *Coleridge's Figurative Language* (Houndmills: Palgrave Macmillan, 1991).

74. Coleridge writes: "These are the Wheels which Ezekiel beheld, when the hand of the Lord was upon him, and he saw visions of God as he sate among the captives by the river of Chebar. *Whithersoever the Spirit was to go, the wheels went, and thither was their spirit to go: for the spirit of the living creature was in the wheels also*" (LS 29).

75. This is why Coleridge goes on to say that, in the Scriptures, "Facts and Persons must of necessity have a two-fold significance, a past and a future, a temporary and a perpetual, a particular and a universal application" (LS 30).

76. See Claude Lefort, "The Permanence of the Theological-Political?," in *Democracy and Political Theory*, 228.

77. I draw here on Derrida's understanding of autoimmunity, which, in the context of sovereignty, involves the way in which the sovereign, by attempting to protect itself against violations of its sovereignty, ends up weakening its own

defenses and destroying what it attempts to safeguard. This notion is developed in various places throughout Derrida's work. For this concept's relation to the question of sovereignty, see Jacques Derrida, *Rogues*, trans. Pascale-Anne Brault and Michael Naas (Stanford, CA: Stanford University Press, 2005). See also both volumes of *Beast and the Sovereign*. For a clear exposition of this concept in Derrida, see J. Hillis Miller, "Derrida's Politics of Autoimmunity," *Discourse* 30:1–2 (Winter & Spring 2008): 208–25.

78. Coleridge, in one of the few examples of the symbol not drawn from Scripture, argues that one must "choose" to be overtaken by a force that transcends the subject, or the "self": "But what the plant *is*, by an act not its own and unconsciously—*that* must thou *make* thyself to *become*!" (LS 71).

3. "TO THE GREAT ENDS OF LIBERTY AND POWER": COMMUNITY AND THE PROBLEM OF SOVEREIGNTY IN WORDSWORTH'S *PRELUDE*

1. M. H. Abrams, *Natural Supernaturalism: Tradition and Revolution in Romantic Literature* (New York: W. W. Norton, 1971), 334.

2. These readings are numerous, but undoubtedly the most influential of them is McGann's watershed book *The Romantic Ideology*, which gave new impetus to historicist approaches to Romanticism. See especially "Wordsworth and the Ideology of Romantic Poems," in *The Romantic Ideology*, 81–92. For a more comprehensive account of Wordsworth's displaced relation to history, see Alan Liu, *Wordsworth: The Sense of History* (Stanford, CA: Stanford University Press, 1989); see also Marjorie Levinson, *Wordsworth's Great Period Poems: Four Essays* (Cambridge: Cambridge University Press, 1986). For a more recent foray into the relationship between Wordsworth and history, see Kevis Goodman, "Making Time for History: Wordsworth, the New Historicism, and the Apocalyptic Fallacy," in *The Wordsworthian Enlightenment*, ed. Helen Regueiro Elam and Frances Ferguson (Baltimore, MD: The Johns Hopkins University Press, 2005), 158–71. For a highly nuanced and convincing argument about Wordsworth's displacement of history, see David Simpson, *Wordsworth's Historical Imagination: The Poetry of Displacement* (New York: Methuen, 1987).

3. McGann, *The Romantic Ideology*, 90.

4. For an excellent formal analysis of Wordsworth's claims about the relationship between metrical language and its relation to passion, see Susan Wolfson, "Wordsworth's Craft," in *Cambridge Companion to Wordsworth* (Cambridge: Cambridge University Press, 2003), 108–24. Wolfson does an excellent job of teasing out the basic problem of the relation between notion of poetic origin, Wordsworth's understanding of the role of meter, and its social effects. She convincingly demonstrates that Wordsworth's basic question (is the production of passion a result of craft or impulse, does it enhance or regulate passion?) has direct political implications.

5. For a particularly astute argument about the way in which aesthetic autonomy or disinterestedness always entails a return back to the realm of the political, see Marc Redfield, "Aesthetic Ideology," in *Phantom Formations: Aesthetic Ideology and the Bildungsroman* (Ithaca, NY: Cornell University Press, 1996), 1–37.

6. I take this term for the episode from Andrzej Warminski's excellent analysis of the passage and its emblematic significance. See his "Missed Crossing: Wordsworth's Apocalypses," *MLN* 99, no. 5 (Dec. 1984): 983–1006.

7. These kinds of figures are strewn throughout the *Prelude* and much of Wordsworth's work, from discharged soldiers, to leech gatherers, to Cumberland Beggars, just to name a few. For a careful reading of these figures and the ethics and politics of Wordsworth's representation of them, see James Averill, *Wordsworth and the Poetry of Human Suffering* (Ithaca, NY: Cornell University Press, 1980); see also Gary Harrison, *Wordsworth's Vagrant Muse* (Detroit, MI: Wayne State University Press, 1994).

8. I borrow this terminology from Frederick Garber's major study *Wordsworth and the Poetry of Encounter* (Urbana: University of Illinois Press, 1971).

9. For an important and careful exposition of this term, see Phillipe Lacoue-Labarthe and Jean-Luc Nancy, "Overture: The System-Subject," in *The Literary Absolute* (Albany: State University of New York Press, 1988), 27–37.

10. I draw here on the work of Phillipe Lacoue-Labarthe. See especially *Typography* (Stanford, CA: Stanford University Press, 1998).

11. See McGann, *Romantic Ideology*. David Simpson argues that Wordsworth's imagination, insofar as it entails a "real" that has been "figured and processed by the mind," becomes ideology once it becomes intersubjective or social. See his *Wordsworth and the Figurings of the Real* (London: Macmillan Press, 1982).

12. Abrams, *Natural Supernaturalism*, 77.

13. Geoffrey Hartman, "A Poet's Progress: Wordsworth and the *Via Naturaliter Negativa*," *Modern Philology* 59, no. 3 (Feb. 1962): 214.

14. See Geoffrey Hartman, *Wordsworth's Poetry: 1787–1814* (New Haven, CT: Yale University Press, 1964), 163–259.

15. Hartman, "A Poet's Progress: Wordsworth and the *Via Naturaliter Negativa*," 216.

16. Paul de Man, "Time and History in Wordsworth," in *Romanticism and Contemporary Criticism* (Baltimore, MD: The Johns Hopkins University Press, 1993), 92.

17. Ibid., 88.

18. Ibid., 93.

19. See de Man, "Time and History in Wordsworth."

20. For a clearly articulated reading of this tendency in Romanticism, see Paul de Man, "The Intentional Structure of the Romantic Image," in *The Rhetoric of Romanticism* (New York: Columbia University Press, 1984), 1–17.

21. For this argument, see Coleridge, *Biographia Literaria*, vol. 2, 40–106.

22. William Wordsworth, "Preface of 1815," in *The Prose Works of William Wordsworth*, vol. 3, ed. W. J. B. Owen and Jane Smyser (Oxford: Clarendon Press, 1974), 36.

23. Wordsworth, *The Thirteen-Book "Prelude,"* vol. 1, 115 (1:353–54). All citations from Wordsworth's *Prelude* are taken from this edition, vol. 1, and will henceforth be cited in text by book number, followed by line numbers. Where the 1850 version is cited, this will be noted in text by adding "1850" before the book and line numbers cited, using this edition: William Wordsworth, *The Fourteen-Book Prelude*, ed. W. J. B. Owen (Ithaca, NY: Cornell University Press, 1985).

24. Alan Liu sees the figure of Napoleon lurking behind this sublime triumphalism. See Alan Liu, *Wordsworth: The Sense of History*, specifically chapters 1 and 8, 3–31 and 359–452.

25. Aside from Hartman, more recent commentators have attempted to challenge a reading of this passage as an inward turn. David Ferris, for example, reads it as a "passage from language to history." See David Ferris, "Where Three Paths Meet: Wordsworth," in *Theory and the Evasion of History* (Baltimore, MD: The Johns Hopkins University Press, 1993), 145.

26. Immanuel Kant, *Critique of the Power of Judgment*, trans. Paul Guyer (Cambridge: Cambridge University Press, 2000), 131–140.

27. For a careful analysis of this pattern see Warminski, "Missed Crossing: Wordsworth's Apocalypse."

28. See Jean-Jacques Rousseau, "Discourse on the Origin and Foundations of Inequality among Men," in *Rousseau's Political Writings*, trans. Julia Conway Bondanella (New York: W. W. Norton, 1988), 3–57.

29. Stephen Gill, *Wordsworth: The Prelude* (Cambridge: Cambridge University Press, 1991), 73.

30. R. F. Storch, "Wordsworth and the City: Social Reason's Inner Sense," *Wordsworth Circle* 1, no. 3 (1970): 114.

31. Anne Janowitz, "The Artifactual Sublime: Making London Poetry," in *Romantic Metropolis*, ed. James Chandler and Kevin Gilmartin (Cambridge: Cambridge University Press, 2005), 251.

32. Alberto Gabriele, "Visions of the City of London: Mechanical Eye and Poetic Transcendence in Wordsworth's Prelude, Book 7," *European Romantic Review* 19, no. 4 (Oct. 2008): 365–84.

33. Richard. J. Onorato long ago remarked that in book seven, "humanity seems sexual to Wordsworth in disturbing ways." See Richard Onorato, *The Character of the Poet: Wordsworth in the Prelude* (Princeton, NJ: Princeton University Press, 1971), 281.

34. Jarvis, *Wordsworth's Philosophic Song*, 140.

35. David Simpson, *Wordsworth, Commodification and Social Concern* (Cambridge: Cambridge University Press, 2009), 56.

36. Jarvis, *Wordsworth's Philosophic Song*, 142.

37. J. Douglas Kneale, for example, reads the episode of the blind beggar as emblematic on several levels at once: the beggar is an emblem of humanity in general and of the project of the *Prelude* itself, becoming ultimately a monument or epitaph for the imagination. See J. Douglas Kneale, "Images of Language: Voice and Letter in *The Prelude*," in *Monumental Writing* (Lincoln: University of Nebraska Press, 1988), 72–99.

38. James Heffernan, "Wordsworth's London: The Imperial Monster," *Studies in Romanticism* 37, no. 3 (Fall 1998): 440.

39. Ibid., 437. Alison Hickey, in a reading of Wordsworth's *Excursion*, extends this sense of Wordsworth's imperialism more broadly "to refer to a kind of imagination that appropriates, incorporates, assimilates, permeates, infuses difference with unity." See her *Impure Conceits: Rhetoric and Ideology in Wordsworth's* Excursion (Stanford, CA: Stanford University Press, 1997), 133. As I go on to suggest, Wordsworth attempts to distinguish a different, less imperial form of being-in-common from its false homogenizing version.

40. Paul Hamilton, *Wordsworth* (Brighton, UK: The Harvester Press, 1986), 113.

41. For a careful exegesis of the many different "texts" in Wordsworth, see Geoffrey Hartman, "Words, Wish, Worth," in *The Unremarkable Wordsworth* (Minneapolis: University of Minnesota Press, 1987), 90–119.

42. For a careful analysis of the city as a semiotic space in Wordsworth's *Prelude*, see Neil Hertz, "The Notion of Blockage in the Literature of the Sublime," in *Psychoanalysis and the Question of the Text*, ed. Geoffrey Hartman (Baltimore, MD: The Johns Hopkins University Press, 1978), 62–85.

43. One could draw many parallels between Wordsworth's description of London and what Walter Benjamin describes as the "shock experience," a trauma that has never fully entered consciousness, and that he claims Baudelaire placed at the center of his writing, associating it strongly with an encounter with the "metropolitan masses." For a discussion of this term, see Walter Benjamin, "On Some Motifs in Baudelaire," in *Walter Benjamin: Selected Writings, vol. 4,1938–1940*, ed. Howard Eiland and Michael W. Jennings (Cambridge, MA: Harvard University Press, 2003), 313–55.

44. Simpson, *Wordsworth's Historical Imagination*, 123.

45. Hartman, "A Poet's Progress: Wordsworth and the *Via Naturaliter Negativa*."

46. Thomas Pfau, *Wordsworth's Profession: Form, Class & the Logic of Early Romantic Cultural Production* (Stanford, CA: Stanford University Press, 1997), 373.

47. Frances Ferguson, *Wordsworth: Language as Counter-Spirit* (New Haven, CT: Yale University Press, 1977), 143. Ferguson's claim that the *Prelude*'s early desire to discover a symbiotic relationship between external nature and the poet's "human nature" entails a continuous "slippage" between external and

internal is realized by the example of the blind beggar because it is only in relation to an outward form (in this case, language or writing) that any internality becomes visible.

48. David Ferris reads a reference to this form of the "now" in the Simplon Pass episode as the "now" of the writing of the poem itself, which becomes the condition of possibility for the very historicity of what is written. See David Ferris, "Where Three Paths Meet: Wordsworth," in *Theory and the Evasion of History*, 170–74.

49. For the origin of this term, see Walter Benjamin, "On the Concept of History," in *Walter Benjamin: Selected Writings, vol. 4, 1938–1940*, ed. Howard Eiland and Michael W. Jennings (Cambridge, MA: Harvard University Press, 2003), 389–400. Benedict Anderson appropriates it to articulate the common or shared time necessary for a concept of the nation to be operative, even in the situation of diaspora. See his *Imagined Communities* (London: Verso, 1983), 1–46.

50. Jarvis, *Wordsworth's Philosophic Song*, 146.

51. Heidegger defines the "world-picture" as a form of making-appear that entails a prior "decision" that is not directly represented in what it allows to become visible: "Every event must be seen so as to be fitted into this ground plan of nature. Only within the perspective of this ground plan does an event in nature become visible as such an event" (119). See Martin Heidegger, "The Age of the World-Picture," in *The Question Concerning Technology and Other Essays*, trans. William Lovitt (New York: Harper and Row, 1977), 115–54.

52. Pyle, *The Ideology of Imagination*, 175.

53. Ibid.

54. John Rieder has argued that "the ideal of an authentic community holds a central place in Wordsworth's poetry throughout his career . . ." (29), but suggests that Wordsworth attempts to form this community through the problem of personal virtue, "which poses the problem as social cohesion at an individual and ethical level" (30). See his *Wordsworth's Counterrevolutionary Turn: Community Virtue and Vision in the 1790s* (Newark: University of Delaware Press, 1997).

55. James Phillips's excellent article on the problem of community in Wordsworth suggests that "the imagination passes from being a faculty of the poet to being an event, an encounter." It is this notion of an "encounter" with something other, with an anteriority that cannot be accounted for, that I retain in my own reading of Wordsworth's political imagination. See his "Wordsworth and the Fraternity of Joy," *New Literary History* 41, no. 3 (Summer 2010): 613–32.

56. William Wordsworth, "Mutability," in *Sonnet Series and Itinerary Poems, 1820–1845*, ed. Geoffrey Jackson (Ithaca, NY: Cornell University Press, 2004),

197. De Man cites this poem as the conclusion to "Time and History in Wordsworth."

57. Jarvis, *Wordsworth's Philosophic Song*, 222.

58. Ibid., 223.

59. William Wordsworth, "Preface to Lyrical Ballads," in *The Prose Works of William Wordsworth*, vol. 1, ed. W. J. B. Owen and Jane Smyser (Oxford: Clarendon Press, 1974), 121.

60. Rebecca Comay gives an extremely lucid account of German Romanticism and Idealism's attempt to invoke a spiritual or cultural revolution in the wake of the failure to enact an event on the scale of the French Revolution in Germany, which has many parallels with Wordsworth's project. See Rebecca Comay, "Missed Revolutions," in *Mourning Sickness: Hegel and the French Revolution* (Stanford, CA: Stanford University Press, 2011), 1–25.

61. For an excellent reading of Wordsworth's theory of community generally, and his understanding of the community of the living and the dead specifically, see Kurt Fosso, *Buried Communities: Wordsworth and the Bonds of Mourning* (Albany: State University of New York Press, 2004).

62. Simpson, *Wordsworth, Commodification and Social Concern*.

63. As Jacques Derrida demonstrates, the metaphor of the sun is a long-standing trope for apodictic certainty. See "White Mythology: Metaphor in the Text of Philosophy," in *Margins of Philosophy*, trans. Alan Bass (Chicago: University of Chicago Press, 1982), 209–271.

64. James Phillips argues, convincingly, that Wordsworth must negotiate the "untranslatableness of fraternity into legal discourse and the vociferous but empty fraternity of political rhetoric, for alongside the failure to embody fraternity in the institutions of laws of the state, there was fraternity's failure to take root in the lives and feelings of the nation." See his "Wordsworth and the Fraternity of Joy," 614.

65. Lucy Newlyn suggests that Wordsworth's sense of community has a biblical or even Puritan origin. See Lucy Newlyn, "'The Noble Living and the Noble Dead': Community in *The Prelude*," in *Cambridge Companion to Wordsworth* (Cambridge: Cambridge University Press, 2003), 55–69.

66. Hegel, *Phenomenology of Spirit*, 58–66.

67. Jarvis, *Wordsworth's Philosophic Song*, 151.

68. Celeste Langan's landmark study poses the question "Why should an encounter with a stranger on the public road become the empirical paradigm of social knowledge, and the social contract?" (13). She goes on to discuss the body politic as a "noumenon" "which the poets encounter in . . . phenomenal form: the impolitic body of the abandoned woman, and the slackened hand of the discharged soldier" (19). See her *Romantic Vagrancy: Wordsworth and the Simulation of Freedom* (Cambridge: Cambridge University Press, 1995).

69. Kant, *Critique of Practical Reason*, trans. Lewis White Beck (New York: Macmillan Publishing, 1956).

70. Mary Jacobus suggests that Wordsworth's earlier reference in book seven might forecast the experiences of "regicide parricide and sacrilege" identified in the section on the French Revolution. See her *Romanticism, Writing and Sexual Difference: Essays on the* Prelude (Oxford: Clarendon Press, 1989), 52.

71. One can see a similar reference to the simulacra of the revolutionary project in Wordsworth's description of the emergence of Napoleon: "when finally, to close/And rivet up the gains of France, a Pope/Is summon'd in, to crown an Emperor;/This last opprobrium when we see the dog/Returning to his vomit, when the sun/That rose in splendour, was alive, and moved/In exultation among the living clouds/Hath put his function and his glory off,/And turn'd into a gewgaw, a machine, Sets like an opera phantom" (10:931–40). The staged or theatrical element is what Wordsworth focuses on here, suggesting that the sun itself, a figure of truth and virtue, has been radically feigned.

72. In fact, Wordsworth revises this poetic phrase himself in the 1850 edition of the *Prelude*, writing: "In what the Historian's pen so much delights/To blazon—power and energy detached? From moral purpose" (1850 13:43–44). The emphasis on "moral purpose" aligns with many of the other revisions he makes that emphasize the fact that the imagination has now become primarily a moral faculty, not unlike Kant's conception of the moral capacities of reason.

73. Wordsworth had earlier in the *Prelude* suggested that the Revolution fails because of a "reservoir of guilt/And ignorance, fill'd up from age to age/That could no longer hold its loathsome charge" (10:436–38). Clearly, Wordsworth sometimes presents multiple, even contradictory claims about the nature of the failure of the Revolution.

74. Rousseau, "Discourse on the Origin and Foundations of Inequality among Men," in *Rousseau's Political Writings*.

75. For a difficult, but important attempt to found the notion of community on something other than a shared identity or homogeneity, see Jean-Luc Nancy, "Being Singular Plural."

76. Jacques Rancière, "The Poet's Voyage," in *Short Voyages to the Land of the People*, trans. James Swenson (Stanford, CA: Stanford University Press, 2003), 17.

77. Schmitt, *Political Romanticism*.

78. Jacques Rancière, "The Poet's Voyage," 21.

4. SHELLEY'S METALEPTIC IMAGINATION AND THE FUTURE OF MODERN SOVEREIGNTY

1. See, for example, Andrew Franta, "Shelley and the Poetics of Political Indirection," *Poetics Today* 22, no. 4 (Winter 2001): 765–93. See also Marc Redfield, "Shelley's Political Poetics," in *The Politics of Aesthetics*, 148–71.

2. See Percy Shelley, "A Philosophical View of Reform," in *Shelley's Prose*, ed. David Lee Clark (Albuquerque: University of New Mexico Press, 1966), 229–61.

3. Percy Shelley, "Queen Mab," in *Shelley's Poetry and Prose*, 21. Henceforth all citations of Shelley's poetry will be from this edition, using the following in-text abbreviations: *Defence of Poetry* cited as "DP" followed by page number; *Mask of Anarchy* cited as "MA" followed by line number; *The Triumph of Life* cited as "TL" followed by line number; and *Prometheus Unbound* cited as "PU" followed by act number, scene if applicable, and line number.

4. See, for example, Percy Shelley, "The Necessity of Atheism," and "Necessity! Thou Mother of the World?" (which is a prose note taken from "Queen Mab") in *Shelley's Prose*, 37–39, 109–12.

5. This claim about Shelley is best expressed in Jerrold Hogle's classic and monumental study, *Shelley's Process* (New York: Oxford University Press, 1988).

6. See, for example Andrew Stauffer, *Anger, Revolution, and Romanticism* (Cambridge: Cambridge University Press, 2005), 110–32; Cian Duffy, *Shelley and the Revolutionary Sublime* (Cambridge: Cambridge University Press, 2005); David Duff, *Romance and Revolution: Shelley and the Politics of a Genre* (Cambridge: Cambridge University Press, 1994); Timothy Clark, *Embodying Revolution: The Figure of the Poet in Shelley* (Oxford: Clarendon Press, 1989); and Betty T. Bennett and Stuart Curran, *Shelley: Poet and Legislator of the World* (Baltimore, MD: Johns Hopkins University Press, 1996).

7. Hogle, *Shelley's Process*, 10.

8. Paul de Man, "Shelley Disfigured," in *The Rhetoric of Romanticism* (New York: Columbia University Press, 1984), 122.

9. Joel Faflak, "The Difficult Education of Shelley's *Triumph of Life*," *Keats-Shelley Journal* 58 (2009): 53–78.

10. Ibid., 72.

11. For examples of the latter, see Jerrold Hogle, *Shelley's Process*; William Keach, *Arbitrary Power*; Deborah White, *Romantic Returns: Superstition, Imagination, History* (Stanford, CA: Stanford University Press, 2000); and Paul de Man's, Jacques Derrida's, and J. Hillis Miller's readingof Shelley in Harold Bloom, ed., *Deconstruction and Criticism* (New York: Continuum Press, 1984). For examples of the former, see M. H. Abrams, *The Mirror and the Lamp* (London: Oxford University Press, 1953), 126–32; and Earl Wasserman, *Shelley: A Critical Reading* (Baltimore, MD: The Johns Hopkins University Press, 1971). For a more recent example that explores the relationship between figural language and Shelley's idealism, see William Ulmer, *Shelleyan Eros: The Rhetoric of Romantic Love* (Princeton, NJ: Princeton University Press, 1990).

12. For a reading of the conception of history in Shelley, see Hugh Roberts, *Shelley and the Chaos of History* (University Park: Pennsylvania State University

Press, 1997). For a reading of the role of metaphor in Shelley's conception of history, see John Wright, *Shelley's Myth of Metaphor* (Athens: University of Georgia Press, 1970). See also Jean Hall, "The Divine and the Dispassionate Selves: Shelley's *Defence* and Peacock's *Four Ages of Poetry*," *Keats-Shelley Journal* 41 (1992): 139–63; and Graham Allen "Transumption and/in History: Bloom, Shelley and the Figure of the Poet," *Durham University Journal* 85 (1993): 247–56.

13. Quintilian, in fact, dismisses the figure as simply another name for abuse of metaphor, or catachresis. See Quintilian, *The Orator's Education*, vol. 3 (8), trans. Donald Russell (Cambridge, MA: Harvard University Press, 2001).

14. *Oxford English Dictionary*, s.v. "metalepsis."

15. Faflak, "The Difficult Education of Shelley's *Triumph of Life*," 66.

16. For two important readings of Shelley that attempt to define his conception of the imagination as something other than a subjective capacity, see Redfield, *The Politics of Aesthetics*, 148–71, and Hogle, *Shelley's Process*.

17. For the differences between a descriptive utterance and a performative utterance, see J. L. Austin, *How to Do Things with Words* (Cambridge, MA: Harvard University Press, 1962).

18. My use of the term "performative" draws on Derrida's notion of a "performative without performative." Since traditional speech act theory requires a stable legal or cultural context against which to determine whether a given speech act has been felicitous (has done what it says), Derrida discusses a performative that is prior to the context in which it is uttered and that sets that context in place to begin with. See Jacques Derrida, *Limited INC*.

19. Kant's articulation of the function of the imagination is split between the transcendental aesthetic of the First Critique, which seeks to discover the *a priori* rules for the possibility of the appearance of objects of experience, and the Third Critique, which locates the imagination as the bridge between the two halves of the Kantian Critical system: the world of experience, and the world of morality. See Immanuel Kant, *Critique of Pure Reason*, and Immanuel Kant, *Critique of the Power of Judgment*.

20. I borrow this term from Paul de Man, which he uses to describe a system of figural substitutions and exchanges that functions as an epistemology of phenomenalization. See Paul de Man, *Aesthetic Ideology* (Minneapolis: University of Minnesota, 1996), in particular, Andrzej Warminski's "Introduction," 1–11.

21. Quintilian describes metalepsis as a form of catachresis. See Quintilian, *The Orator's Education*.

22. See Aristotle, "Poetics," in *The Complete Works of Aristotle*, ed. Jonathan Barnes (Princeton, NJ: Princeton University Press, 1984), 2316, 1447A10.

23. Austin, *How to Do Things with Words*.

24. I am relying here, once again, on Derrida's use of this term. See Jacques Derrida, *Limited INC.* Derrida's use of the performative should be understood in relation to what Geoffrey Bennington calls the "quasi-transcendental" aspect of Derrida's use of terms (such as "*différance*") that appear to be concepts, but never achieve the status of a meta-linguistic operators. They are rather conditions of possibility that simultaneously "make impossible the purity of the phenomenon made possible." See Geoffrey Bennington, *Jacques Derrida*, trans. Geoffrey Bennington (Chicago: University of Chicago Press, 1993), 267–84.

25. Shelley describes Dante's words as "a burning atom in inextinguishable thought" that "may yet lie covered in the ashes of their birth, and pregnant with a lightning which has yet found no conductor" (DP 528).

26. Homer's inimitability is what separates him from the authors that Shelley describes as a "flock of mock-birds," none of whom "sought to fulfill a single condition of epic truth." The one exception appears to be Virgil, who "affected the fame of an imitator even whilst he created anew all that he copied" (DP 527).

27. Shelley makes a point to single out both Dante and Milton as important religious reformers on the same order of Luther (DP 528).

28. The notable exception here is Susan Wolfson's important study, *Formal Charges.*

29. On August 16, 1819, a crowd of approximately eighty thousand pro-reform protestors gathered at St. Peter's Field near Manchester to hear reformist orator Henry Hunt speak. Government militia, ordered to disperse the unarmed crowd, charged them with sabers drawn, maiming an estimated five hundred to eight hundred people and murdering between eight and eleven.

30. Richard Cronin, *The Politics of Romantic Poetry* (New York: Macmillan Press, 2000), 179.

31. Wolfson, *Formal Charges*, 193–226.

32. Redfield, *The Politics of Aesthetics*, 161.

33. For an argument about the connection between Shelley's understanding of language and his conception of political power, see Keach, *Arbitrary Power*, 1–23. Keach's argument in the first chapter of his book articulates a connection between the arbitrary nature of the signifier and the arbitrary (or the illegitimate) in the political realm.

34. Austin, *How to Do Things with Words.* Austin tries to separate constatives (utterances that describe the world and therefore are subject to questions of truth or falsity) from performatives (utterances that are themselves an act and are therefore not judged in terms of their descriptive accuracy, but in terms of whether they have carried out an action or not).

35. Redfield, *The Politics of Aesthetics*, 159.

36. Stephen Jones, *Shelley's Satire: Violence, Exhortation and Authority* (De Kalb: Northern Illinois University Press, 1994), 112.

37. Jones, *Shelley's Satire*, 112.

38. Keach, *Arbitrary Power*, 147.

39. Susan Wolfson, "Something Must Be Done: Shelley, Hemans, and the Flash of Revolutionary Female Violence," in *Fellow Romantics: Male and Female British Writers, 1790–1835*, ed. Beth Lau (Surrey, UK: Ashgate, 2009), 99–122.

40. Paul de Man, "Shelley Disfigured," in *The Rhetoric of Romanticism*, 116.

41. For a discussion of the Kantian "schema-image" as a crucial transition in the modern period from image as representation to image as presentation, see Jean-Luc Nancy, *Ground of the Image*, trans. Jeff Fort (New York: Fordham University Press, 2005), 80–99.

42. A number of commentators have linked the Shape's indeterminacy to the vision of non-violent resistance that emerges in the third section of the poem. See for example, Michael Henry Scrivener, *Radical Shelley* (Princeton, NJ: Princeton University Press, 1982), 207–10.

43. In "Shelley Disfigured" de Man analyzes the illusion of continuity created by the light imagery in *Triumph of Life*. Each new figure metaleptically transposes the next into itself as the ground of its apparently inaugural commencement. See de Man, "Shelley Disfigured," 105–12.

44. For a useful discussion of this distinction between Shelley's "exoteric" and "esoteric" poems, see Stephen Behrendt, "The Exoteric Political Poems," in *Shelley*, ed. Michael O'Neill (New York: Longman, 1993), 122–39.

45. This important observation is made clearly and effectively by Alan Weinberg in "The Limits of Super-Rationality: A New Look at the Conception of Jupiter in *Prometheus Unbound*," *European Legacy: Toward New Paradigms* 14, no. 4 (July 2009): 253–67.

46. Tilottama Rajan productively reads Demogorgon's as an "empty schema" that complicates hermeneutic assurances of a unity of meaning behind his figurality and therefore the text as a whole. In her argument he becomes "the means by which we recognize that the inner core of the work is absent, its voice 'lacking,' its cryptic and contradictory text all that there is." See Tilottama Rajan, *The Supplement of Reading* (Ithaca, NY: Cornell University Press, 1990), 311.

47. More than one commentator has suggested that that the exchange between Asia and Demogorgon reveals the way Demogorgon echoes back Asia's assumptions evident in her form of questioning about power. Carol Jacobs, for instance, argues persuasively that Asia's desire that Demogorgon name the ultimate source of authority entails a desire for a form of "control that accompanies naming, domination through the curse, language as authority." See Carol Jacobs, *Uncontainable Romanticism* (Baltimore, MD: The Johns Hopkins University Press, 1989), 44.

48. Carol Jacobs offers a careful and persuasive reading of this line by linking the "deep truth" Demogorgon mentions to the "abysm" he represents. This means that "the deep truth" cannot "be voiced as Asia wishes, as a presence, as the present, as a here and now that endures." See Carol Jacobs, *Uncontainable Romanticism*, 46. One should add that this "deep truth" is also incapable of being incarnated in a particular figure, except a thoroughly ambivalent one like Demogorgon himself.

49. For an in-depth discussion of this concept, see Claude Lefort, "The Permanence of the Theological-Political?," in *Democracy and Political Theory*, 213–55.

50. Carol Jacobs rightly claims that "'Eternity' here implies anything but a state of permanence, for it operates rather as the perpetual disruption of temporal and spatial stasis." See Carol Jacobs, *Uncontainable Romanticism*, 57.

51. See Jean-Jacques Rousseau, "Discourse on the Origin and Foundations of Inequality among Men," in *Rousseau's Political Writings*, 3–57.

52. Percy Shelley, "Queen Mab," in *Shelley's Poetry and Prose*, Canto 6, line 105.

53. For some other examples of a reading of this phrase, see P. M. S. Dawson, *The Unacknowledged Legislator: Shelley and Politics* (Oxford: Oxford University Press, 1980); Timothy Clark, *Embodying Revolution*; and Betty T. Bennett and Stuart Curran, *Shelley: Poet and Legislator of the World*.

54. I draw here on the work of Jacques Rancière, who discusses what he calls a "distribution of the sensible," which is both a "system of self-evident facts" and "the system of *a priori* forms determining what presents itself to sense experience." What disrupts a given "distribution of the sensible" is the power of a form of thought "that has become foreign to itself: a product identical with something not produced, knowledge transformed into non-knowledge. . . ." See Jacques Rancière, *The Politics of Aesthetics*, trans. Gabriel Rockhill (London: Continuum Press, 2004), 20–30.

55. Schmitt famously defines the modern sovereign as "he who decides on the exception." See Carl Schmitt, *Political Theology*, 5.

EPILOGUE: "UPPING THE ANTE"

1. This commentary on Celan occurs in two main texts. The revised published version appears in Jacques Derrida, "Majesties," in *Sovereignties in Question*, ed. Thomas Dutoit and Outi Pasonen (New York: Fordham University Press, 2005), 108–34. It also forms part of Derrida's lectures published as Jacques Derrida, *Beast and the Sovereign*, vol. 1, 216–35.

2. Derrida, *Beast and the Sovereign*, vol. 1, 230.

3. This phrase renders a difficult word to translate from the French: *surenchère*. It is meant to designate something like an n+1, a gesture toward something hyperbolic, "more than" or in excess of every figure of sovereignty.

4. See Giorgio Agamben, *State of Exception*, 39.

5. One could argue that Nancy's work as a whole involves an attempt to think a politics that is non-sovereign, that is, a politics organized around something other than a common subjectivity. Nancy develops the specific concept of a "non-sovereign politics" most explicitly in the "Complements" section of *The Creation of the World*. See Jean-Luc Nancy, *The Creation of the World*, trans. Francois Raffoul and David Pettigrew (Albany: State University of New York Press, 2007), 93–112.

6. See Giorgio Agamben, *Homo Sacer*, 59.

7. See both volumes of Derrida's *Beast and the Sovereign*.

BIBLIOGRAPHY

Abrams, M. H. *The Mirror and the Lamp*. London: Oxford University Press, 1953.

———. *Natural Supernaturalism: Tradition and Revolution in Romantic Literature*. New York: W. W. Norton, 1971.

Agamben, Giorgio. *Homo Sacer: Sovereign Power and Bare Life*. Translated by Daniel Heller-Roazen. Stanford, CA: Stanford University Press, 1998.

———. *The Kingdom and the Glory*. Translated by Lorenzo Chiesa. Stanford, CA: Stanford University Press, 2011.

———. *State of Exception*. Translated by Kevin Attell. Chicago: University of Chicago Press, 2005.

Allen, Graham. "Transumption and/in History: Bloom, Shelley and the Figure of the Poet." *Durham University Journal* 85 (1993): 247–56.

Anderson, Benedict. *Imagined Communities*. London: Verso, 1983.

Aristotle. *The Complete Works of Aristotle*. Edited by Jonathan Barnes. Princeton, NJ: Princeton University Press, 1984.

Austin, J. L. *How to Do Things with Words*. Cambridge, MA: Harvard University Press, 1962.

Averill, James. *Wordsworth and the Poetry of Human Suffering*. Ithaca, NY: Cornell University Press, 1980.

Balfour, Ian. *The Rhetoric of Romantic Prophecy*. Stanford, CA: Stanford University Press, 2002.

Barth, J. Robert. *Coleridge and Christian Doctrine*. Cambridge, MA: Harvard University Press, 1969.

———. *The Symbolic Imagination: Coleridge and the Romantic Tradition*. 2nd ed. New York: Fordham University Press, 2001.

Bataille, Georges. "Sovereignty." In *The Accursed Share*, vols. 2 and 3, translated by Robert Hurley, 197–361. New York: Zone Books, 1993.

Behrendt, Stephen. "The Exoteric Political Poems." In *Shelley*, edited by Michael O'Neill, 122–39. New York: Longman, 1993.

Benjamin, Walter. "On the Concept of History." In *Walter Benjamin: Selected Writings, Vol. 4, 1938–1940*, edited by Howard Eiland and Michael W. Jennings, 389–400. Cambridge, MA: Harvard University Press, 2003.

———. "On Some Motifs in Baudelaire." In *Walter Benjamin: Selected Writings, Vol. 4, 1938–1940*, translated by Howard Eiland and Michael W. Jennings, 313–55. Cambridge, MA: Harvard University Press, 2003.

Bennett, Betty T., and Stuart Curran. *Shelley: Poet and Legislator of the World*. Baltimore, MD: The Johns Hopkins University Press, 1996.

Bennington, Geoffrey. *Jacques Derrida*. Translated by Geoffrey Bennington. Chicago: University of Chicago Press, 1993.

———. "X." In *Interrupting Derrida*, 76–92. London: Routledge Press, 2000.

Berkeley, Richard. *Coleridge and the Crisis of Reason*. Houndmills, UK: Palgrave Macmillan, 2007.

Blake, William. *The Complete Poetry and Prose*. Edited by David V. Erdman. Rev. ed. New York: Anchor Books, 1988.

Bloom, Harold. *Blake's Apocalypse: A Study in Poetic Argument*. Ithaca, NY: Cornell University Press, 1963.

———, ed. *Deconstruction and Criticism*. New York: Continuum Press, 1984.

———. *Visionary Company*. Ithaca, NY: Cornell University Press, 1961.

Christensen, Jerome. "The Method of *The Friend*." In *Coleridge's Blessed Machine of Language*, 186–269. Ithaca, NY: Cornell University Press, 1981.

Clark, Timothy. *Embodying Revolution: The Figure of the Poet in Shelley*. Oxford: Clarendon Press, 1989.

Coleman, Deirdre. *Coleridge and the Friend (1809–1810)*. Oxford: Oxford University Press, 1988.

Coleridge, S. T. *Biographia Literaria*. 2 vols. Edited by James Engell and W. Jackson Bate. Princeton, NJ: Princeton University Press, 1983.

———. *The Friend*. Edited by Barbara E. Rooke. Princeton, NJ: Princeton University Press, 1969.

———. *Lay Sermons*. Edited by R. J. White. Princeton, NJ: Princeton University Press, 1972.

———. *Logic*. Edited by J. R. de J. Jackson. Princeton, NJ: Princeton University Press, 1981.

———. *On the Constitution of Church and State*. Edited by John Colmer. Princeton, NJ: Princeton University Press, 1976.

———. *Poetical Works I*. Edited by J. C. C. Mays. Princeton, NJ: Princeton University Press, 2001.

Comay, Rebecca. *Mourning Sickness: Hegel and the French Revolution*. Stanford, CA: Stanford University Press, 2011.

Cronin, Richard. *The Politics of Romantic Poetry*. New York: Macmillan Press, 2000.

Damon, S. Foster. *A Blake Dictionary*. Hanover, NH: University Press of New England, 1988.

Damrosch, Leopold. *Symbol and Truth in Blake's Myth*. Princeton, NJ: Princeton University Press, 1980.

Dawson, P. M. S. *The Unacknowledged Legislator: Shelley and Politics*. Oxford: Oxford University Press, 1980.

De Luca, Vincent. *Words of Eternity: Blake and the Poetics of the Sublime*. Princeton, NJ: Princeton University Press, 1991.

de Man, Paul. *Aesthetic Ideology*. Minneapolis: University of Minnesota Press, 1996.

———. "The Intentional Structure of the Romantic Image." In *The Rhetoric of Romanticism*, 1–17. New York: Columbia University Press, 1984.

———. "A New Vitalism: Harold Bloom." In *Critical Writings: 1953–1978*, edited by Lindsay Waters, 90–96. Minneapolis: University of Minnesota Press, 1989.

———. "The Rhetoric of Temporality." In *Blindness and Insight*, 187–228. Minneapolis: University of Minnesota Press, 1983.

———. "Shelley Disfigured." In *The Rhetoric of Romanticism*, 93–123. New York: Columbia University Press, 1984.

———. "Time and History in Wordsworth." In *Romanticism and Contemporary Criticism*, 74–94. Baltimore, MD: The Johns Hopkins University Press, 1993.

Derrida, Jacques. *Beast and the Sovereign*. Translated by Geoffrey Bennington. 2 vols. Chicago: University of Chicago Press, 2009–2011.

———. "Faith and Knowledge: The Two Sources of 'Religion' as the Limits of Reason Alone." In *Acts of Religion*, edited by Gil Anidjar, 42–101. New York: Routledge Press, 2002.

———. *The Gift of Death*. Translated by David Wills. Chicago: University of Chicago Press, 1999.

———. *Limited INC*. Translated by Samuel Weber. Evanston, IL: Northwestern University Press, 1988.

———. *The Politics of Friendship*. Translated by George Collins. London: Verso Press, 1997.

———. *Rogues*. Translated by Pascale-Anne Brault and Michael Naas. Stanford, CA: Stanford University Press, 2005.

———. *Sovereignties in Question*. Edited by Thomas Dutoit and Outi Pasonen. New York: Fordham University Press, 2005.

———. "White Mythology: Metaphor in the Text of Philosophy." In *Margins of Philosophy*, translated by Alan Bass, 207–71. Chicago: University of Chicago Press, 1982.

DiSalvo, Jackie, G. A. Rosso, and Christopher Z. Hobson, eds. *Blake, Politics, and History*. New York: Routledge, 1998.

Duff, David. *Romance and Revolution: Shelley and the Politics of a Genre*. Cambridge: Cambridge University Press, 1994.

Duffy, Cian. *Shelley and the Revolutionary Sublime*. Cambridge: Cambridge University Press, 2005.

Eilenberg, Susan. *Strange Power of Speech: Wordsworth, Coleridge, and Literary Possession*. Oxford: Oxford University Press, 1992.

Engell, James. *The Creative Imagination*. Cambridge, MA: Harvard University Press, 1981.

Erdman, David V. *Blake: Prophet against Empire*. Princeton, NJ: Princeton University Press, 1954.

Essick, Robert N. "Coleridge and the Language of Adam." In *Coleridge's* Biographia Literaria, edited by Frederick Burwick, 62–74. Columbus: Ohio University Press, 1989.

Esterhammer, Angela. "Calling into Existence: *The Book of Urizen*." In *Blake in the Nineties*, edited by Steve Clark and David Worrall, 114–32. New York: St. Martin's Press, 1999.

———. *Creating States: Studies in the Performative Language of John Milton and William Blake*. Toronto: University of Toronto Press, 1994.

———. *The Romantic Performative: Language and Action in British and German Romanticism*. Stanford, CA: Stanford University Press, 2000.

Faflak, Joel. "The Difficult Education of Shelley's *Triumph of Life*." *Keats-Shelley Journal* 58 (2009): 53–78.

Ferguson, Frances. "Coleridge on Language and Delusion." *Genre* 2 (Summer 1978): 191–207.

———. *Wordsworth: Language as Counter-Spirit*. New Haven, CT: Yale University Press, 1977.

Ferris, David. "Coleridge's Ventriloquy: The Abduction from the *Biographia*." *Studies in Romanticism* 24 (Spring 1985): 41–84.

———. *Theory and the Evasion of History*. Baltimore, MD: The Johns Hopkins University Press, 1993.

Fichte, J. G. *The Science of Knowledge*. Translated by Peter Heath and John Lachs. Cambridge: Cambridge University Press, 1970.

Fosso, Kurt. *Buried Communities: Wordsworth and the Bonds of Mourning*. Albany: State University of New York Press, 2004.

Foucault, Michel. "Truth and Power." In *Power/Knowledge*, edited by Colin Gordon, 109–33. New York: Pantheon Books, 1977.

Franta, Andrew. "Shelley and the Poetics of Political Indirection." *Poetics Today* 22, no. 4 (Winter 2001): 765–93.

Freud, Sigmund. "Dissection of the Psychical Personality." In *New Introductory Lectures on Psychoanalysis*, translated by James Strachey, 88–112. New York: Penguin, 1983.

Frye, Northrop. *Fearful Symmetry*. Princeton, NJ: Princeton University Press, 1947.

Fulford, Tim. *Coleridge's Figurative Language*. Houndmills, UK: Palgrave Macmillan, 1991.

Gabriele, Alberto. "Visions of the City of London: Mechanical Eye and Poetic Transcendence in Wordsworth's *Prelude*, Book 7." *European Romantic Review* 19, no. 4 (Oct. 2008): 365–84.

Garber, Frederick. *Wordsworth and the Poetry of Encounter.* Urbana: University of Illinois Press, 1971.

Gill, Stephen. *Wordsworth: The Prelude.* Cambridge: Cambridge University Press, 1991.

Goodman, Kevis. "Making Time for History: Wordsworth, the New Historicism, and the Apocalyptic Fallacy." In *The Wordsworthian Enlightenment*, edited by Helen Regueiro Elam and Frances Ferguson, 158–71. Baltimore, MD: The Johns Hopkins University Press, 2005.

Gregory, Alan. *Coleridge and the Conservative Imagination.* Macon, GA: Mercer University Press, 2003.

Grimes, Ronald. "Time and Space in Blake's Major Prophecies." In *Blake's Sublime Allegory*, edited by Stuart Curran and Joseph Wittreich Jr., 59–81. Madison: University of Wisconsin Press, 1973.

Hall, Jean. "The Divine and the Dispassionate Selves: Shelley's *Defence* and Peacock's *Four Ages of Poetry*." *Keats-Shelley Journal* 41 (1992): 139–63.

Halmi, Nicholas. *The Genealogy of the Romantic Symbol.* Oxford: Oxford University Press, 2007.

Hamilton, Paul. *Coleridge and German Philosophy.* New York: Continuum Press, 2007.

———. *Coleridge's Poetics.* Oxford: Blackwell Publishing, 1983.

———. *Wordsworth.* Brighton, UK: The Harvester Press, 1986.

Harding, Anthony John. *Coleridge and the Inspired Word.* Kingston, ON: McGill University Press, 1985.

Hardt, Michael, and Antonio Negri. *Empire.* Cambridge, MA: Harvard University Press, 2000.

Harrison, Gary. *Wordsworth's Vagrant Muse.* Detroit, MI: Wayne State University Press, 1994.

Hartman, Geoffrey. "A Poet's Progress: Wordsworth and the *Via Naturaliter Negativa*." *Modern Philology* 59, no. 3 (Feb. 1962): 214–24.

———. "Words, Wish, Worth." In *The Unremarkable Wordsworth*, 90–119. (Minneapolis: University of Minnesota Press, 1987.

———. *Wordsworth's Poetry: 1787–1814.* New Haven, CT: Yale University Press, 1964.

Heffernan, James. "Wordsworth's London: The Imperial Monster." *Studies in Romanticism* 37, no. 3 (Fall 1998): 421–43.

Hegel, G. W. F. *Introduction to the Philosophy of History.* Translated by Leo Rausch. Indianapolis, IN: Hackett Publishing, 1988.

———. *The Phenomenology of Spirit.* Translated by A. V. Miller. Oxford: Oxford University Press, 1977.

Heidegger, Martin. "The Age of the World-Picture." In *The Question Concerning Technology and Other Essays*, translated by William Lovitt, 115–54. New York: Harper and Row, 1977.

———. *Kant and the Problem of Metaphysics*. Translated by Richard Taft. Bloomington: Indiana University Press, 1990.

Hertz, Neil. "The Notion of Blockage in the Literature of the Sublime." In *Psychoanalysis and the Question of the Text*, edited by Geoffrey Hartman, 62–85. Baltimore, MD: The Johns Hopkins University Press, 1978.

Hickey, Alison. *Impure Conceits: Rhetoric and Ideology in Wordsworth's* Excursion. Stanford, CA: Stanford University Press, 1997.

Hodgson, John A. "Transcendental Tropes: Coleridge's Rhetoric of Allegory and Symbol." In *Allegory, Myth and Symbol*, edited by Morton W. Bloomfield, 233–92. Cambridge, MA: Harvard University Press, 1981.

Hogle, Jerrold. *Shelley's Process*. New York: Oxford University Press, 1988.

Jackson, J. R. de J. *Method and Imagination in Coleridge's Criticism*. Cambridge, MA: Harvard University Press, 1969.

Jacobs, Carol. *Uncontainable Romanticism*. Baltimore, MD: The Johns Hopkins University Press, 1989.

Jacobus, Mary. *Romanticism, Writing and Sexual Difference: Essays on the* Prelude. Oxford: Clarendon Press, 1989.

Janowitz, Anne. "The Artifactual Sublime: Making London Poetry." In *Romantic Metropolis*, edited by James Chandler and Kevin Gilmartin, 246–60. Cambridge: Cambridge University Press, 2005.

Jarvis, Simon. *Wordsworth's Philosophic Song*. Cambridge: Cambridge University Press, 2007.

Jasper, David. *Coleridge as Poet and Religious Thinker*. London: Macmillan Press, 1985.

Jones, John H. *Blake on Language, Power, and Self-Annihilation*. Houndmills, UK: Palgrave Macmillan, 2010.

Jones, Stephen. *Shelley's Satire: Violence, Exhortation and Authority*. De Kalb: Northern Illinois University Press, 1994.

Kaiser, David Aram. *Romanticism, Aesthetics, Nationalism*. Cambridge: Cambridge University Press, 1999.

Kant, Immanuel. *Critique of the Power of Judgment*. Translated by Paul Guyer. Cambridge: Cambridge University Press, 2000.

———. *Critique of Practical Reason*. Translated by Lewis White Beck. New York: Macmillan Publishing, 1956.

———. *Critique of Pure Reason*. Translated by Werner Pluhar. Indianapolis, IN: Hackett Publishing Company, 1996.

Kantorowicz, Ernst. *The King's Two Bodies: A Study in Medieval Political Theology*. Princeton, NJ: Princeton University Press, 1957.

Keach, William. *Arbitrary Power: Romanticism, Language, Politics*. Princeton, NJ: Princeton University Press, 2004.

Kitson, Peter J. "Coleridge as Political Thinker." In *Cambridge Companion to Coleridge*, edited by Lucy Newlyn, 156–69. Cambridge: Cambridge University Press, 2002.

Kneale, J. Douglas. *Monumental Writing*. (Lincoln: University of Nebraska Press, 1988.

Lacoue-Labarthe, Phillipe. *Heidegger, Art and Politics*. Translated by Chris Turner. Cambridge, MA: Blackwell Publishing, 1990.

———. *Typography*. Stanford, CA: Stanford University Press, 1998.

Lacoue-Labarthe, Phillipe, and Jean-Luc Nancy. *The Literary Absolute*. Albany: State University of New York Press, 1988.

Langan, Celeste. *Romantic Vagrancy: Wordsworth and the Simulation of Freedom*. Cambridge: Cambridge University Press, 1995.

Leask, Nigel. *The Politics of Imagination in Coleridge's Critical Thought*. London: Macmillan Press, 1988.

Lefort, Claude. *Democracy and Political Theory*. Translated by David Macey. Minneapolis: University of Minnesota Press, 1988.

Levinson, Marjorie, ed. *Rethinking Historicism: Critical Readings in Romantic History*. Oxford: Oxford University Press, 1989.

Levinson, Marjorie. *Wordsworth's Great Period Poems: Four Essays*. Cambridge: Cambridge University Press, 1986.

Lincoln, Andrew. "Politics and Desire in Blake's *The French Revolution*." In *Blake, Politics and History*, edited by Jackie DiSalvo, G. A. Rosso, and Christopher Z. Hobson, 187–95. New York: Routledge, 1998.

Liu, Alan. *Wordsworth: The Sense of History*. Stanford, CA: Stanford University Press, 1989.

Makdisi, Saree. *William Blake and the Impossible History of the 1790s*. Chicago: University of Chicago Press, 2003.

Malebranche, Nicolas. "The Search after Truth." In *Philosophical Selections*, edited by Steven Nadler, 3–144. Indianapolis, IN: Hackett Publishing, 1992.

McFarland, Thomas. "Aspect of Coleridge's Distinction Between Reason and Understanding." In *Coleridge's Visionary Languages*, edited by Tim Fulford and Morton Paley, 165–80. Cambridge: D. S. Brewer, 1993.

———. *Coleridge and the Pantheist Tradition*. Oxford: Oxford University Press, 1969.

———. "Involute and Symbol in the Romantic Imagination." In *Coleridge, Keats and the Imagination*, edited by J. Robert Barth, S. J. and John L. Mahoney, 29–57. Columbia: University of Missouri Press, 1990.

McGann, Jerome. *The Romantic Ideology*. Chicago: The University of Chicago Press, 1983.

Mee, Jon. "Blake's Politics in History." In *Cambridge Companion to William Blake*, 133–49. Cambridge: Cambridge University Press, 2003.

———. *Dangerous Enthusiasm: William Blake and the Culture of Radicalism in the 1790s*. Oxford: Oxford University Press, 1992.

Mill, John Stuart. *Mill on Bentham and Coleridge*. Cambridge: Cambridge University Press, 1980.

Miller, J. Hillis. "Derrida's Politics of Autoimmunity." *Discourse* 30, no. 1–2 (Winter & Spring 2008): 208–25.

Milton, John. *Complete Poems and Major Prose*. Edited by Merritt Hughes. Saddle River, NJ: Prentice Hall, 1957.

Morrow, John. *Coleridge's Political Thought*. London: Macmillan Press, 1990.

Nancy, Jean-Luc. "Being Singular Plural." In *Being Singular Plural*, translated by Robert D. Richardson and Anne E. O'Byrne, 1–99. Stanford, CA: Stanford University Press, 2000.

———. *The Creation of the World*. Translated by Francois Raffoul and David Pettigrew. Albany: State University of New York Press, 2007.

———. *Ground of the Image*. Translated by Jeff Fort. New York: Fordham University Press, 2005.

———. *The Inoperative Community*. Translated by Peter Connor. Minneapolis: University of Minnesota Press, 1991.

Newlyn, Lucy. "'The Noble Living and the Noble Dead': Community in *The Prelude*." In *Cambridge Companion to Wordsworth*, 55–69. Cambridge: Cambridge University Press, 2003.

Onorato, Richard. *The Character of the Poet: Wordsworth in* The Prelude. Princeton, NJ: Princeton University Press, 1971.

Orsini, G. N. G. *Coleridge and German Idealism*. Carbondale: Southern Illinois University Press, 1969.

Perry, Seamus. *Coleridge and the Uses of Division*. Oxford: Oxford University Press, 1999.

Pfau, Thomas. *Wordsworth's Profession: Form, Class & the Logic of Early Romantic Cultural Production*. Stanford, CA: Stanford University Press, 1997.

Phillips, James. "Wordsworth and the Fraternity of Joy." *New Literary History* 41, no. 3 (Summer 2010): 613–32.

Pyle, Forest. *The Ideology of Imagination*. Stanford, CA: Stanford University Press, 1995.

Quintilian. *The Orator's Education*. Translated by Donald Russell. Cambridge, MA: Harvard University Press, 2001.

Rajan, Tilottama. *The Supplement of Reading*. Ithaca, NY: Cornell University Press, 1990.

Rancière, Jacques. "The Poet's Voyage." In *Short Voyages to the Land of the People*, translated by James Swenson, 9–24. Stanford, CA: Stanford University Press, 2003.

———. *The Politics of Aesthetics*. Translated by Gabriel Rockhill. London: Continuum Press, 2004.

Redfield, Marc. *Phantom Formations: Aesthetic Ideology and the Bildungsroman*. Ithaca, NY: Cornell University Press, 1996

———. *The Politics of Aesthetics: Nationalism, Gender Romanticism*. Stanford, CA: Stanford University Press, 2003.

Reid, Nicholas. *Coleridge, Form and Symbol: Or the Ascertaining Vision*. Burlington, VT: Ashgate Publishing, 2006.

———. "Coleridge and Schelling: The Missing Transcendental Deduction." *Studies in Romanticism* 33 (Fall 1994): 451–79.

Rieder, John. *Wordsworth's Counterrevolutionary Turn: Community Virtue and Vision in the 1790s*. Newark: University of Delaware Press, 1997.

Roberts, Hugh. *Shelley and the Chaos of History*. University Park: Pennsylvania State University Press, 1997.

Robespierre, Maximilien. *Virtue and Terror*. Translated by John Howe. London: Verso, 2007.

Rousseau, Jean-Jacques. "Discourse on the Origin and Foundations of Inequality among Men." In *Rousseau's Political Writings*, translated by Julia Conway Bondanella, 3–57. New York: W. W. Norton, 1988.

———. "On Social Contract." In *Political Writings*, translated by Julia Bondanella, 84–173. New York: W. W. Norton, 1988.

Rovira, James. "Creation Anxiety and *The (First) Book of Urizen*." In *Blake and Kierkegaard: Creation and Anxiety*, 121–43 New York: Continuum Press, 2010.

Schelling, F. W. J. *System of Transcendental Idealism*. Translated by Peter Heath. Charlottesville: University Press of Virginia, 1993.

Schmitt, Carl. *Political Romanticism*. Translated by Guy Oakes. Cambridge, MA: MIT Press, 1986.

———. *Political Theology*. Translated by George Schwab. Chicago: University of Chicago Press, 1985.

———. *Politische Romantik*. München: Verlag von Duncker & Humblot, 1925.

Scrivener, Michael Henry. *Radical Shelley*. Princeton, NJ: Princeton University Press, 1982.

Shelley, Percy. *Shelley's Poetry and Prose*. Edited by Donald H. Reiman and Neil Fraistat. New York: W. W. Norton, 2002.

———. *Shelley's Prose*. Edited by David Lee Clark. Albuquerque: University of New Mexico Press, 1966.

Simpson, David. *Wordsworth, Commodification and Social Concern*. Cambridge: Cambridge University Press, 2009.

———. *Wordsworth and the Figurings of the Real*. London: Macmillan Press, 1982.

———. *Wordsworth's Historical Imagination: The Poetry of Displacement*. New York: Methuen, 1987.

Spivak, Gayatri. "The Letter as Cutting Edge." *Yale French Studies* 55/56 (1977): 206–26.

Stauffer, Andrew. *Anger, Revolution, and Romanticism.* Cambridge: Cambridge University Press, 2005.

Storch, R. F. "The Politics of the Imagination." *Studies in Romanticism* 21 (Fall 1982): 448–56.

———. "Wordsworth and the City: Social Reason's Inner Sense." *Wordsworth Circle* 1, no. 3 (1970): 114–22.

Swearingen, James E. "William Blake's Figural Politics." In *Blake, Politics, and History*, edited by Jackie DiSalvo, G. A. Rosso, and Christopher Z. Hobson, 80–96. New York: Routledge, 1998.

Thomson, E. P. *Witness against the Beast: William Blake and the Moral Law.* Cambridge: Cambridge University Press, 1993.

Ulmer, William. *Shelleyan Eros: The Rhetoric of Romantic Love.* Princeton, NJ: Princeton University Press, 1990.

Wageknecht, David. *Blake's Night: William Blake and the Idea of Pastoral.* Cambridge, MA: Harvard University Press, 1973.

Warminski, Andrzej. "Missed Crossing: Wordsworth's Apocalypses." *MLN* 99, no. 5 (Dec. 1984): 983–1006.

Wasserman, Earl. *Shelley: A Critical Reading.* Baltimore, MD: The Johns Hopkins University Press, 1971.

Weinberg. Alan. "The Limits of Super-Rationality: A New Look at the Conception of Jupiter in *Prometheus Unbound.*" *European Legacy: Toward New Paradigms* 14, no. 4 (July 2009): 253–67.

Wheeler, Kathleen. *Sources, Processes and Methods in Coleridge's* Biographia Literaria. Cambridge: Cambridge University Press, 1980.

White, Deborah. *Romantic Returns: Superstition, Imagination, History.* Stanford, CA: Stanford University Press, 2000.

Williams, Nicholas. *Ideology and Utopia in the Poetry of William Blake.* Cambridge: Cambridge University Press, 2006.

Wolfson, Susan. "Blake's Language in Poetic Form." In *Cambridge Companion to William Blake*, 63–84. Cambridge: Cambridge University Press, 2003.

———. *Formal Charges: The Shaping of Poetry in British Romanticism.* Stanford, CA: Stanford University Press, 1997.

———. "Something Must Be Done: Shelley, Hemans, and the Flash of Revolutionary Female Violence." In *Fellow Romantics: Male and Female British Writers, 1790–1835*, edited by Beth Lau, 99–122. Surrey, UK: Ashgate, 2009.

———. "Wordsworth's Craft." In *Cambridge Companion to Wordsworth*, 108–24. Cambridge: Cambridge University Press, 2003.

Wordsworth, William. *The Fourteen-Book Prelude.* Edited by W. J. B. Owen. Ithaca, NY: Cornell University Press, 1985.

———. "Preface of 1815." In *The Prose Works of William Wordsworth*. Vol. 3. Edited by W. J. B. Owen and Jane Smyser, 23–39. Oxford: Clarendon Press, 1974.

———. "Preface to Lyrical Ballads." In *The Prose Works of William Wordsworth*. Vol. 1. Edited by W. J. B. Owen and Jane Smyser, 111–65. Oxford: Clarendon Press, 1974.

———. *Sonnet Series and Itinerary Poems, 1820–1845*. Edited by Geoffrey Jackson. Ithaca, NY: Cornell University Press, 2004.

———. *The Thirteen-Book "Prelude."* Edited by Mark Reed. 2 vols. Ithaca, NY: Cornell University Press, 1991.

Wright, John. *Shelley's Myth of Metaphor*. Athens: University of Georgia Press, 1970.

Wright, Luke Savin Herrick. *Samuel Taylor Coleridge and the Anglican Church*. Notre Dame, IN: University of Notre Dame Press, 2010.

INDEX